Englisch als 2. Fremdsprache

English G 21

A1

für Gymnasien

Cornelsen

English G 21 • Band A 1 • Zweite Fremdsprache

Im Auftrag des Verlages herausgegeben von
Prof. Hellmut Schwarz, Mannheim

Erarbeitet von
Laurence Harger, Wellington, Neuseeland
Barbara Derkow Disselbeck, Köln
Allen J. Woppert, Berlin
sowie Susan Abbey, Nenagh, Irland

unter Mitarbeit von
Wolfgang Biederstädt, Köln
Joachim Blombach, Herford
Helmut Dengler, Limbach
Dr. Jens-Peter Green, Oldenburg
Dr. Ursula Mulla, Germering
Jörg Rademacher, Ilvesheim
Jennifer Seidl, München
Sabine Tudan, Erfurt
Mervyn Whittaker, Bad Dürkheim

in Zusammenarbeit mit der Englischredaktion
Kirsten Bleck (Projektleitung);
Dr. Christian v. Raumer (verantwortlicher Redakteur);
Susanne Bennetreu (Bildredaktion); Christiane Bonk;
Dr. Philip Devlin; Gareth Evans; Bonnie S. Glänzer;
Uwe Tröger; Klaus G. Unger sowie Britta Bensmann

Beratende Mitwirkung
Helga Estor, Darmstadt; Anette Fritsch, Dillenburg;
Dr. Helga Hämmerling, Jena; Patrick Handschuh, Köln;
Martina Kretschko-Ulbrich, Dresden; Wolfgang
Neudecker, Mannheim; Birgit Ohmsieder, Berlin; Albert
Rau, Brühl; Angela Ringel-Eichinger, Bietigheim-
Bissingen; Dr. Jana Schubert, Leipzig; Siegbert
Sonnenberg, Mühlacker; Sieglinde Spranger, Chemnitz;
Harald Weißling, Mannheim

Illustration
Graham-Cameron Illustration, UK: Fliss Cary, Grafikerin
sowie Roland Beier, Berlin

Fotos
Rob Cousins, Bristol

Layoutkonzept und technische Umsetzung
Aksinia Raphael; Korinna Wilkes

Umschlaggestaltung
Klein und Halm Grafikdesign, Berlin

Für die freundliche Unterstützung danken wir der
Cotham School, Bristol.

www.cornelsen.de
www.EnglishG.de

2. Auflage, 1. Druck 2016

Alle Drucke dieser Auflage sind inhaltlich unverändert und können im Unterricht nebeneinander verwendet werden.
Einige der in diesem Druck verwendeten Bilder können sich von denen in der vorherigen Auflage unterscheiden. Der Austausch dieser Bilder war aus urheberrechtlichen Gründen notwendig, um Ihnen die Inhalte auch digital zur Verfügung stellen zu können.

Druck: Mohn Media Mohndruck, Gütersloh

ISBN 978-3-06-031868-1

PEFC zertifiziert
Dieses Produkt stammt aus nachhaltig bewirtschafteten Wäldern und kontrollierten Quellen.
www.pefc.de
PEFC/04-31-1033

Dein Englischbuch enthält folgende Teile:

Hello/Bonjour; Welcome	Einstieg in das Buch
Units	die sechs Kapitel des Buches
Topics	besondere Themen – z.B. „Weihnachten in Großbritannien"
Skills File (SF)	Beschreibung wichtiger Lern- und Arbeitstechniken
Grammar File (GF)	Zusammenfassung der Grammatik jeder Unit
Vocabulary	Wörterverzeichnis zum Lernen der neuen Wörter jeder Unit
Dictionary	alphabetische Wörterverzeichnisse zum Nachschlagen

Die Units bestehen aus diesen Teilen:

Lead-in	Einstieg in das neue Thema
A-Section	neuer Lernstoff mit vielen Aktivitäten
Practice	Übungen
Text	eine spannende oder lustige Geschichte

In den Units findest du diese Überschriften und Symbole:

I can ...	Hier kannst du zeigen, was du auf Englisch schon sagen kannst.
Looking at language	Hier sammelst du Beispiele und entdeckst Regeln.
STUDY SKILLS	Einführung in Lern- und Arbeitstechniken
DOSSIER	Schöne und wichtige Arbeiten kannst du in einer Mappe sammeln.
ACTIVITY	Aufgaben, bei denen du etwas vorspielst, malst oder bastelst
GAME	Spiele für zwei oder für eine Gruppe – natürlich auf Englisch
GETTING BY IN ENGLISH	Alltagssituationen üben; Sprachmittlung
LISTENING	Aufgaben zu Hörtexten auf der CD
Now you	Hier sprichst und schreibst du über dich selbst.
POEM	Gedichte
PRONUNCIATION	Ausspracheübungen
REVISION	Übungen zur Wiederholung
SONG	Lieder zum Anhören und Singen
WORDS	Übungen zu Wortfamilien und Wortfeldern, Wortverbindungen
Checkpoint	Im Workbook kannst du dein Wissen überprüfen.
Extra	Zusätzliche Aktivitäten und Übungen
	Partnerarbeit/Gruppenarbeit
/	Nur auf CD / Auf CD und im Schülerbuch
>	Textaufgaben

Inhalt

Inhalt

Hello!
Bonjour!

My favourite colour is
What about you?
My favourite song is "Frère Jacques".
My favourite song is "Frère Jacques".
My favourite song is "Bruder Jakob". What about you?
And I like
I don't like
What about you?
What about you?

Welcome

I can ...

... talk to my partner in English.

Hi! My name is ... What's your name?
I'm ... years old. How old are you?
I'm from ... Where are you from?

Talk to different partners.

•••

This is *Sophie Carter-Brown.*
She's new in Bristol. She's 11 years old.

This is *Jack Hanson.*
Jack is 11 years old. He's from Bristol.

This is *Dan Shaw* – with his twin brother *Jo.*
They're 12 years old. They're from Bristol.

This is *Ananda Kapoor.*
She's 11 years old. She's from Bristol too.

I can ...

... talk about my partner in English.

This is ...
He's/She's ... years old.
He's/She's from ...

Tell the class about your partner.

•••

▸ WB 1–2 (pp. 3–4)

1 Welcome to Bristol

Bristol is in England. It's a great place!

a) *Talk about the photos.*
I can see ... in photo number ...

a band • a boat • boys •
a football • girls • a kite •
a skateboard • trees • water

b) *Now listen and act out the four activities.*

► *WB 3 (p. 5)*

1

2

3

4

2 Welcome to Cotham Park Road

17 Cotham Park Road is a big, old house in Bristol.

a) *Is the house empty? Listen and find out.*

b) *Complete the sentences. You can listen and check.*
When the house is empty, Prunella is ...
When the house is full, Prunella is ...

happy • not happy

3 SONG Prunella's song

Sing the song and act it out.

I'm Prunella the poltergeist,
Hee, hee, hee!
I close things and I open things,
I push things and I pull things,
I drop things
And then I laugh:
Hee, hee, hee!

I'm Prunella the poltergeist,
Hee, hee, hee!
I can see you, you can't see me.
You look, but you can't find me,
I drop things
And then I laugh:
Hee, hee, hee!

Prunella the poltergeist,
That's me.
Prunella the poltergeist,
Hee, hee, hee!

4 Sophie and Prunella

a) *Match the letters and numbers:*

A: I think picture number 1 is B.
B: Yes, I think that's right. And I think number 2 is A.
A: No, I think it's ...

A This is very nice!

B Emily, you can take baby Hannah

C Sophie, you can help me in here.

D Oh! Who are you?

E That's your room there.

F What? You can see me?!

b) *Listen and check your answers.*

c) *Who is in the pictures?*
Picture 1: Sophie, Sophie's mum, ...
Picture 2: ...
Listen and check.

baby Hannah • Emily • Prunella • Sheeba • Sophie • Sophie's dad • Sophie's mum • Toby

▸ *WB 4 (p. 5)*

5 Welcome to Hamilton Street

The twins Dan and Jo Shaw live at 7 Hamilton Street, Bristol, with their father.
Today is the last day of the summer holidays.

Mr Shaw — Sorry, I'm late, boys.
Jo — OK, Dad.
Dan — I've got the shopping list.
Mr Shaw — Thank you, Dan. Let's look at the list ... 'school bag'. Jo, you need a school bag, right?
Jo — Yes, Dad.
Dan — Me too, Dad.
Mr Shaw — Pencil case. Dan, you need a pencil case, right?
Dan — Yes, Dad.
Jo — Me too, Dad.
Mr Shaw — OK, OK. Two bags, two pencil cases, two ... rubbers, two pencil sharpeners, two pens – felt tips?
Jo — Yes, Dad.
Mr Shaw — Two exercise books, two rulers, two glue sticks, two MP3 players ... hey, what's this?!
Jo — We need MP3 players, Dad.
Mr Shaw — Not for school! This is a school shopping list. Let's go, you two!

I can ...

... say what's in my school bag.

a) *Say what's in the network and write the words.*
I can see a ...

b) *Then draw a network with things in your school bag. Swap networks with a partner. Label the network and say what he/she has got in his/her network.*
You've got a ...

...

▸ WB 5 (p. 6)

6 My favourite colour

Dan My favourite colour is blue:
the blue school bag for me, please.
Jo And the red school bag for me.
Mr Shaw OK. What about pencil cases?
Jo Orange for me, please.
Dan The blue pencil case for me.
And I need a rubber: the green rubber, please.
Jo Ugh! A green rubber!
Yellow for me.
Mr Shaw Right ... pencil sharpeners ...
Dan A blue pencil sharpener, please.
Jo Black for me, please.
Dan And we need the glue sticks.
Jo And the MP3 players!

7 Now you

a) *Act out the dialogue.*

b) *Act out a new dialogue with your favourite colours.*

I can ...

... talk about colours in English.

A: What colour is your house/
your school bag/...?
B: It's yellow/pink/purple/...

Talk to different partners.

...

8 SONG Prunella's plates

Listen. Then sing the song and act it out.

I like red,
Red, red, red.
Here's my red plate.
Ooops!
Crash! Bang! Wallop!
Aaaaw. Oh well ...

I like green,
Green, green, green.
Here's my green plate.
Ooops!
Crash! Bang! Wallop!
Aaaaw. Oh well ...

I like brown,
...

► *WB 6–7 (pp. 6–7)*

9 Welcome to Paul Road

The Kapoors have got a shop at 13 Paul Road in Bristol. They live in a flat over the shop.

Ananda — Well, is my new school uniform OK?
Mrs Kapoor — Very nice, Ananda, very nice.
Dilip — Monday today, Tuesday tomorrow ... the big day for my baby sister ... first day at the new school ...
Mrs Kapoor — It's a nice school, Ananda.
Dilip — It's a big school, Ananda.
Mrs Kapoor — Stop that, Dilip! You can go to the shop and help your father.
Dilip — OK, OK, Mum. But why me? It's the last day of my holidays too.

10 POEM The days of the week

a) *Listen to the poem. Then write it down with the days from the box.*

The days of the week

Day one of the week is ...,

Two ..., three ..., OK?

Then ... and ... and then: Hooray!

..., ... : we can play.

Tuesday
Saturday
Wednesday
Thursday
Friday
Monday
Sunday

b) *Read the poem to a partner. Are the days right?*

c) *Listen to the poem again. Can you say it?*

▸ *WB 8 (p. 7)*

11 Two newspapers for number 19

Mark Good morning, Mr Kapoor.
Mr Kapoor Good morning, Mark.
You need the newspapers for ...?
Mark Cotham Park Road, Mr Kapoor.
Mr Kapoor Right ... Cotham Park Road: one 'Times' for number 2, one for number 3, one for number 8, two for number 19 ... Ah, Dilip! Very good. You can help Mark now. And I can have breakfast.

12 The numbers

1	one	11	eleven	21	twenty-one
2	two	12	twelve	22	twenty-two
3	three	13	thirteen	30	thirty
4	four	14	fourteen	40	forty
5	five	15	fifteen	50	fifty
6	six	16	sixteen	60	sixty
7	seven	17	seventeen	70	seventy
8	eight	18	eighteen	80	eighty
9	nine	19	nineteen	90	ninety
10	ten	20	twenty	100	a hundred

13 Telephone numbers

14 POEM Numbers

Say the poem and act it out.

Numbers

One, two, three,
I can see.

Four, five, six,
I can do tricks.

Seven, eight,
Oh, I'm late!

Nine, ten,
Goodbye, then.

► *WB 9–10 (p. 8)*

15 Welcome to the Pretty Polly Bed and Breakfast

Mary, Peter and Jack Hanson
(and Polly, the parrot)
welcome you to

The
PRETTY POLLY
Bed & Breakfast
28 Cooper Street Bristol BS6 6PA
(0117) 969 22 00

Wheelchairs Families Pets

It's Monday.
Mrs Hanson is at work.
Mr Hanson is at work too.
He's at work in the Pretty Polly Bed and Breakfast.

Jack Morning, Dad.
Mr Hanson Morning? It's 12.15, Jack!
Polly 12.15! 12.15!
Jack Well, it is the last day of the holidays, Dad.
Mr Hanson Yes, half past seven tomorrow, Jack!

16 Good luck!

Mrs Schmidt Excuse me, can I say goodbye?
Mr Hanson Oh, Mrs Schmidt ...
Mrs Schmidt Your B&B is great. Thank you, Mr Hanson, and goodbye.
Polly Goodbye. Goodbye.
Mrs Schmidt Goodbye, Polly. And goodbye, Jack.
Jack Goodbye ... and a nice trip back to Germany, Mrs Schmidt.
Mrs Schmidt Thank you, Jack. And good luck with your new school.
Mr Hanson Thank you, Mrs Schmidt.
Polly Good luck! Good luck!

I can …

… say what the time is.

It's eleven o'clock.

It's quarter past …

It's half past …

It's quarter to …

It's five to …

It's eleven o'clock.

It's eleven fifteen.

It's eleven thirty.

It's eleven forty-five.

It's eleven fifty-five.

It's eleven o nine.

It's eleven twenty.

It's eleven twenty-five.

It's eleven thirty-seven.

It's eleven fifty-two.

…

DOSSIER *About me*

Start your dossier like this:

My name is …
I'm … old.
I'm from …
My favourite colours are …
My favourite day of the week is …
I like … and …
My telephone number is …

17 Now you

a) *What's the time? Say these times:*
6.05, 9.15, 4.25, 7.45, 3.40, 8.30, 12.18, 10.55, 2.36, 5.00

b) *Draw five different times on five clocks. Ask and answer.*

A: Excuse me, what's the time, please?
B: It's …
A: Thank you.
B: You're welcome.

c) *Listen. What's the time? Choose the right clock on this page. One clock is missing. Can you draw it?*

► *WB 11–13 (p. 9)*

Unit 1

New school, new friends

D

I can ...

... say lots of things in English.

What can you see in the photos?
A: I can see an apple in photo A.
B: Yes, and there's a comic in photo ...
C: And there are two bananas in ...
...

A

B

C

1 In the morning

It's 8 o'clock in the morning in Bristol and day one of the new school year.

a) *Copy the chart:*

	Ananda	Dan + Jo	Jack	Sophie
Photo				
Words				

b) *Listen. Match the photos and the names.*

c) *Listen again.*
Match words from the box to each name.

apple • baby • book • box • boy • breakfast • chair • girl • glue stick • milk • mobile phone • pen • pencil • pencil case • poltergeist • school bag • table

d) **Extra** *Try to find more words for your chart.*

2 Extra GAME

Draw one thing from the box in ***1c****. Who can guess what it is?*

A: It's a chair!

B: Yes, it is. / No, it isn't.

DOSSIER ***My school bag/My room***

What have you got in your school bag or in your room at home? Choose one. Draw and label lots of things on a piece of paper.

► P 1 (p. 25) • WB 1 (p. 10)

1 Before lessons

It's 8.30 and the new students are at school.

Dan — Look, Jo. Room 14!
Jo — OK. – You're nervous, right?
Dan — Me? No! You're nervous.
Jo — No, no.
Dan — OK. Then you go first.
Jo — No, you go first.
Dan — No, you.
Jo — No, you.
Dan — Oh, OK.

Ananda — Hi! Oh, you're twins!
Dan — Hi. Yes, we're Dan and Jo. I'm Dan, the clever twin. He's Jo, the mad twin.
Jo — Don't listen to Dan. *He's* the mad twin.

Ananda — Come and sit with me and Jack. – Hey, Jack! Here are Dan and Jo. They're twins. This is ... er ...
Dan — It's OK. I'm Dan and he's Jo.
Jack — Well, *I'm* Jack. And *she's* Ananda.

2 ACTIVITY

Write your name on a piece of paper. Put all the pieces of paper in a box. Take a piece of paper and make one or two sentences about the student.

Anton — Max: He's 11 years old. ... from Bonn.
Max — Yes, that's right. / No, that's wrong. I'm ... My turn. Eva: She's ...

Looking at language

Copy and complete.

		Singular	Plural	
First person		I'... Dan, the clever twin.	Yes, we'... Dan and Jo.	
Second person	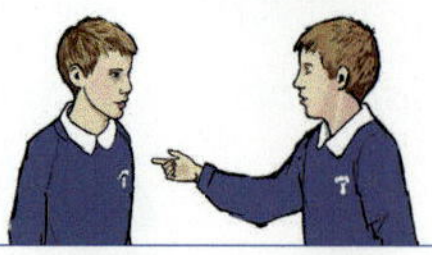	You'... nervous, right?	Oh, you'...	
Third person		He'... Jo, the ... She'... Ananda. It'...	They'...	

▸ GF 1: Personal pronouns (p. 127) • P 2–3 (pp. 25–26) • WB 2–3 (p. 11)

3 Ananda is a nice name

Dan Ananda is a nice name. Is it Indian?
Ananda Yes, it is.
Jo Are your mum and dad from India?
Ananda No, they aren't. My mum is from Bristol. My dad is from Uganda.
Jack And how old are you?
Ananda I'm 11. What about you, Jack? Are you 11 too?
Jack Yes, I am.
Jo We aren't 11. We're 12.
Jack And you're from Bristol, right?
Dan Yes, that's right.
Ananda Are your mum and dad from Bristol?
Dan Our dad, yes. But our mum ...
Jo Our mum isn't here. She's in New Zealand with her new partner. Our mum and dad aren't together.
Jack Oh, I'm sorry.
Dan I'm sorry too.
Ananda Oh look. Here's the teacher.

▸ *GF 2: (to) be (p. 128) • P 4–6 (pp. 26–27) • WB 4–6 (pp. 11–13)*

4 ACTIVITY

Make a 'be' poster for your classroom.

5 GAME

Mime things from the box.
Can your group guess?
A: Are you nervous/...?
B: Yes, I am. / No, I'm not.

a baby • a dog • happy • a house • a kite • mad • nervous • a parrot • a poltergeist • a teacher • a tree • a twin

6 Meet Mr Kingsley

Mr Kingsley — Good morning. Welcome to Cotham School. I'm your form teacher *and* your English teacher. My name is Paul Kingsley, K–I–N–G–S–L–E–Y. And you're Form 7PK: P for Paul, K for Kingsley. And now please tell me your names. Oh, and can you play football? I'm your PE teacher too! – Yes, you please.

Ananda — I'm Ananda Kapoor. I can't play football, but I can play hockey.

Mr Kingsley — Thank you, Ananda. Now you.

Sophie — My name is Sophie Carter-Brown.

Jo — Carter-Brown? One name isn't enough?

Form 7PK — Ha ha ha.

Mr Kingsley — Quiet, please. – And who are you?

Jo — I'm Jo. Jo Shaw.

Mr Kingsley — Can you play football, Jo?

Jo — Yes, I can, Mr Kingsley.

Mr Kingsley — Good. Football is good. Jokes about names are bad. Can you remember that, Jo?

Jo — Yes, Mr Kingsley.

▸ *GF 3: can (p. 129) • P 7 (p. 27) • WB 7–9 (pp. 13–14)*

7 Now you

A: Can you play football/hockey/...?
B: Yes, I can. And I can play ... too. / No, I can't. But I can play ...

badminton • basketball • ice hockey • tennis • ...

8 SONG Alphabet rap

A B C D E F G

Throw a ball, climb a tree.

H I J K L M N

Write your name, drop your pen.

O P Q R S T U

Yes, that's right. Do what I do.

V W X Y Z

Enough, enough, your face is red.

9 GAME

Write a name on a piece of paper and put it in a box. Take a piece of paper. Spell the name for your group. Can the group guess the name before you finish?

10 Timetable time

Mr Kingsley — OK, quiet please. Now, take out your exercise books. Listen and write down the timetable for today, Tuesday.
At 8.45 on Tuesday it's English with me, here in Room 14.
Then it's Geography in Room 16.

Jo — Mr Kingsley? I'm sorry. Can you spell 'Geography', please?

Mr Kingsley — That's OK, Jo. I can write it on the board:
G–E–O–G–R–A–P–H–Y.

Jo — Thank you, Mr Kingsley.

Mr Kingsley — You're welcome, Jo. After the morning break it's …

11 Form 7PK's timetable

a) *Copy the timetable and look at the subjects:*

Drama • Maths • Music • PE • RE • Science

You don't understand the words? Look in the Vocabulary.

Timetable, Form 7PK

TUESDAY

Time	Subject	Room
8.45	English	14
9.40	Geography	16
10.35	Morning break	–
10.50	…	…
11.45	…	…
12.40	Lunch break	–
1.40	…	…
2.35	…	…

b) *Now listen and complete the timetable.*

c) *Swap timetables with your partner. Listen again and check.*

► GF 4: Imperatives (p. 130) • P 9–11 (pp. 28–29) • WB 10–13 (pp. 14–16)

STUDY SKILLS Wörter lernen

Finden *Das Vocabulary (ab S. 148) gibt dir viele Informationen zu den neuen Wörtern einer Unit und hilft dir, diese Wörter zu lernen.*

Anwenden *Schau dir Seite 156 an.*
Welche Schulfächer findest du dort?
Weitere Tipps zum Wörter lernen findest du im Skills File auf den Seiten 118–119.

► SF 1 (pp. 118–119) • P 8 (p. 27) • WB 14–15 (p. 17)

12 Extra SONG Wonderful World

Listen to 'Wonderful World'.
Which school subjects from the board can you hear?

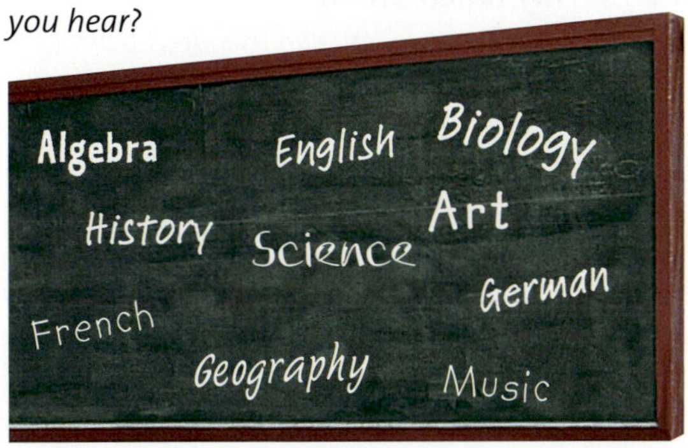

13 Lunch break

Ananda — Let's sit here.
Sophie — OK.
Jack — Hi! Can we sit with you?
Ananda — Yes, you can.
Jo — Is the food OK?
Sophie — Mmm, I've got the lasagne. It's OK.
Ananda — I've got the pizza. It's really good.
Dan — Oh, I haven't got a chair.
Ananda — Look, there's an empty chair at that table.
Sophie — Jack, do you like the Geography teacher?
Jack — The bank robber?
All — What?!
Ananda — Mr Barker isn't a bank robber!
Jack — Well, no, but he has got a face like a bank robber. I can see him on a poster: 'Wanted: bank robber'.
Sophie — Your ideas are really mad, Jack!
Jo — Hey, what have we got next?
Sophie — Music, and then Maths.
Ananda — Oh, I like Maths.
Dan + Jo — You're mad!

▸ *GF 5: have got (pp. 130–131) • P 12–15 (pp. 30–31) • WB 16–21 (pp. 18–20)*

14 My lunch break

a) *Prepare a dialogue. You can use ideas from* ***13*** *and these phrases.*

He's/She's very nice/boring/OK/…
Can I sit with you?
It's …
Yes, …
Me too. / And me.
You're mad.
Do you like …?
I like …
Is the food OK?
What have we got next?

b) *Practise your dialogue and act it out in class.*

DOSSIER ***My school***

Write about your friends, your form, your school, sports, … for your dossier.

Extra *Write your timetable in English and put it in your dossier too.*

I'm in class … at … School.
My class teacher is …
My friends are …
My favourite subjects are …
I like …, but I hate …
I can play …
…

▸ *P 16 (p. 31) • WB 22 (p. 20)*

1 WORDS What's different?

Partner B: Look at page 114.
Partner A: Look at the picture.
Find out what's different in your partner's picture.

A: There's one apple in my picture.
B: Oh, there are ... in my picture. They're green.
A: Yes, my apple is green too.
B: There are two plates in my picture.
A: Oh, there are ...
...

2 Photos (Personal pronouns)

a) *Complete the sentences with I, you, he, she, it, we or they.*

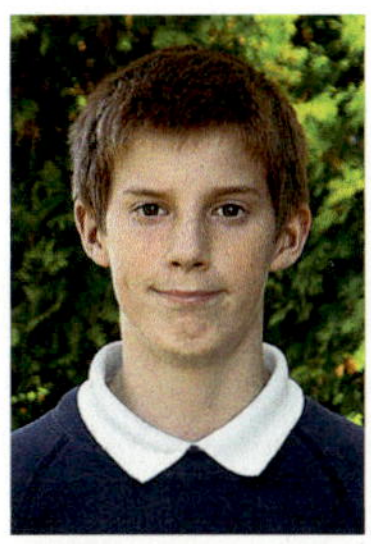
This is Jo.
He's in my form.

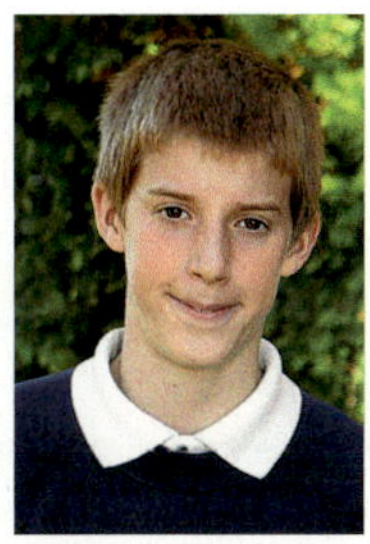
This is Dan. ...'s in my form too.

This is Dan with Jo. ...'re twins.

This is my school. ...'s very big.

This is me. ...'m at school here.

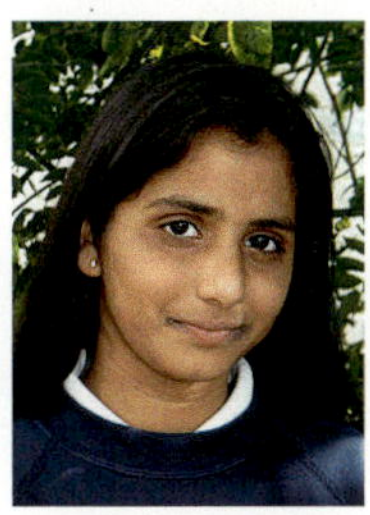
This is Ananda. ...'s very nice.

This is me with Ananda. ...'re friends.

And this is you, Dad. ...'re with Polly!

b) *Bring photos of your family and talk to your partner.*

A: This is ...
B: I'm/He's/She's/We're/They're ...
B: Who's that?
A: Is that ...?
A: Are you ...?
B: Is he/she ...?

3 The new school (Personal pronouns; be: positive statements)

a) *Complete the sentences with the correct pronouns and form of* **be** (*I'm, you're, he's, …*).
1 The new school is in Bristol. *It's* a good school.
2 Dan and Jo are at school. … nervous.
3 Ananda is there too. … nice.
4 Jo: 'Hi, … Jo. That's Dan. … my brother. … twins.'
5 Dan: '… the clever twin.'
6 Dan: 'Jo, … mad!'
7 Jack and Ananda are nice. … new friends.
8 Ananda: 'This is Jack. … my new friend.'

b) *Now complete these sentences.*
1 My school's name is … It's …
2 My new friend … He/She …

4 Prunella isn't a parrot (be: negative statements)

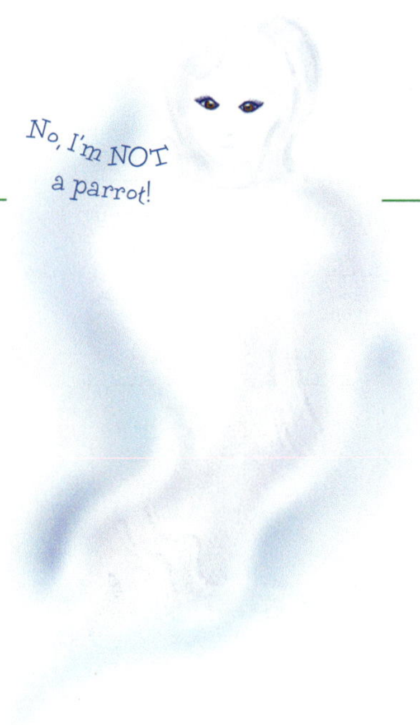

a) *Use the lists and write negative statements.*

1 *Prunella*		from Bristol
2 Polly		brother and sister
3 Dan and Jo Shaw	'm not	brothers
4 Sophie and Emily		a poltergeist
5 The new school	*isn't*	in London
6 Dilip and Ananda		sisters
7 Mr and Mrs Hanson	aren't	*a parrot*
8 I		very old
9 My friend and I		teachers

b) *Now add positive statements.*
1 Prunella isn't a parrot, *she's a poltergeist*.
2 Polly isn't …
…

5 Yes, he is. No, he isn't (be: questions and short answers)

a) *Partner A: ask your partner the questions. Partner B: choose the right answers.*

1 *Is Dilip Ananda's brother?*	Yes, she is.
2 Is Emily Sophie's sister?	*Yes, he is.*
3 Is the school a big school?	Yes, they are.
4 Are the Carter-Browns new in Bristol?	Yes, I am.
5 Are you in Form 5?	Yes, it is.

b) *Partner B: ask your partner the questions. Partner A: choose the right answers.*

1 *Is Dilip Sophie's brother?*	No, they aren't.
2 Is the house at 17 Cotham Park Road empty now?	No, she isn't.
3 Is Mrs Hanson in a wheelchair?	No, we aren't.
4 Are the twins from London?	*No, he isn't.*
5 Are you and your family in Bristol now?	No, it isn't.

6 About you (be: questions and short answers)

a) *Answer the questions.*

1 Is your mum 42?	Yes, she is. / No, she isn't.
2 Are you 12?	Yes, I am. / No, I'm not.
3 Are you and your mum friends?	Yes, we ... . / No, we ... .
4 Is your English teacher from England?	...
5 Is your school big?	
6 Are your exercise books in your school bag?	
7 Is your father a teacher?	
8 Are your mum and dad from Bristol?	
9 Are you and your friend from Germany?	

b) *Think of more questions with* **Is ...?** *and* **Are ...?** *and ask your partner.*

7 Can your English teacher sing? (can/can't)

a) *Work in groups of four. Two of you write the names of students and teachers on cards. The other two write activities on cards. The box below can help you.*

do tricks • find their/his/her school things • open and close things • play football • play hockey • sing • talk • ...

b) *Take a name card and an activity card. Ask and answer questions:*

Mr Meyer

do tricks

sing

Mrs Urban

A: Can Mr Meyer sing?
B: Yes, he can. / No, he can't.

A: Can Hanna and Paul do tricks?
B: Yes, ... / No, ...

A: Can Mrs Urban ...
B: ...

c) *Report to your form what the people on your cards can/can't do.*

Mr Meyer can't sing.
Hanna and Paul can do tricks.
Mrs Urban can't find her school things. ...

8 STUDY SKILLS Das Vocabulary

a) *Finde im Vocabulary (S. 148–153) folgende Informationen heraus.*

1 Welches Wort benutzt man mit „welcome" (S. 8) für das deutsche „willkommen *in*"?
to ▸ *S. 148: „Welcome (to Bristol). Willkommen (in Bristol)."*
2 Wie sagt man auf Englisch „auf dem Foto"? ('photo', S. 9)
3 An welcher Stelle des Satzes steht „too" (S. 8)?
4 Was ist das Gegenteil von „empty" (S. 10)?
5 Wo liegt die Betonung bei „exercise book" (S. 12)?
6 Welches ungewöhnliche Zeichen steht für die Aussprache von „th" im Wort „think" (S. 11)?
7 Was sollst du bei der Aussprache von „talk" (S. 8) beachten?
8 Welche Silbe wird im Wort „wheelchair" (S. 16) hauptsächlich betont?

b) **Extra** *Partner/in A: Schreibe drei bis vier Fragen zu den Vocabulary-Einträgen zu den Seiten 18–19. Partner/in B: Schreibe drei bis vier Fragen zu den Vocabulary-Einträgen zur Seite 20. Kannst du alle Fragen deiner Partnerin/deines Partners beantworten?*

9 LISTENING Classroom English

a) *Read the phrases. You can hear them in classrooms every day. Then listen to the CD.*

Quiet, please! • What's that in English? • Can I open/close the window, please? • Sorry, I haven't got my exercise book. • Can I help you? • Look at the picture. • What page are we on, please? • Sorry? • It's your turn. • Can I go to the toilet, please? • Write down the words on the worksheet. • Can we work with a partner? • What's for homework? • Write five sentences in your exercise book. • Can we go now, please?

b) *Who can say what? Put ticks (✔) in a copy of the chart.*

	teachers can say	students can say	students or teachers can say
Quiet, please!	✔		
What's that in English?			✔
Sorry, I haven't got my exercise book.		✔	
...			

c) *Listen again and check.*

d) *Act out little classroom scenes. One of you is the teacher. Use phrases from the box in a).*

- Es ist heiß in der Klasse.
- Es ist zu laut in der Klasse.
- Jemand hat sein Heft vergessen.
- ...

e) *ACTIVITY Make English 'classroom ladders'.*

10 Do this! Don't do that! (Imperatives)

a) *Look at the picture and complete the sentences in the speech bubbles. Use words from the box.*

1 *Sing* the song for me, please.
2 No, … to the CD.
3 …

be • climb • eat • listen • open • play • push • sing

b) **Extra** *Draw a picture. Write three sentences like in a). Can your partner complete the sentences?*

11 WORDS The new timetable

a) *Partner B: Look at page 114.*
Partner A: Not all the subjects are in your timetable. Ask your partner what they are.

A: What's lesson 1 on Monday?
B: Lesson 1 on Monday is Maths.

b) *Now answer your partner's questions.*

	Monday	Tuesday	Wednesday	Thursday	Friday
1	…	German	…	…	…
2	Science	Geography	Maths	Maths	Drama
3	Science	RE	English	English	Science
4	Drama	…	…	PE	PE
5	…	PE	Geography	PE	Music
6	English	Music	…	German	Maths

12 Jo has got a twin brother (have got/has got)

a) *Make sentences with **have got/has got**.*

1 Jo
2 The twins
3 Sophie
4 Prunella
5 The Kapoors
6 Jack
7 Ananda
8 Mr and Mrs Hanson

a nice name.
a shop.
mad ideas.
a twin brother.
a B&B.
a great dad.
a nice room.
two sisters.

1 Jo *has got* a twin brother.
2 The twins *have got* a ...
3 ...

b) *Say what they've got (✓) and what they haven't got (✗).*

	brother	*sister*
Dan	✓	✗
Jack	✗	✗
Ananda	✓	✗

Dan *has got* a brother. He *hasn't got* a sister.

c) **Extra** *Make a chart like in b). Talk to different people in your class. Find out what they've got or haven't got. Report to the class.*

You — Have you got a brother?
Partner — Yes, I have. I've got two. What about you?
You — I've got one brother. Have you got a sister?
Partner — No, I haven't. ...

Hannah *has got* two brothers.
But she *hasn't got* a sister. And she ...

13 GAME What have you got?

Nils — I've got a blue pencil case. Laura, have you got a blue pencil case too?
Laura — Yes, I have. Malek, have you got a blue pencil case too?
Malek — No, I haven't. But I ... a blue school bag. Maja, ... you ... a blue school bag too?
Maja — No, I ... But ... a red school bag. Lukas, ...?

14 PRONUNCIATION 'a' [ə] or 'an' [ən]?

a) *Listen and read:*

An apple, a green apple, an English apple, a red English apple, an old apple, a brown apple: Ugh!

*When is it **a**? When is it **an**?*

Before a vowel sound it's ...
Before a consonant sound it's ...

b) *Write these words with **a** or **an**:*

rubber • English teacher • blue ball • orange chair • pencil case • felt tip • happy mum • exercise book • old house • student • empty box

c) *Listen and check your answers.*

d) *Is it **a** or **an** before **MP3 player**? And before **uniform**? Why?*

15 PRONUNCIATION 'the' with [ə] or [i]?

a) *When is* **the** *with* [ə]*? When is* **the** *with* [i]*?*
Before … it's … and before … it's …

Listen.

For **the** *with* [ə]:

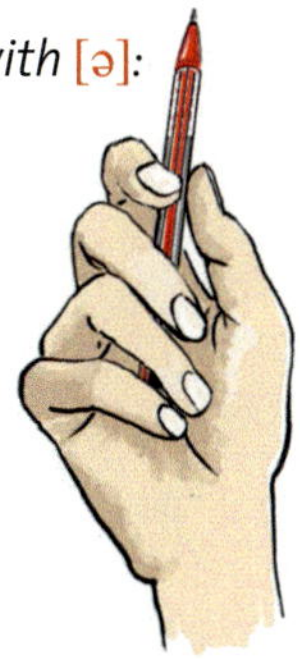

For **the** *with* [i]:

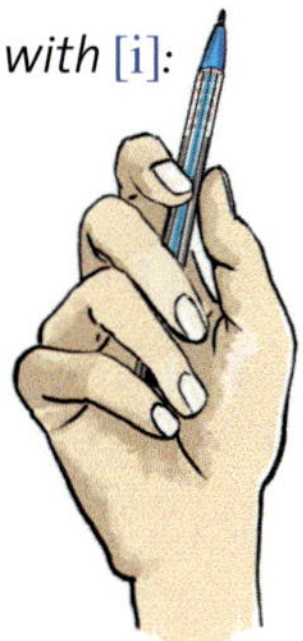

b) *Listen to the poem. Can you say it too?*

Going to school

An English breakfast, a boy and a girl,
An orange school bag, a big red bus,
The empty classroom, the exercise books,
The chairs, the tables, the board – and us!

16 GETTING BY IN ENGLISH Meeting new friends

a) *Can you say these things in English?*

1 Hallo, ich bin Dan. (p. 20)
2 Danke. – Gern geschehen. (p. 23)
3 Können wir uns zu euch setzen? (p. 24)
4 Magst du den Erdkundelehrer? (p. 24)
5 Ich mag Mathe. (p. 24)
6 Du bist verrückt. (p. 24)

b) *Make a dialogue. Use the words from a).*

A: Grüße B und sag, wie du heißt.
B: Grüße zurück und sag, wer du bist.
A: Schlag vor, dass ihr zusammensitzt.
B: Bedanke dich.
A: Frag B, wie alt er/sie ist.
B: Antworte und frag dasselbe.
A: Antworte. Frag, ob er/sie Englisch mag.
B: Sag, dass du Englisch magst, aber dass dein Lieblingsfach Mathe ist.
A: Sag, dass er/sie verrückt ist.

c) *Act out your dialogue.*

STUDY SKILLS Stop – Check – Go

*Es ist wichtig, dass du manchmal kurz anhältst (**Stop**) und dich fragst, was du gelernt hast (**Check**). Dann überlege, wie es am besten weitergeht (**Go**). Also etwa so:*

Stop *Einmal pro Unit, z.B. jetzt für Unit 1.*

Check *Kenne ich wirklich die Vokabeln aus Unit 1? (Lass dich zehn Wörter abfragen!)*
Kann ich die Grammatik von Unit 1?
Kann ich jemandem sagen, dass er etwas nicht tun soll?
Kann ich einen Mini-Dialog zum Thema „New friends" schreiben?

Damit du nicht vergisst, dich zu „checken", wirst du am Ende jeder Unit daran erinnert: **Checkpoint** ► *im Workbook*

Go *Was kannst du besser machen?*
Tipps dafür findest du auf Seite 120.

► *SF 2 (p. 120)*

Checkpoint 1 ► *WB (p. 23)*

How's the new school?

It's 3.30 and it's the end of school for today.

1

2

3

4

5

6

Ananda, how was the first day at your new school?
They're great! Jo and Dan are twins – they're very nice, and you really can't see who is Jo and ...
7
Good, thank you, Mrs Smith.
Hello, Mrs Smith. 'Computer World'?
I like the uniform! Thank you, Mrs Kapoor. See you.
8
Well, go on, go on. Jo and Dan and ...?
Then there's Jack. He's very nice and his mad ideas are great!
9
A packet of mints, please. Oh, your little girl is at Cotham now!
Yes, first day today.
Bye, then.
10
Bye, Mr Brown, and thank you. Now, Ananda, tell me more: Are there girls in your form too?
Little girl, tell Mum everything!
11
There's a very nice girl. Her name is Sophie. Her sister Emily isn't nice, but she's very pretty and Dilip likes her ... a lot!
12

Working with the text

1 Who is it?

Match the speech bubbles to the photos. Then put everything in the right order.

Mrs Kapoor

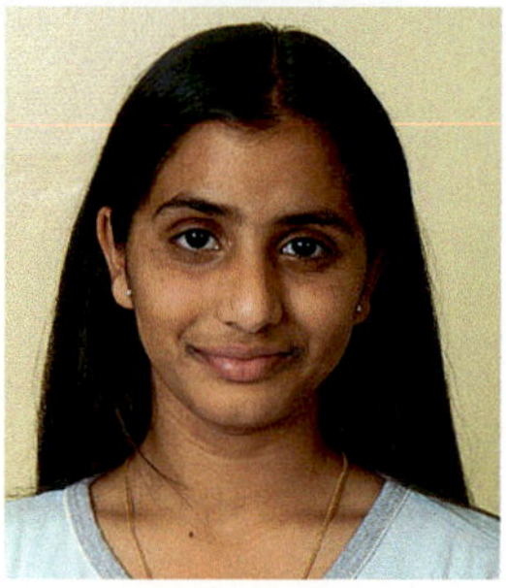
Ananda

A He's very nice too.

B Jo and Dan are twins.

C Hi, Mum. I need my tea.

D Are there girls in your form too?

E Is the teacher nice?

F First tell me about your classmates.

G Dilip, who is this Emily?

H There's a very nice girl.

2 After the first day at the new school

a) *Write a dialogue for Jack and his dad. You can use phrases from* **1**.

Mr Hanson ___ Tell me about your new form.
Jack ___ The form is ...
Mr Hanson ___ And who is your form t...?
Jack ___ His name ...

b) **Extra** *Write a dialogue for Sophie and Prunella.*

c) *Act out your dialogue(s) for the class.*

3 Extra Now you

Write about your school. You can look at p. 24 (DOSSIER) and the photo story for ideas.

► WB 23 (p. 21)

Make a birthday calendar

I can ...

... say when my birthday is.

My birthday is in May. When's your birthday?
My mum's/brother's/sister's/dad's/friend's/ ... birthday is in ...

...

1 Months of the year

a) *Find the missing letters and write the months in the right order. Use a nice colour for your birthday month. Check with a partner.*

A: What's month number one?
B: Number one is January. What's month number two?

Mark where the words are different from the German words. January

Janu__ • Mar__ • Jun__ • O__ber • De__ber • Ma__ • Feb__ • Sep__ • Nov__ • Ap__ • Jul__ • Aug__

__ust • __ril • __ary • __cem__ • __y • __cto__ • __ember • __y • __e • __ch • __tember • __ruary

b) *Now listen to the 'Calendar Song' and check: is the order right? Can you say the months in English? Say a month with A__, J__, M__, ...*

2 Dates

a) *Listen. Then read out loud.*

1st	first	12th	twelfth
2nd	second	13th	thirteenth
3rd	third	14th	fourteenth
4th	fourth	...	
5th	fifth	20th	twentieth
6th	sixth	21st	twenty-first
7th	seventh	22nd	twenty-second
8th	eighth	23rd	twenty-third
9th	ninth	...	
10th	tenth	30th	thirtieth
11th	eleventh	31st	thirty-first

You write:	You say:
9th April	the ninth of April
on 31st May 1998	on the thirty-first of May nineteen ninety-eight
2005	two thousand and five

b) *Say these dates:*
12th February, 18th July, 20th May, 3rd April, 2007, 22nd September, 1899

3 GAME When's your birthday?

Talk to different students:

A: My birthday is on 13th June. When's your birthday?
B: It's on ...
A: What's the date today?
B: It's ...

► WB 24–26 (p. 22), Activity page 1

4 ACTIVITY The birthday calendar

Make a card about yourself for the class birthday calendar.

A weekend at home

I can …

… talk to my partner about my home:

- I live in a … What about you?
- There are … rooms in my/our … What about your home?
- In my/our room there's …/there are …
- I've got a nice/big/… room.
- I share a bedroom with my sister/… What about you?

…

Homes for people …

1 House or flat?

a) Can you remember?

The Shaws live in a …
The Kapoors live in a …
The Hansons …
The Carter-Browns …

b) **Extra** *Listen and check.*

2 Now you

Bring a picture of your room to school. Tell different partners about it.

DOSSIER ***My room***

Label your picture.
Put it in your dossier.

► WB 1–2 (p. 24)

A a hutch in the garden

B a cage in the living room

… and homes for pets

C a cage in the living room

D a basket in the kitchen

E a basket in the bedroom

3 Where are the pets?

a) *Say where the pets are.*

The rabbits are in a hutch …

The dog is in …

b) *Listen. Put ticks (✓) in a copy of the chart. Then fill in the name of the owner.*

	cat	parrot	rabbit	dog	hamster	owner
Sheeba				✓		Sophie
Hip and Hop						
Harry						
Polly						
Bill and Ben						

c) **Extra** *Write three sentences about the Bristol pets. Compare with a partner.*

4 Now you

Talk to a partner about pets.

budgie • cat • dog • fish • guinea pig • hamster • horse • mouse • parrot • rabbit • tortoise

A: We've got a/two …
His/Her name is … / Their names are …
He's/She's two years old/…
They are black/…
What about you?

B: We haven't got a pet, but my friend has got a …
His/Her name is …

► *WB 3–4 (p. 25)*

I can …

… sing and act the song 'This is the way I …'

• • •

1 Friday afternoon

Ananda Have you got plans for the weekend?

Jack Well, we've got that essay for Mr Kingsley: 'A day in the life of …'

Jo Oh, that's easy! Listen: 'A day in the life of Jo Shaw. I get up at 7.15 every morning. Then I clean my teeth.'

Dan No, no, no. I get up at 7.15, you sleep. I clean my teeth, you sleep. I wash my hands and face, you sleep. You get up at 7.45.

Jo OK, OK. 'We go to the kitchen and have breakfast. Then we go to school.' The end.

Jack You two write boring essays. – Oh, there's my bus! Bye!

All Bye, Jack.

▸ *GF 6: Plural (pp. 131–132) • P 1–2 (p. 42) • WB 5–6 (p. 26)*

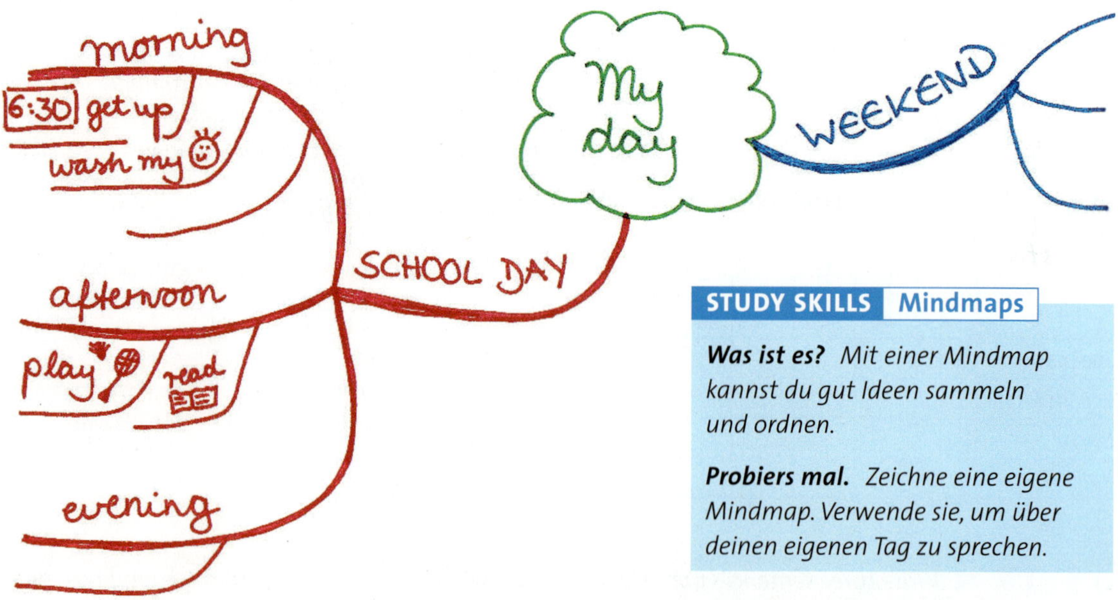

STUDY SKILLS Mindmaps

Was ist es? *Mit einer Mindmap kannst du gut Ideen sammeln und ordnen.*

Probiers mal. *Zeichne eine eigene Mindmap. Verwende sie, um über deinen eigenen Tag zu sprechen.*

▸ *SF 3 (p. 121) • P 3 (p. 42) • WB 7 (p. 27)*

2 On Saturday mornings

On Saturday mornings Sophie gets up at 9 o'clock. She gets dressed and tidies her room. Then she gives the pets their breakfast. Every Saturday – boring!
First she feeds Sheeba, the dog. Sheeba eats meat and drinks water. I push Sheeba's bowl and – splash! – there's water everywhere. 'Bad dog!' says Sophie.
Then she goes to the living room and feeds Harry, the hamster. He likes toast and carrots and water. Sometimes Toby tries to help Sophie. He cleans the cage and puts hay in it. I put the carrots in the hay. 'Oh, Toby, don't put the carrots there!' says Sophie.
After that Sophie goes to the rabbit hutch.

It's in the garden. Sophie feeds Hip and Hop. They like rabbit food, carrots and water. Sophie watches the pets. Then she has *her* breakfast. Please, Sophie, not the pets this Saturday! Let's play!

Looking at language

a) *Copy the chart and complete the sentences from **1** and **2**.*

	Singular	Plural
1st person	I ... up at 7.15 every morning.	Then we ... to school.
2nd person	You ... up at 7.45.	You two ... boring essays.
3rd person	Sophie ... up at 9 o'clock.	They ... rabbit food and carrots.

b) *What's different in the 3rd person singular (he, she, it)?*

▸ *GF 7a–b: Simple present (pp. 132–133) • P 4–8 (pp. 43–44) • WB 8–10 (pp. 27–28)*

3 POEM My fish Wanda

My fish Wanda

My fish Wanda, she's OK.
She lives in a bowl and she plays all day.
She eats fish food and drinks and drinks.
I really wonder what she thinks.

Practise the poem with a partner. Then read it to the class.

4 Extra Now you

Write a poem about a pet. Learn your poem and say it in class. Make a 'poems poster' for your classroom wall or put your poem in your DOSSIER.

My	dog hamster ...	Hasso Hannelore ...	he's she's	OK.

He She	lives in	our house a cage ...	and ...	he she	sleeps plays ...	all day.

He She	eats	meat carrots ...	and drinks and drinks.

I really wonder what	he she	thinks.

5 Saturday afternoon

Prunella — Can I help you with your homework, Sophie?
Sophie — No thanks, Prunella. I don't need your help.
Prunella — You don't like me.
Sophie — Of course I like you, Prunella. But I really don't need your help.
Prunella — Well, can I see your essay?
Sophie — Yes, here you are.
Prunella — 'A day in the life of the Carter-Brown family.' Hmm ... This is all wrong, Sophie.
Sophie — Wrong? Why?
Prunella — Look here: 'My sister Emily and I sometimes argue.' Sometimes? You don't argue sometimes – you argue all the time.
Prunella — And here: 'My brother Toby does judo on Saturdays.' He doesn't do judo on Saturdays – he plays football on Saturdays.
And here: 'My mum and dad go to bed early.' They don't go to bed early. They watch TV till 11.30 every night! Sorry, Sophie. This isn't very good.
Sophie — No?
Prunella — No. Let's write a new essay. We don't need the old essay.
Sophie — No?
Prunella — No!

Looking at language

a) *Complete these sentences from **5**:*
I ***don't need*** your help.
You ... me.
He ... judo on Saturdays.
We ... the old essay.
You ... sometimes.
They ... to bed early.

b) *How do you make the negative sentences? What's different in the 3rd person singular?*

6 GAME My friend Nora

Play the game like this:
A: My friend Nora likes numbers. But she doesn't like letters. Your turn.
B: My friend Nora likes November. But she doesn't like December.
C: My friend Nora likes no. But she doesn't like yes.

Go on.
You can play the game with different names:
Heike, Patrick, ...

► *GF 7c: Negative statements (p. 134) • P 9–11 (p. 45) • WB 11–14 (pp. 28–30)*

7 Sunday afternoon: Tea at the Shaws' house

Grandma — Well boys, here's your family tree. Look. Your grandparents are at the top: Grandpa and me, and your Grandpa and Grandma Shaw.

Dan — And the cross is there because Grandpa Shaw is dead, right?

Grandpa — Right.

Grandma — And here are our children: one son, two daughters.

Jo — Oh yes, here's Uncle Harry, Mum's brother. And here's Aunt Elizabeth, her sister. And here's our mum, Catherine.

Grandpa — Yes, Jonah.

Grandma — And Harry is married to your Aunt Jane, and here are your cousins, Anne and Mark.

Dan — And you're their grandparents too. So you've got five grandchildren.

Grandpa — Yes: all one big happy family.

Dan — One big happy family?

Grandpa — Yes, Daniel: children and parents – married, single or divorced – they're all family.

Dan — A family without a mum!

Jo — We've got a mum. She just isn't here.

Dan — Yeah, right.

► *GF 8–9: Possessive determiners, possessive form (pp. 134–135) • P 12–14 (p. 46) • WB 15–18 (pp. 30–32)*

8 Now you

a) *Bring photos of your family to school and talk to different partners about them.*

This is my … / Here's a photo of my …
That's …
Is that your …?
Who's the man/woman/boy/girl in …?
Who's that? / What's his/her name?

b) **Extra** *Use your photos and make your family tree and label it. You can put it in your DOSSIER. Or make your 'dream-family tree' with photos of you and your favourite stars.*

► *P 15–16 (p. 47)*

1 REVISION Bristol people (Personal pronouns)

Match these sentences.

1. 'My name is Mr Kingsley.'
2. This is Sophie.
3. The house is quiet.
4. 'Ananda and I are at Cotham School.'
5. 'No, Dan and Jo!'
6. Mr Kingsley is Ananda's form teacher.
7. Dan and Jo are twins from Bristol.

'We're in Form 7PK.'
'You can't have MP3 players.'
'I'm your new English teacher.'
He's nice.
They're twelve years old.
She's new in Bristol.
It's empty.

2 PRONUNCIATION Plurals

a) *Is the '-s' like this?*

Or is it like this?

Or is the end of the word like the word 'is'?

Copy the chart. Say the words from the box and put them in the chart.

[-s]	[-z]	[-ɪz]
boats	beds	boxes

beds • boats • books • boxes • boys • budgies • cats • cages • colours • dogs • friends • hutches • months • pages • pencil cases • plans • raps • shops • streets • things

b) *Swap charts. Listen and check.*

3 STUDY SKILLS Mind maps

a) *Make a mind map about pets. Start with these words.*

cage • cat • do tricks • fish • hamster • homes • hutch • play • what they do • what they eat and drink

b) *Talk to a partner about pets. You can use ideas from your mind map.*

Lots of students in our class have got pets.
There are dogs and cats and ...
Rabbits/... live in .../do tricks/...
You can ... with a dog/...
Hamsters/... eat ...

4 Weekends (Simple present: positive statements)

a) *Make sentences.*

We	play football in the park	
Our friends	watch TV	every weekend.
I	play computer games	every Saturday.
My mum and dad	go to bed late	every Sunday.
They	do boring things	

b) *Write four sentences about your weekends.*

5 PRONUNCIATION The '-s' in the simple present

a) *Read the poem.*

b) *Copy the poem. Use different colours for the different '-s' sounds:*
[-s] [-z] [-ɪz]

c) *Listen and check.*

6 Every day after school (Simple present: positive statements)

a) *Say what these people do every day after school.*

1 Jo *plays* *(play)* football every day after school.

2 Jack ... *(feed)* Polly ...

3 Ananda ... *(eat)* an apple ...

4 Dan ... *(play)* computer games ...

5 Sophie ... *(read)* a book ...

6 Dilip ... *(listen to)* music ...

7 Jack ... *(write)* e-mails ...

8 Prunella ... *(open)* and ... *(close)* things every day.

b) *What about you? Work in groups of six. Make a chain.*
Timo: I play football every day.
Anna: Timo plays football and I talk to my friends every day.
Lena: Timo plays football and Anna talks to her friends and I ... every day. ...

7 What they do every day (Simple present: positive statements)

a) *Partner B: Go to page 114. Partner A: Look at the chart below. Find out about Ananda.*

A: Jack gets up at 7 o'clock.
What about Ananda?

B: Ananda gets up at …

b) *What about you? Complete a copy of the chart. Then talk to your partner.*

A: I get up at … What about you?

B: I get up at … I get dressed at …
What …

c) **Extra** *Write about your partner's day.*

	Jack	*Ananda*	*You*	*Your partner*
get up	*at 7.00*	…	…	…
get dressed	*at 7.15*	…	…	…
have breakfast	*at 7.20*	…	…	…
clean teeth	*at 7.45*	…	…	
come home from school	*at 4.00*	…		
listen to CDs	*at 6.15*			
go to bed	*at 9.00*			

8 LISTENING At the pet shop

a) *Look at the picture for two minutes. Then close your book. What's in the window?*

A: There are three rabbits in a hutch.

B: And a brown dog in …

b) *Make a list of the pets in the window.*
3 rabbits, 2 …

c) *The next day six pets aren't there. What are they? Listen to Dan and Jo.*

9 WORDS Clean a sandwich?

Which words can go with these verbs? Which can't? Write three sentences like these:
Our teacher cleans the board. I clean my pet's cage. You can't clean a sandwich.

1 clean | a cage / a sandwich / the board

2 write | an essay / a book / a picture

3 listen to | the teacher / a lamp / a CD

4 go to | the shops / homework / school

5 play | a book / a computer game / football

6 live | in a house / at 13 Paul Road / on a shelf

10 I don't, he doesn't (Simple present: negative statements)

***a)** Complete the dialogue with **don't** + verb.*

Ananda I *don't like* *(like)* our Drama teacher.
Dilip You ... *(like)* him? But he's nice.
Ananda Well you ... *(see)* him for Drama every day.
Dilip No, we ... *(do)* Drama with him. We've got him for football.
Ananda Well, the girls at Cotham ... *(play)* football. They play hockey.
Dilip Of course you ... *(play)* football. You're girls.
Ananda Dilip! I really ... *(like)* big brothers!
Dilip Sorry, Ananda.

***b)** Complete the dialogue with **doesn't** and one of these verbs:*

eat • live • like • need • sleep • work

1 Prunella is a poltergeist. She *doesn't sleep* in a bed.
2 Ben is a cat. He ... in a hutch.
3 Polly is a parrot. She ... hamburgers.
4 Sophie ... Prunella's help.
5 Prunella is Sophie's friend, but she ... Emily.
6 Sophie's mum is a doctor. She ... at home.
7 Dan and Jo's mum is in New Zealand. She ... in England.

11 Can you remember? – A quiz (Simple present: positive and negative statements)

***a)** Correct the sentences. Use **doesn't** or **don't** + verb.*

1 Mrs Hanson lives in New Zealand.
Mrs Hanson doesn't live in New Zealand. She lives in England.
2 The Kapoors live in a flat over a B&B.
The Kapoors don't ...
3 Mr Shaw sits in a wheelchair.
4 Jo likes Maths.
5 Polly sleeps in a hutch in the garden.
6 Sophie gives the pets their breakfast after her breakfast.
7 Toby helps Emily with the pets on Saturdays.
8 Sophie and Emily sometimes argue.
9 Jo gets up at 7.15.
10 Ananda plays football at school.

***b)** Make a quiz with a partner. Write three wrong sentences about people in the book and three wrong sentences about your classmates. Swap quizzes with different partners. Can you correct all the sentences?*

12 WORDS The right word

Complete the sentences with words from the box.

about • at • in • of • on • over • to • with

1 Please listen *to* this CD. Then we can talk ... it.
2 Can I talk ... you? I need help ... my homework.
3 The Kapoors live ... 13 Paul Road. They live ... a flat ... the shop.
4 Let's go ... the shops and look ... T-shirts.
5 Welcome ... Cotham. I play ... the school band.
6 It's an essay: A day ... the life ... Polly the Parrot.
7 We've got Science ... Tuesdays ... Room 6.

13 WORDS The fourth word

a) *Find the fourth word.*

1 father – mother
son – *daughter*
2 grandpa – grandma
uncle – ?
3 Mr Hanson – married
Mr Shaw – ?
4 mum – mother
dad – ?
5 cousin – aunt and uncle
child – ?
6 play – hockey
? – judo
7 fish – bowl
rabbit – ?
8 one – first
three – ?
9 April – May
? – January

b) *Put more words in groups of four like in a). Use words from the box.*

ball • carrots • climb • close • drink • eat • open • pull • push • throw • tree • water

1 open – close
push – p...

2 throw – ...

3 eat – ...

14 My home, your home (Possessive determiners)

a) *Fill in* **my** *(3x),* **your**, **his** *(3x),* **her**, **its**, **our**, **their**

1 The Hansons have got a B&B. ... name is Pretty Polly Bed and Breakfast.
2 They've got five bedrooms in ... house.
3 Jack can see lots of houses from ... room.
4 Jack: 'I like ... room. It's little. But ... house is big. What about ... house, Sophie?'
5 Sophie: 'We live in a big house too. ... room is pink and very nice.'
6 Jack: 'Have you got a pet? ... pet is a parrot.'
7 Sophie: 'Yes, we've got a hamster. ... name is Harry. And a dog – ... name is Sheeba. Oh, here's my brother. ... name is Toby.'

*b) Write about your home, your room, your pet(s), your family. Use possessive determiners (**my, your, his, her, ...**).*
We live in a flat. Our flat is ... My brother has got a dog. His name is ...

c) **Extra** *Tell your class or different partners about your house, room and pets.*

15 The Shaws' garden (Possessive form)

Follow the lines and write down what's what.
That's the Shaws' garden. That's Polly's ...

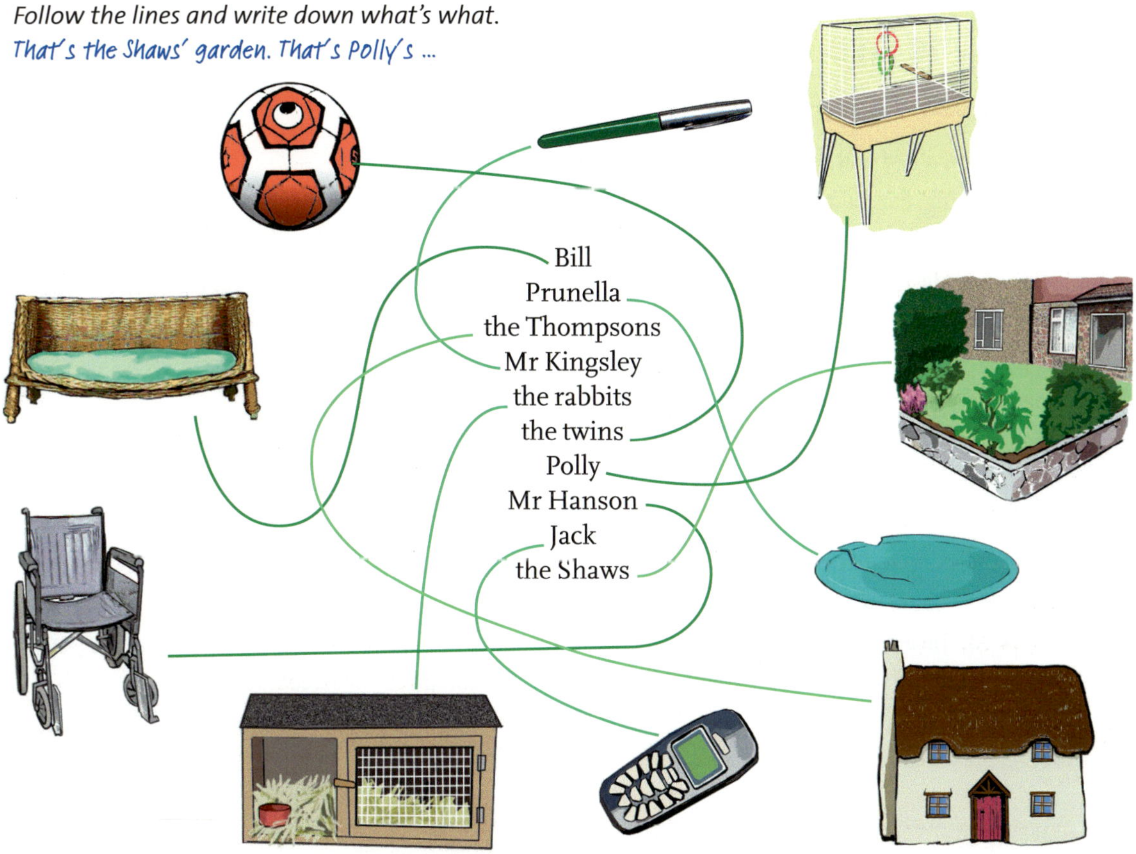

16 GETTING BY IN ENGLISH English guests

a) *Can you say these things in English?*

1 Hast du am Wochenende etwas vor? (p. 38)
2 frühstücken (p. 38)
3 Kann ich dir bei deinen Hausaufgaben helfen? (p. 40)
4 Nein danke. Ich brauche deine Hilfe nicht. (p. 40)

b) *Partner A: English guests are at your home. You are there when they come.*
Partner B: You and your parents are English guests at Partner A's home.
Use words from a) and make a dialogue.

A: Heiße die Familie willkommen.
B: Bedanke dich.
A: Frag, ob du ihnen mit ihren Taschen helfen kannst.
B: Sag danke, aber ihr braucht keine Hilfe.
A: Frag, ob sie am Wochenende etwas vorhaben.
B: Sag, dass ihr keine Pläne habt. Frage, ob A eine gute Idee hat.
A: Sag ja, und deine Eltern haben auch gute Ideen.
B: Sag, dass du das großartig findest.
A: Sag, dass ihr samstags um halb neun frühstückt.
B: Sag, dass das eine gute Zeit ist.

c) *Practise your dialogue and act it out in class.*

A day in the life of ...

A day in the life of Jack Hanson

by Jack Hanson

My family has got a bed and breakfast. We get up early every morning. First I make my bed and have my shower. And then I get things ready for breakfast: the table in the kitchen for the family, the table in the living room for the guests.

After breakfast I go to school. I'm at home again at 4 o'clock. Then I do my homework, or I help my parents.

Lots of interesting people come to the Pretty Polly B&B: families from other countries, film stars and bank robbers. We've got a new guest, Mr Green. I think he's a bank robber. Or a spy. He wears sunglasses all day! And he doesn't talk to us. It all fits.

After my homework I watch TV. Then I play games on my computer or listen to music or write stories. I go to bed at 9 o'clock.

A day in the 'life' of a poltergeist

by Prunella the poltergeist

I don't get up in the morning. I don't sleep. I'm a poltergeist!

At 1 o'clock in the morning I go to Mr and Mrs Carter-Brown's room. I open the window. At 2 o'clock, Mr Carter-Brown gets up and closes it. Then he and Mrs Carter-Brown argue. 'You open the window every night,' he says. 'You're mad,' she says. Hee, hee, hee!

At 3 o'clock I go to Emily's room. I don't like Emily. She isn't nice to her sister Sophie. Sophie is my friend. I open Emily's school bag. Then I drop it. After that, Emily can't sleep. Hee, hee, hee!

At 7.30 I go to Sophie's room. 'Sophie, get up! It's time for school!' But she can't hear me. She just sleeps and sleeps. Then I push and pull her bed. Or I drop her books. Or her alarm clock. She doesn't need an alarm clock. She has got me! Hee, hee, he

Extra

A day in the life of Bill and Ben

by Daniel Shaw

Bill and Ben are cats. Every morning after breakfast I open the door for them. Then Bill and Ben go out.

First the two cats go to the park. They play their favourite game, 'Chase the birds'.

After the game, Bill and Ben are hungry and thirsty. They find lots of water in the park, but no food. Then they go to the shops. Their favourite shop is Mr King's fish shop. Bill and Ben like fish a lot.

They watch Mr King. They watch and watch. Then Ben gives the signal. He goes to Mr King and miaows. 'I'm hungry,' he miaows. But Mr King doesn't give Ben a fish. He chases him.

Ben runs away. Bill runs too. But he runs to the shop. He takes a fish before Mr King sees him. And then he runs to the park again. Bill and Ben have a great lunch. Then they sleep. And after that they go home and wait for Jo and me.

Working with the text

1 Right or wrong?

Correct the wrong statements.

Jack's essay

1. Jack's family has got a little shop.
   Wrong. They've got a B&B.
2. Jack helps at the B&B before school.
3. Jack doesn't help the guests.
4. The Hansons have got a new guest.
5. Jack thinks Mr Green is a spy.

Prunella's essay

1. Prunella gets up early every day.
2. Mr and Mrs Carter-Brown argue. That makes Prunella happy.
3. Sophie needs a new alarm clock.

Extra Dan's essay

1. Bill and Ben play 'Chase the dogs' in the park.
2. Mr King likes cats in his shop.
3. After lunch Bill and Ben sleep in the park.

2 Now you

Say what you think about the essays. Use words from the box. Start like this:

I think Jack's/… essay is/isn't …

I like/don't like it because it's/it isn't …

boring • clever • mad • difficult • easy • good • interesting

3 Extra Imagine

Imagine you're one of these people and write an essay: Mr Green, Emily, Bill, Ben.

Don't say who you are. Can your classmates guess?

4 Your essay

a) *Write an essay: 'A day in the life of …'. Use words and phrases like* ***first, then, after that, at 9.15, in the morning/afternoon/evening****, …*

Use your mind map from p. 38 again for help.

b) *Swap essays with a partner. Correct your partner's essay with a pencil. You can draw a picture for your essay and put it in your DOSSIER.*

► WB 19 (p. 33) **Checkpoint 2** ► WB (p. 35)

A tour of the house

Go on a tour of the Carter-Browns' house with Prunella and her uncle, Sir Henry. Then you can tell a partner about your dream house.

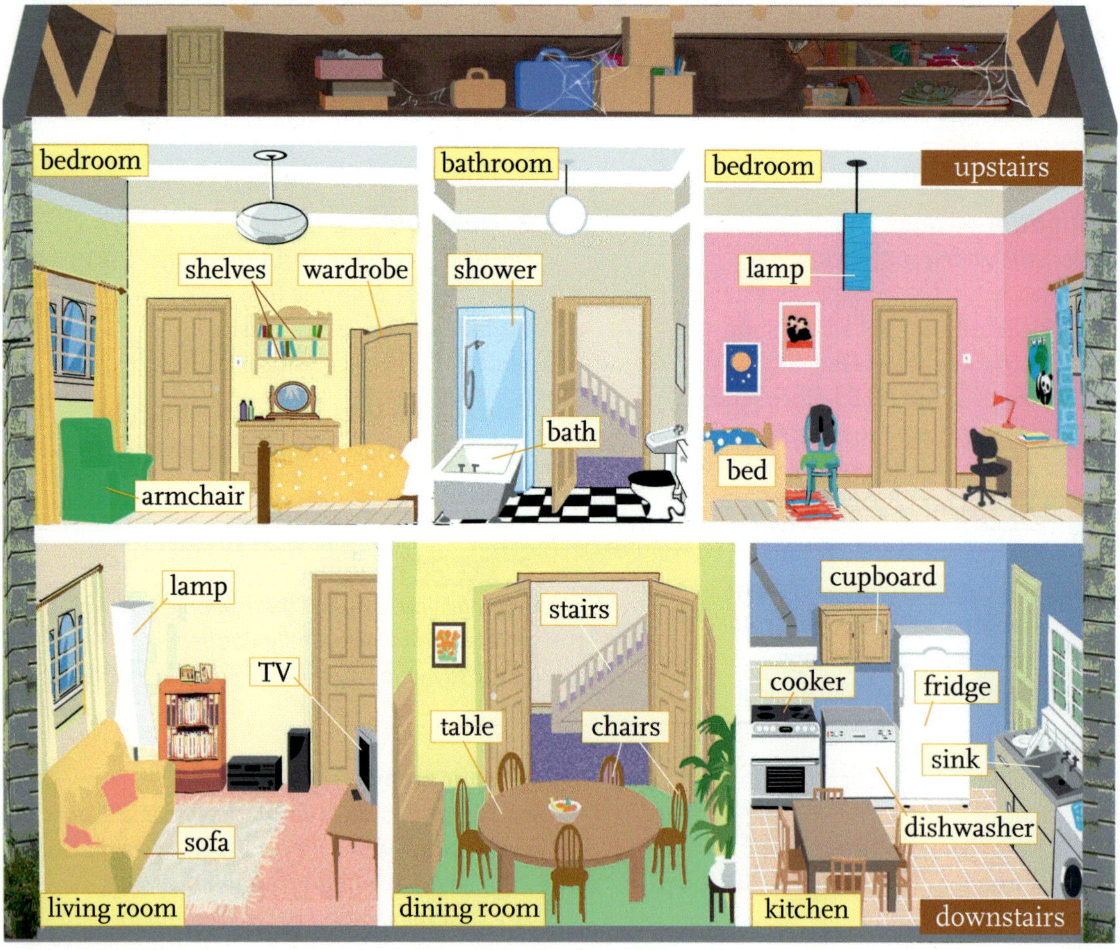

1 Sophie's home

Ask a partner questions about the Carter-Browns' house:
What colour is the bedroom/fridge/...? / Where is the dishwasher/...? / What can you find in the ... room? / What's upstairs/...?

2 Prunella's tour of the house

a) *Look at Prunella's dialogue with her uncle. What are the missing words ★?*

Sir Henry – Can I see the house then?
Prunella – Yes, Uncle Henry. Come with me. This is the living room. The family sits here in the evenings. They talk, listen to music or watch ★.
Sir Henry – ★? What's that?
Prunella – That box there. That's the ★.
Sir Henry – And they sit and watch the box? Very strange!
Prunella – Well, not really. You see, er ... well, yes, it is strange.
Sir Henry – I like the yellow ★. It looks very comfortable.
Prunella – Yes, Mrs Carter-Brown sits on the yellow ★. The children sometimes sit on the floor.
Sir Henry – When they watch the box?
Prunella – Yes, that's right. And this is the kitchen.
Sir Henry – Oh! This looks very different. Is that big white thing a wardrobe?
Prunella – The big white thing? Oh, that's the ★.
Sir Henry – The what?
Prunella – The ★. You put food in there. It's cold.
Sir Henry – But why? I like my food hot.
Prunella – You like your food hot? Then you can put it on the ★.
Sir Henry – The ★?! Is that that thing over there?
Prunella – Yes, Uncle Henry. That's the ★.
Sir Henry – Hmm ... A ★ – interesting: ★ ... And after they eat, they do the dishes here in the sink, right?
Prunella – No, they don't. They put them in the ★. That's this box here.
Sir Henry – ★? *People* don't do the dishes?
Prunella – Well, now people have got ★. You put the dishes in the ★ and, after an hour, they're clean.
Sir Henry – That's great! So why have they got a sink?

b) *Listen and check.*

3 Your dream house

a) *Draw or paint your dream house. You can have a fridge in the bedroom – it's your dream!*

b) *Collect words for your dream house from page 50 and **2**. Put them in a network.*

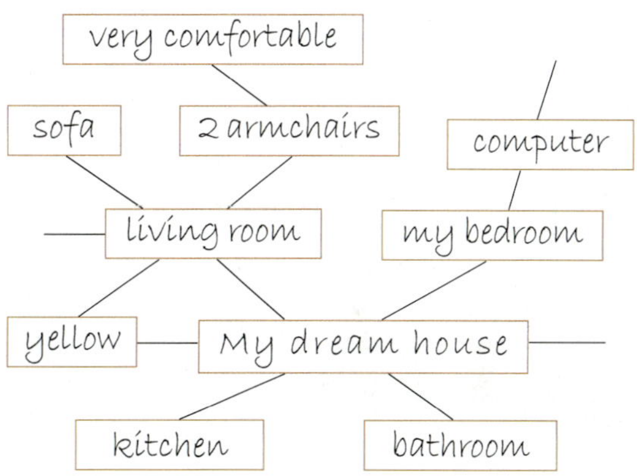

c) *Use your picture and your network and take Sir Henry (your partner) on a tour of your dream house. Answer Sir Henry's questions about your dream house. Look at Prunella's tour and below for help.*

Come with me, please.
This is the ...
This is my/my sister's/...
My bedroom is ...
Look at ...
It's very nice/warm/big/comfortable/...
What's a ...?
A computer/... – what's that?
That's funny/strange/...

▸ *WB 20 (p. 34)*

Sports and hobbies

I can ...

... talk to a partner about my sports and hobbies.

A: After school I play ... And on Mondays I go to ... What about you?
B: I play/read/listen to/watch/go to ... in my free time.
A: And your friend/brother/...?
B: Oh, he/she ...
...

Form 7PK

Our sports and hobbies

1

2

4

3

5

6

7

8

1 Form 7PK's hobbies

a) *Write the numbers 1–8. Then look at the pictures. Match the activities from the blue box to the numbers and then to the verbs from the green box.*

dancing lessons • football • the guitar • hockey • models • riding • stamps/cards • swimming

collect • go (2x) • go to • make • play (3x)

1 – play football
2 – ...

b) *Listen and check.*

c) *Listen again and add the names to your list from a).*

Ananda • Anne • Dan and Jo • Jack • Jo • Michelle • Simon • Sophie

d) *Write a sentence for each picture.*
1 – Jo plays football a lot.

e) *Check your sentences with a partner.*

▸ P 1–3 (p. 58) • WB 1–2 (p. 36)

2 ACTIVITY

a) *Bring a photo of yourself and one of your hobbies to school. Use the photos and make a classroom poster like 7PK's.*

b) **Extra** *Tell your class about your photo.*
In the photo I'm at my judo lessons. I go to judo lessons on Monday afternoons. I like judo a lot.

DOSSIER *My sports and hobbies*

Make a page for your dossier. You can use your mind map from P 3 (p. 58).

MY SPORTS AND HOBBIES

I play basketball at the weekend.
I'm in a team.
I like swimming too.

1 The Kapoors at the sports shop

Shop assistant	Good afternoon. Can I help you?
Mrs Kapoor	Yes, please. We need hockey shoes for my daughter.
Shop assistant	What size?
Mrs Kapoor	Size four, please.
Shop assistant	Here you are, a size four hockey shoe.
Mrs Kapoor	Thank you. Try it on, Ananda. Does it fit?
Ananda	Yes, it does.
Shop assistant	Does she like the colour?
Mrs Kapoor	Do you like the colour, Ananda?
Ananda	No, I don't.
Mrs Kapoor	No, she doesn't.
Shop assistant	What about these red and white shoes? Does she ...?
Ananda	I can talk too, you know.
Mrs Kapoor	Ananda!
Ananda	Can I try them on, please?
Shop assistant	Yes, of course. Well?
Ananda	Do they look nice, Mum?
Mrs Kapoor	Yes, they do. Do you want them?
Ananda	Do I want them? Oh yes, I do!
Mrs Kapoor	OK, let's buy them then.

> *Can you find Ananda? She's number ...*

2 Now you

Who does it? You? Or your mum/dad/...?
Ask your partner.

A: Do you buy your shoes? Or does your mum buy them?
B: My mum buys them. What about you?
A: ...

- buy your shoes/clothes/...
- make your lunch/...
- wash your clothes/sports stuff/...
- choose your T-shirts/shoes/school stuff/...
- ...

Looking at language

Copy the chart and complete the questions from 1.

	Singular	Plural
1st person	... I ... them?	Do we need an assistant?
2nd person	... you ... the colour?	Do you two need help?
3rd person	... she ... the colour?	... they ... nice?

▸ *GF 10a–b: Simple present: questions/short answers (p. 136) • P 4–8 (pp. 59–60) • WB 3–7 (pp. 37–38)*

3 Prunella plays tennis

Prunella — Sophie, come and play with me!
Sophie — I can't. I've got homework. It's an English project: 'What do people do in their free time?'
Prunella — Great, you can ask me!
Sophie — You? Oh ... OK. What do you do in your free time, Prunella?
Prunella — I sing, and I play the piano, and I collect plates and I play tennis.
Sophie — You play tennis? Alone?
Prunella — No. I play with Uncle Henry. He hasn't got a head, so I always win.
Sophie — How do you play tennis?
Prunella — With your racket, of course!
Sophie — Oh! And when do you play tennis?
Prunella — At night, when you're all in bed.
Sophie — And where do you play?
Prunella — We play in the garden.
Sophie — But the neighbours ...?
Prunella — Oh, they think your family is mad anyway.

▸ *GF 10c: wh-questions (p. 137) • P 9 (p. 60)*

STUDY SKILLS **Wörter nachschlagen**

Was ist es?
Wenn du ein Wort vergessen hast und es auch nicht aus dem Zusammenhang verstehst, kannst du es im Dictionary ab S. 179 nachschlagen.

Probier's mal
*Schlag diese Wörter im Dictionary nach: **about**, **plate**, **know**, **racket**. Auf welchen Seiten stehen sie? Dann finde heraus:*
- *In welcher Reihenfolge stehen die Wörter im Dictionary?*
- *Welche Informationen gibt es zu den Wörtern?*
- *Was bedeuten die Zahlen am Ende jedes Eintrags?*
- *Wo in deinem Buch kannst du mehr über ein Wort herausfinden? Schlag dieselben vier Wörter dort nach. Was hast du erfahren?*

▸ *SF 4 (p. 122) • P 10 (p. 61) • WB 8–9 (p. 39)*

4 ACTIVITY

Find three words from the Dictionary and write them down for a partner. Can your partner find the words and write down the German words in one minute?

5 Now you

a) *Ask a classmate. Look at **3** for ideas.*

A: What do you do in your free time?
B: I ...
A: Where do you ...?
B: I ...
A: Do you ... alone?
B: No, I ... with ... / Yes, I do.
A: When do you ...?
B: ...

b) *Write about your classmate and tell the class.*
Tobias goes skating in the park with his sister and her friends every Saturday.

6 An e-mail to Jay

Ananda has got a cousin in New York. She often writes to him.

Send | Save | Attach | Tools

To: jay.gupta@newyork-ny.com

Subject: Your hobbies

Dear Jay

Just a quick e-mail today …
Here are some questions. Can you answer them for me? It's for an English project.
- What are your hobbies?
- How often do you do them?
- Do you go to school matches?
- Have you got a bike? How often do you ride it?

Thanks a lot!

Love
Ananda

The next morning Ananda finds an answer from her cousin.

Hi, Ananda

Here's a quick answer to your e-mail.
- My hobbies are basketball, basketball and basketball.
- I play every day (I play for the school basketball team).
- I sometimes go to school baseball games. But I NEVER go to football games – they're boring! (American football of course!)
- Yes, I've got a bike. But I don't often ride it …
  I usually walk.

Say hi to Dilip for me.

Jay

► *GF 11: Adverbs: word order (p. 137)* • *P 11–14 (pp. 61–63)* • *WB 10–12 (pp. 40–41)*

7 Now you

Imagine Ananda sends you the same e-mail. Answer her e-mail and tell her about your hobbies and sports. You can put your e-mail to Ananda in your DOSSIER.

8 Extra Lazy Larry

Listen and do what Larry does.

9 I hate sport

On Wednesdays Jack's mum does yoga after work, and his dad plays basketball. Jack has to do his homework.
'At least I don't have to do yoga or play basketball,' Jack says. 'I hate sport!'
'Hate sport, hate sport,' Polly says.
'And now we have to do our English project. It's about free time. And what do most people do in their free time? Sport!'
'Hate sport, hate sport.'
'At least you understand me, Polly. Oh no, it's 5.30: I have to go shopping. Then I have to lay the table for dinner. I have to do everything in this house! Because Mum and Dad do sport.'
'Hate sport, hate sport.'
'Does Mum have to do yoga? And does Dad have to play basketball?'
'Basketball, basketball!' Polly says. 'Go team! Go team!'
'Oh no, Polly. Not you too!'

10 SONG I have to get up

I have to get up, I have to get up,
I have to get up in the morning.
(S)he has to get up, (s)he has to get up,
(s)he has to get up right now.
I have to get dressed, I have to get dressed,
I have to get dressed in the morning.
(S)he has to get dressed, (s)he has to get
dressed, (s)he has to get dressed right now.
The teacher has to teach things.
The students have to learn things.
The teacher has to shout a lot.
And then we can all go home.

a) *Listen to the song. Then make two groups (for the green and red lines) and sing it.*

b) **Extra** *Write your own song.*
Here are some ideas:
... do sport
... go and play
trainer ... train us
players ... play ball

11 GAME Busy Betty

a) *Busy Betty is always busy. Here are her jobs for Saturday morning:*

clean her room • do her homework • help her mum • make her bed

Make a timetable for her from 8 to 11 o'clock.

b) *Can your partner guess your timetable for Busy Betty?*

B: Does your Betty have to make her bed at 8?
A: Yes, she does. | *A:* No, she doesn't.
B: Does your ...? | *B:* My turn. Does ...?
A: ... | *B:* ...

Busy Betty: Saturday

8 make her bed
9 clean her room
10

▸ GF 12: (to) have to (p. 138) • P 15–18 (pp. 63–64) • WB 13–15 (pp. 42–43)

1 REVISION Jo plays football, he doesn't ... (Simple present statements)

a) *Complete the sentences.*

1. Jo ... (play) football every day after school. He .. (~~play~~) the guitar.
   Jo plays football every day after school. He doesn't play the guitar.
2. Dan ... (read) in the evenings, but he .... (~~like~~) big books.
3. Jack sometimes ... (make) model boats, but he ... (~~collect~~) stamps.
4. The girls in Form 7PK .... (~~play~~) football. They ... (play) hockey.

b) *On a card, write two sentences about yourself like this:*

I like apples
but I don't eat bananas.
I play football
but I don't play for the school.

Now collect all the cards in a box.
One student takes a card and reads it to the class like this:

This student likes *apples* but doesn't eat bananas. He or she plays football but he or she doesn't play for the school.

Who can guess who it is?

2 WORDS A word snake

a) *Find ten words about sports and hobbies.*

b) *Find five verbs. Match them to the words in a).*

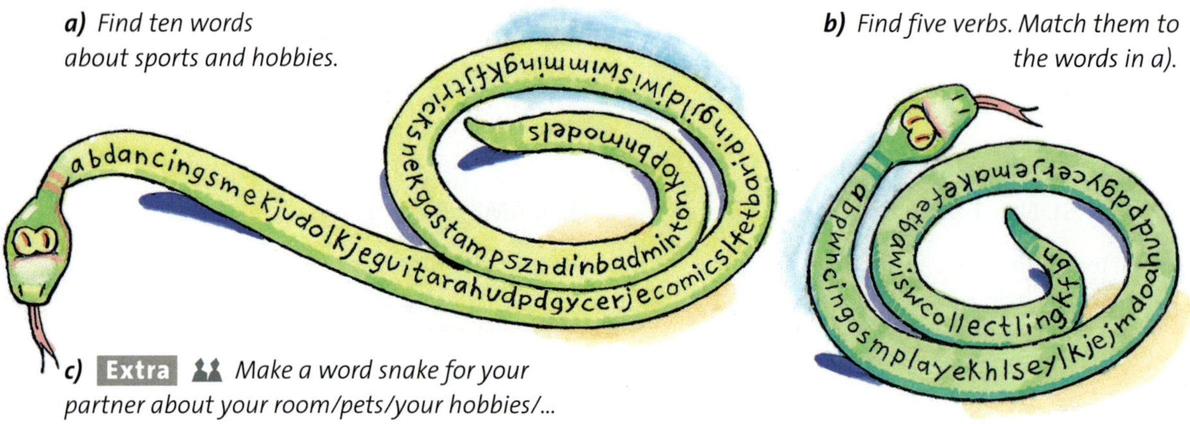

c) **Extra** *Make a word snake for your partner about your room/pets/your hobbies/...*

3 WORDS A sports and hobbies mind map

Copy the mind map.
Look at 'I can ...' on page 52 and add words to the mind map.
Add more words to it when you do other parts of the unit.

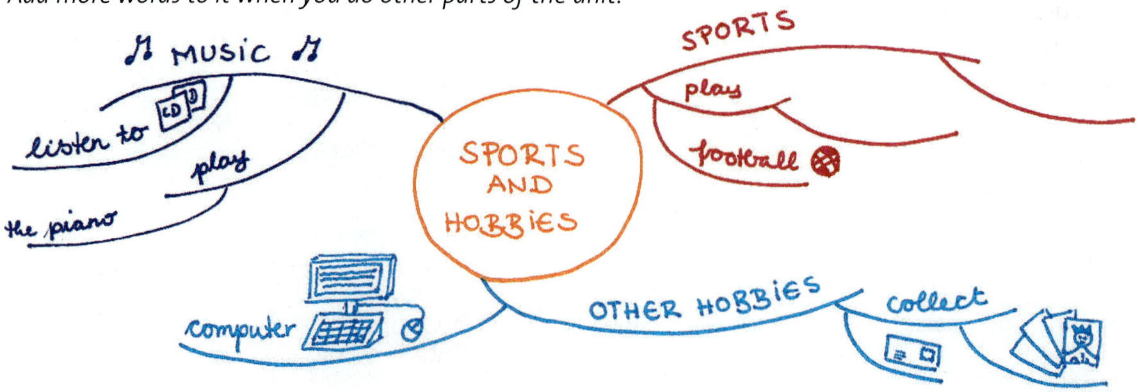

4 The questions game (Simple present: questions)

a) *Make two groups. Group A writes people on green cards:*

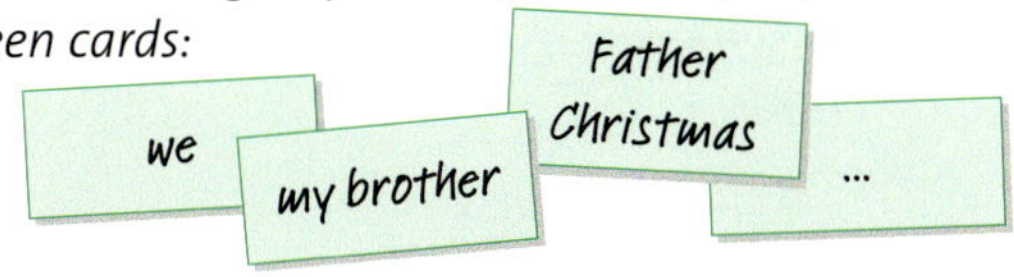

Group B writes verbs and things on blue cards:

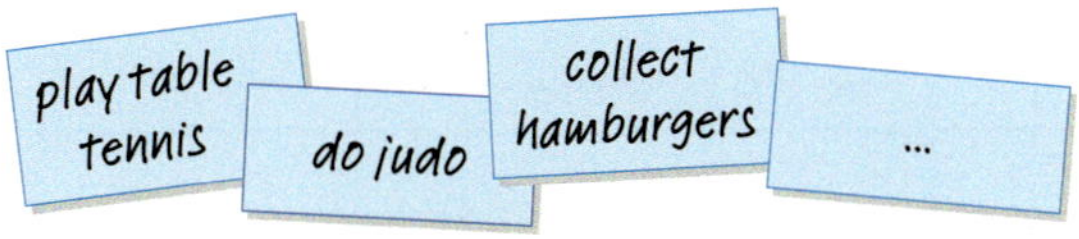

*The teacher makes a **Do** card and a **Does** card.*

b) *Three students come to the front. The first student takes a green card, the second student takes a blue card and the third student has to choose the right card (**Do** or **Does**).*
The students stand in the right order with the cards and read out the question, e.g.
Does my brother play table tennis?
Word order correct: the next group comes to the front. Word order wrong: try again.

5 Does it fit? (Simple present: questions)

Ananda needs more things. Make Mrs Kapoor's questions.

1 'The T-shirt fits.' < sweatshirt? >
Mrs Kapoor: *Does the sweatshirt fit too?*
2 'This dress is the wrong size.' < a different? >
Do you ...?
3 'I like the shoes.' < jeans? >
4 'I don't want this T-shirt in "S".' < in "M"? >
5 'The green top looks nice.' < black top? >
6 'We need white T-shirts for tennis.' < shorts? >

6 Shopping (Simple present: questions)

a) *Prepare a shopping dialogue. You can use your ideas, ideas from page 54 and ideas from the box.*

A: Good ... Can I help you?
B: Yes, please. I/We need ..., size ...
A: Here you are, ... Do they fit? / Does it fit?
B: Yes, they do. / No, they don't.
Yes, it does. / No, it doesn't.

dress • tennis shoes • shoes • shorts • socks • top • T-shirt

A: Do you like ...?
B: Yes, I do./No, I don't.

b) *Practise your dialogues and act them out in class.*

7 A quiz (Simple present: questions)

Think of questions for a quiz about the families in your English book. Ask your partner questions. Then answer his/her questions.

Do Does	Ananda Jack Sheeba Prunella Mr and Mrs ... the twins ...	live in a flat? live with Sophie? sleep in a basket? do sport? like music? like his/her brother? ...

8 Do you know your classmates? (Simple present: questions and short answers)

a) *Make appointments with three classmates.*
'Can we meet at 1/2/3 o'clock?'
Write their names in a list.

My appointments
1 o'clock ___ Marco
2 o'clock ___ Sandra
3 o'clock ___ ...

b) *Are the sentences below right for you?*
Write 'Y' (for Yes) in a copy of the chart. Not true?
Write 'N' (for No).

1 I play football in a team.
2 I make models.
3 I watch sport on TV.
4 I collect stamps.
5 I know lots of sports stars.
6 I go to the shops every Saturday.
7 I play the guitar.
8 I like books: I read a lot.

What do you think? Are the sentences true for your appointment partners? Write Y or N under their names.

	me	Marco	...	...
1				
2				
3				
4				
5				
6				
...				

c) *When the teacher says it's 1 o'clock, go to your first appointment.*
A: Marco, do you play football in a team?
B: Yes, I do. / No, I don't.

d) *Tell your class about your partners. Don't say their names. Can the class guess who they are?*
This boy doesn't play football in a team, but he makes models.

9 Sport in different countries (Simple present: wh-questions)

a) *Partner B: Go to p. 115. Partner A:*
Look at the people below. Which of these questions can you answer about them?
Where ... come from?
What sport ... do?
When ... do sport?

b) *Ask your partner questions about the missing information and write it in your exercise book.*
A: What sport does Sophie do?
B: She goes riding.
A: Where does Yoko ...?
Then answer your partner's questions.

10 STUDY SKILLS Wörter nachschlagen

a) *Write the words in alphabetical order.*

1. dialogue, divorced, difficult, different, dining room
2. classmate, clever, climb, class, clean
3. plan, place, plate, please, play
4. weekend, well, welcome, wear, Wednesday
5. think, third, thing, throw, this

b) *Where can you find these words in a dictionary?*

bowl • at • act • band • bye • activity • because • aunt • all • again • baby • ask • back • begin • bus • almost • bedroom • breakfast

Put them in the right list between about *and* animal, answer *and* bag, *or* ball *and* break. *Be careful: three words don't fit!*

about – animal	*answer – bag*	*ball – break*
act	*at*	*bowl*
...		

c) *Find the words in the Dictionary (pp. 179–191) and answer the questions.*

1. ***hobby:*** What word comes before it, what word comes after it?
2. ***climb:*** What letter don't you say in the word?
3. ***eat, sweatshirt:*** How do you say 'ea' in the two words?
4. ***get dressed:*** Can you find this under 'g', under 'd' or under 'g' and 'd'?
5. ***match:*** What meanings can you find?
6. ***sunglasses:*** Where can you find this word first in the book? Check the page and find the sentence.
7. ***invite:*** What is it in German?
8. ***group, about, colour:*** How do you say 'ou' in the three words?

11 Sports and hobbies in my class

a) *Write 4–6 questions for a survey on hobbies and sport.*
Look at pages 54–56 again for ideas or think of your own questions. You can ask questions like:
Do you like/play/do/go ...?
Where/What/When/How often/... do you ...?

b) *Write your questions in a chart. Then ask five partners your questions. Write down their answers.*

Questions	*Answers*
Do you do sport?	
How often do you play computer games every week?	
Where do you do it?	
When do	

c) *Show what you find out in a chart. Then tell the class.*

Four people do sport, one person doesn't.
One person plays computer games every day, ...

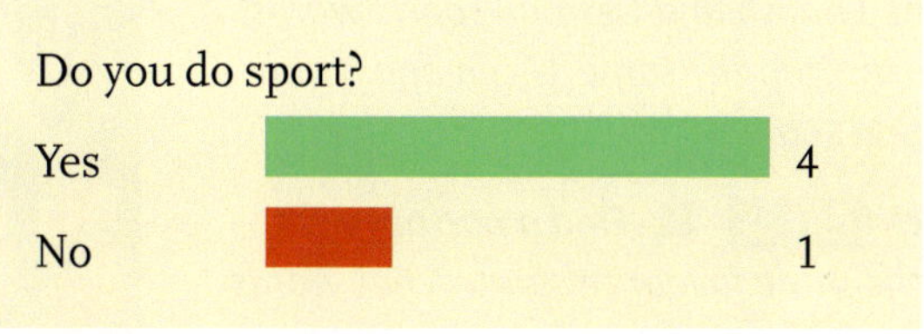

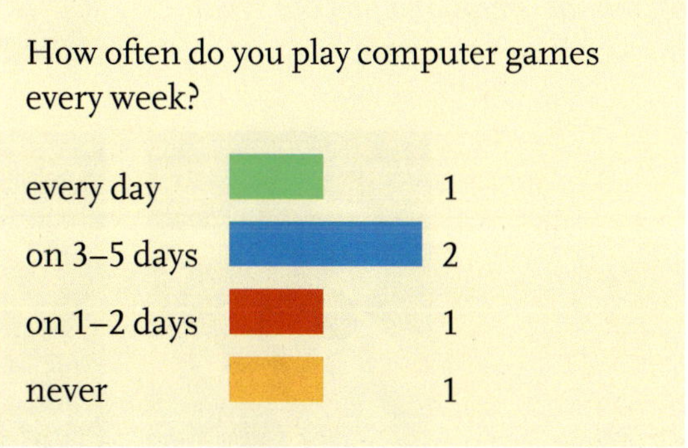

12 PRONUNCIATION [æ] and [eɪ]

a) *Listen to the poem. Then practise it.*

b) *Listen and practise.*

Happy rabbit in a hat,
Where's the mad black cat?
At the bank?
Bad, bad, bad!

c) *Now say these words. Which is the odd one out?*

1	bank	baby	band
2	date	day	dad
3	take	thank	that
4	make	May	mad
5	play	plan	page
6	mad	make	match
7	packet	great	name
8	eight	happen	hey

d) *Listen and check.*

e) *Put the words from c) in a copy of the chart.*

'black' [æ] words	'skate' [eɪ] words
bank	baby
band	…
…	

13 LISTENING Sport on the radio

a) *Listen. Write down what sports you can hear. The pictures can help you – four are right.*

b) *English and German sports words are often the same. Listen again and find some.*

c) **Extra** *Find a partner with the same favourite sport. What words are important in this sport? Write a list of German words and find out what the words are in English.*

14 Prunella and Sophie's computer (Adverbs: word order)

a) *Prunella sometimes plays with Sophie's computer and mixes up Sophie's e-mails. Correct the sentences.*

1 often – go dancing – I
I often go dancing.
2 sometimes – tennis – plays – my brother
3 the news – on TV – Dad – watches – always
4 don't often – we – play – hockey at school
5 doesn't – usually – write – my sister – letters
6 computer games – plays – never – my mum
7 she – always – to work – walks
8 talk – on the phone – sometimes – and I – my aunt
9 usually – goes swimming – our class – on Friday
10 never – sport – our rabbits – do

b) **Extra** *Now you write 3–5 sentences. Use one of these words in each sentence:*
always – usually – often – sometimes – never
Write the sentences again, but this time mix up the words. Swap with a partner. Write his/her sentences in the right order. Swap the sentences again. Check your partner's word order.

15 WORDS Link the words

a) *Which nouns from the yellow box go with the verbs from the orange box?*
clean – shoes, teeth, CDs

clean • come • do • have • like • listen to • make • play • write

bed • breakfast • CDs • computer games • e-mails • home • homework • judo • music • shoes • stories • teacher • teeth • television

b) *Now complete these sentences.*

1 Jack cleans his *teeth* every morning.
2 Before he has ... in the morning, he makes his ...
3 When he comes ... from school, he does his ...
4 Jack likes books, so he sometimes writes ... after school.

c) *Write two more sentences about Jack. Use a verb from the orange box and a noun from the yellow box in each sentence.*

16 Who has to wash the car? (have to/has to)

a) *The Carter-Brown family has got a job timetable. Who has to do what this week?*
Mr Carter-Brown *has to* wash the car.
Emily and Toby *have to* ...

Week of 4th December

wash the car	Dad
clean the bathroom	Emily + Toby
feed the pets	Sophie + Toby
take Toby to judo	Mum
go shopping	Mum + Emily
go to the park with Sheeba	Emily
help Mum with tea	Sophie
help Dad in the garden	Toby

b) *Prunella is a poltergeist, not a person. What doesn't she have to do?*
Prunella doesn't have to eat.
She doesn't have to ...

17 My partner and I (have to/has to)

a) *Write questions for your partner.*

1 make your bed in the morning
Do you have to make your bed in the morning?
2 help your mum at home
3 walk to school
4 have sandwiches for lunch
5 feed the pets in your home
6 do your homework before you meet your friends
7 drink tea in the evening
8 go to bed at eight o'clock

b) *Ask your partner the questions. Put 'Y' or 'N' for his/her answers. Then answer his/her questions.*

c) *What do you and your partner both have to do? Copy this window and write all the answers from 1 to 8 in the correct boxes.*

	My partner has to ...	*My partner doesn't have to ...*
I have to ...		
I don't have to ...		

d) *Now tell your class about you and your partner.*

I have to ..., and Sven has to ... too.
I have to ..., but Sven doesn't have to ...
I don't have to ..., but Sven has to ...
I don't have to ..., and Sven doesn't have to ...

18 GETTING BY IN ENGLISH Shopping

a) *How can you do these things in English? Do you need help? Look at page 54.*

1 jemanden begrüßen und fragen, ob du ihm/ihr helfen kannst
2 einen Hockeyschuh in einer bestimmten Größe verlangen
3 fragen, ob du etwas anprobieren kannst
4 „Ja, natürlich" sagen
5 fragen, ob Schuhe oder ein Kleidungsstück passen
6 fragen, ob etwas gut aussieht
7 fragen, ob jemand etwas haben/kaufen will

b) *Partner A: You're the shop assistant in a shop. Partner B: You need help.*

A: Grüße B und biete Hilfe an.
B: Sag, dass du das rote T-Shirt magst. Frag, ob du es anprobieren kannst.
A: Sag ja, natürlich.
B: Frag A, ob es gut aussieht.
A: Sag ja.
B: Sag, dass du die Farbe doch nicht magst. Frag, welche anderen Farben es gibt.
A: Sag, du hast das T-Shirt auch in Blau und Grün.
B: Frag, ob du es in Grün anprobieren kannst.
A: Gib B das grüne T-Shirt. Frag, ob es passt.
B: Sag ja. Sag, dass es dir gut gefällt.
A: Frag A, ob er/sie das T-Shirt haben will.
B: Bejahe dies.

c) *Write your own shopping dialogue and act it out for the class.*

The SHoCK Team

Before you read the story about the SHoCK Team, look at the pictures. What do you think?
- *Is the man at the Pretty Polly B&B Mr Green/a spy/a bank robber/...?*
- *Who's in the SHoCK Team – the man or Jack and his friends?*

It's 7.45 on Wednesday night. Mr and Mrs Hanson aren't at home. Mr Green, the only guest at the Pretty Polly B&B, is out too. Jack is alone in his room.
Suddenly he hears a noise downstairs. He stops and listens. Yes, there's the noise again. He goes to the stairs and looks down. Outside room number 3 – Mr Green's room – there's a man in black jeans and a black sweatshirt. Jack can't see his face, but he looks very scary.

'Er, excuse me!' Jack says. 'Can I help you?'
The man sees Jack and runs away.
Polly calls, 'Hurry up! Hurry up!' and Jack runs downstairs. Outside, he looks left and right, but he can't see the man in black. The street is empty.
'Where is he?' Jack thinks. 'I have to call the police!'
Jack runs back into the Pretty Polly B&B.
He goes to room 3 and tries the door.
'Hmmm,' Jack thinks, 'it's locked. Maybe I don't have to call the police.'

The next day at lunch Jack tells his friends about the scary visitor.
'You have to tell your parents,' Ananda says.
'No,' Dan says, 'you have to phone the police.'
Jo agrees with his brother. 'Yes, and you have to tell Mr Green.'
'No,' Jack tells them. 'You see, I think this is about Mr Green.'
'What do you mean, about Mr Green?' Sophie asks.
'I think maybe he's a spy,' Jack says. 'Or a bank robber ... or ... I know! This is what we have to do: we have to find out about Mr Green. We have to be detectives.'
'Yes!' Jo agrees. '"Detective Jo Shaw" – I like it!'

Sophie thinks it's a great idea too. 'Who's got a piece of paper?' she asks.
'I have,' Dan answers.
'Good. And a pencil?'
'I've got a pencil,' Jo says. 'Why do you need it?'
'Well,' Sophie says, 'we need a name for our detective group.'
Sophie writes and writes. The others watch. Suddenly she says, 'I've got it. We're the SHoCK Team.'
'We're what?!' Jack asks.

Sophie shows them what she means. 'Look, S for Shaw, H for Hanson, C for Carter-Brown and K for Kapoor. Add one little o and you've got SHoCK: The SHoCK Team.'
'Great, Sophie!' Jack says. 'The SHoCK Team: I like it. Right, team, when we aren't at school, we watch Mr Green. We start today at five o'clock. Synchronize watches!'

Working with the text

1 Extra What do you know?

Write down what you know about:
- the man in black
- the SHoCK Team

Here's some help:

... detectives • outside ... room • runs ... • scary • SHoCK comes from ... • watch ... • sweatshirt • ...

2 Right or wrong?

a) *Read this sentence and correct it.*
On Wednesday night Mr and Mrs Hanson hear a noise downstairs.

b) *Now think of two more wrong sentences. Swap with a partner and correct his/her sentences.*

3 The SHoCK Team's first job

a) *Listen to the CD and answer these questions about the SHoCK Team's first job.*
1 Where's the Pretty Polly B&B?
2 Where do Ananda and Jo wait? And Sophie and Dan?
3 Where is Jack?
4 Where is Mr Green?

b) *Complete Jack's message for the SHoCK Team.*

c) **Extra** *The next day the SHoCK Team get Jack's message. What do they do next? Write a dialogue and act it out.*

► WB 16 (p. 44)
Checkpoint 3 ► WB (pp. 46–47)

An English jumble sale

At a jumble sale in England people sell old, used things and then give the money to a charity like Oxfam or a local hospital or youth group.
How is a jumble sale different from a 'Flohmarkt' in Germany?

1 The money

▸ *WB: Activity page 2*

Pounds [paʊndz] and pence [pens]

	You say:
1p	one p [piː]
45p	forty-five p
£1	one pound/a pound
£1.25	one (pound) twenty-five (p)
£2	two pounds
£2.50	two (pounds) fifty (p)
£3.79	three (pounds) seventy-nine (p)

Euros ['jʊərəʊz] and cents [sents]

	You say:
1c	one cent
20c/€0.20	twenty cents
€1	one euro/a euro
€50	fifty euros
€49.55	forty-nine (euros) fifty-five (cents)

Listen to these people at an English jumble sale. What does the woman buy? Write down all the prices. What is the price in the end?

2 Your jumble sale

a) *Bring jumble (e.g. old clothes, games, books) to school for your jumble sale. Or you can make a cake, make a model, ...*

b) *In groups of five talk about the prices.*
A: What about €1.50 for this?
B: Good idea! / No, that's too much.
Write a price list on a piece of paper. Or put the prices on your jumble.

red T-shirt	€1
Madonna CD	€1.20
Hitchcock book	50c

c) *When all groups are ready, start your jumble sale. One person from each group sells the things. The others walk around and buy things from the other groups.*
A: Excuse me, how much is the .../this?
B: Let's see: it's €1.10/...
A: Oh, no, that's too much. / I've only got ...
B: Well, I can take 10c off. / You can have it for ... / Sorry, that isn't enough.
A: Good, I'll take it. Here's one euro.
B: Thank you. Here's your change.

▸ *WB 17 (p. 45)*

Party, party!

I can ...

... talk to my partner about food and drink.
My favourite food/drink is ... What's your favourite food/drink?
I usually/always/... have ... for breakfast/lunch/tea/dinner.
What do you have?
I like ..., but I don't like ... What about you?
My favourite party food is ...
...

1 Food and drink

a) *Match words from the box to the numbers 1–14 in the photo.*

birthday cake • cheese • chicken • chips • chocolate biscuits • cola • crisps • fruit salad • lemonade • orange juice • salad • sandwiches • sausages • sweets

b) *Tell your partner where things are in the photo. You can use words from a) and from these two boxes. Can your partner guess what the food is?*

behind the ...	bottle (of)
in front of the ...	bowl (of)
in the ...	glass (of)
next to the ...	jug (of)
on the ...	plate (of)

A: It's on a big yellow plate. It's brown.
B: It's ...
A: That's right. Your turn. / That's wrong, try again.

2 ACTIVITY Your dream party

a) *Make a list of food and drink for your dream party. You can have seven things. Then work with a partner. Agree on a new list of seven things together.*

A: Let's have a fruit salad/pizza/...
B: Yes, good idea./No, I hate fruit salad.

Then make a group of four with two other students. Agree on a list together.

b) *Make a poster of food and drink for your dream party. Draw pictures or use pictures from magazines or packets.*

c) *With a partner prepare a dialogue like this to go with your poster.*

A: Would you like some food/a drink?
B: Yes, please. I'm really hungry/thirsty. What's that on the big white plate?
A: What, next to the orange juice? That's chicken/milkshake ... Would you like some?
B: Yes, please./No, thanks. I don't like ... I'd like some ... And can I have ..., please?
A: Of course you can.

► P 1–2 (p. 75) • WB 1–3 (pp. 48–49)

1 A party invitation

Sophie — Now, where's the invitation list for my birthday party? Let's look at it.
Prunella — It's a very long list! Why do you want to invite Ananda?
Sophie — Because I like her, of course.
Prunella — And Jack?
Sophie — Because I like him too.
Prunella — And Jo and Dan?
Sophie — Prunella, I like them too. They're my friends.
Prunella — And I'm your friend, so I want an invitation too.
Sophie — Well, no, Prunella. I can't invite you – you're a poltergeist.
Prunella — What about Uncle Henry?
Sophie — No!
Prunella — You don't like us! Just because we're different ...
Sophie — I like you both, Prunella, but my party is for real people. I'm sorry.

> *Who is on Sophie's list? Who isn't? Why?*

2 ACTIVITY

Make an invitation to ...

a barbecue • a disco • a fancy-dress party • a sleepover • a Halloween party

You can put your invitation in your DOSSIER.

3 SONG The invitation rap

Listen. Then do the rap.

Looking at language

Look at these sentences from **1**.

1 'Let's look at **it**.'
2 'Because I like **her**, of course.'
3 'Prunella, I like **them** too.'

*What is **it**? Who are **her** and **them**?*
*What are **it**, **her** and **them** in German?*

▸ GF 13: Personal pronouns (pp. 38–39) • P 3–5 (pp. 75–76) • WB 4–6 (pp. 49–50)

4 A present for Sophie

Sophie's birthday party is today. Ananda and Jack still need a present.

Jack — Let's buy her some soap.
Ananda — No, soap is boring.
Jack — What about socks? Let's buy her some funny socks.
Ananda — No, too expensive.
Jack — OK, OK. Have you got any ideas?
Ananda — Yes, let's buy her some earrings. She hasn't got any earrings.
Jack — But they're expensive too.
Ananda — Well, then what about ...
Jack — Hey, look. There's Mr Green. And he's in a hurry! Can you follow him, Ananda? He knows me.
Ananda — OK. Good luck with the present. Bye!

STUDY SKILLS Notizen machen

Wenn du dir etwas merken willst oder über etwas berichten musst, schreibst du dir Stichworte (key words) auf. Zum Beispiel:
Let's buy her some funny socks. – No, too expensive.

In Stichworten: funny socks: too expensive

Man notiert also nur, was man für das eigene Verständnis braucht.
Lies nochmal **4** *und schreibe dir Stichworte zu den Geschenkvorschlägen auf.*

► SF 5 (p. 123)

Looking at language

Find sentences with **some** *and* **any** *in* **4**.

Positive statements	Negative statements	Questions
Let's buy her some soap.	She hasn't got ...	...
...		

When do you use **some**? *When do you use* **any**?

5 Another present for Sophie

a) *Copy the chart. Listen and write down Dan's ideas.*

b) *Listen again. Why doesn't Jo like Dan's ideas? Write down key words.*

Dan's ideas	Jo's reasons
DVD	not enough money
...	

c) *Swap your charts. Listen again and check.*

► P 6 (p. 76) • WB 7–8 (p. 51)

6 Now you

a) *What presents can you buy for a friend? Make a list.*

b) *Prepare a dialogue and act it out.*
A: Let's buy a/some ...
B: No, he's/she's got lots of ...
A: Have you got any ideas?
B: Yes, I have. Let's buy him/her a/some ...

► GF 14: some/any (p. 139) • P 7–8 (p. 77) • WB 9–10 (p. 52)

7 The Carter-Browns are getting ready for the party

It's 12 o'clock on Saturday. Sophie's dad is cleaning the bathroom. Her mum is in the kitchen. She's making the birthday cake. Sophie is tidying her room.

Prunella I'm helping too!
Sophie No, Prunella! You aren't helping, you're making a mess. Please go away!

It's 2.30 now. Sophie's mum is making the sandwiches.

Mum Where's baby Hannah?
Toby She's with me, Mum! We're taking the hamster up to my room.
Emily Mum, I'm going to Jenny's now, OK?
Mum No, Emily, it isn't OK. The others are helping.
Emily Dad is watching sport on TV. He isn't helping!
Mum And you aren't going to Jenny's! You can go later. Now please put the sandwiches on the table. Dennis! Are you ...?
Dad I'm not watching TV, dear! I'm ... cleaning the living room.

> *Find a sentence in **7** for each picture. Say what the people are doing.*

Looking at language

Complete a copy of the chart.
*Use sentences from **7**.*

Subject	form of 'be'	-ing form
The Carter-Browns	are	getting ...
Sophie's dad	is	cleaning ...
Her mum	is	making ...
Sophie	...	...
I	...	...

▸ *GF 15–16a: Present progressive (p. 140) • P 9–12 (pp. 78–79) • WB 11–14 (pp. 53–54)*

8 Extra Now you

Imagine what your mother is doing now. And your father/brother/sister/grandma/pet?

is dancing • is drawing • is eating • is listening to • is playing • is reading • is making • is teaching • is working • is writing • ...

Tell the class.

– I think my grandpa is playing with my little brother now, and my mum is teaching her class.
– I think my rabbit is eating now.

9 What's he doing now?

Ananda — Jack, is that you?
Jack — Yes, Ananda. Are you still following Mr Green?
Ananda — Yes, of course I am.
Jack — I can hear trains. Are you calling from the station?
Ananda — Yes, I am. Mr Green is waiting for the train from London ... here it is now ...
Jack — And?
Ananda — I think he's meeting somebody. A woman is getting off the train.
Jack — Sorry, I can't hear you, Ananda ... Ananda?
Ananda — A woman is getting off the train! Now he's talking to her ... she's giving Mr Green a little parcel. Now he's looking round ... oops ...
Jack — Ananda! What's happening?
Ananda — I'm hiding! Now they're running.
Jack — Where are they running?
Ananda — They're running to another train ... she's getting on the train back to London! But he isn't getting on.
Jack — So what's he doing?
Ananda — He's walking out of the station ... see you at the party, Jack.
Jack — Ananda, about our present ... I've got this idea and Mrs Carter-Brown says it's OK. Sophie would like a ... Ananda? Ananda!

> *Where is Ananda? What's she doing there? What's Mr Green doing? Where is Jack?*

10 Which picture?

a) *Which pictures are right for text* ***9*** *on p. 73 – a or b?*

b) *Put the pictures in the right order and write titles for them. Use words and phrases from* ***9****.*
The first picture is 4b: 'Ananda is following Mr Green.'

► *GF 16b: Present progressive: (p. 141) • P 13 (p. 79)*

11 Extra What's Mr Green doing?

a) *Mr Green is leaving the station. What can you hear next? Write the numbers 1–7. Listen and take notes.*

b) *Compare your notes.*

A: What's Mr Green doing in number 1?
B: He's running.
A: I've got that too. / No, I think he's ...

12 GAME Musical statues

Write an activity on a card. Put the cards in a box.
Make two groups.
Group 1: take a card.
Group 2: close your eyes. The teacher starts the music.

Group 1: mime to the music.
When the music stops, you stop too.
Group 2: open your eyes and guess the activity.
Swap after three times.

I'm swimming.

I'm singing.

I'm riding my bike.

► *P 14–16 (p. 80) • WB 15–17 (p. 55)*

1 WORDS Food and drink

a) Match these phrases to words in the box.

a basket of *apples, bananas, ...*

a bowl of ...	a packet of ...
a bottle of ...	a piece of ...
a glass of ...	a plate of ...

apples • bananas • biscuits • cake • carrots • cheese • chicken • chips • chocolate • cola • crisps • fish • juice • lemonade • meat • milk • mints • oranges • pizza • salad • sandwiches • sausages • sweets • toast • water

b) Make new combinations of words for new food and drinks.

apple cake, cheese sandwich, ...

DOSSIER *My favourite party food*

Make a list of food and drinks for your party. Use or draw pictures too.

Food
Carrot salad
Chicken
Chocolate cake

2 REVISION A quiz (Subject pronouns + be)

a) Can you answer these questions?

1 Is Dilip Ananda's brother?
– Yes, he is.
2 Are Ananda's parents from Germany?
– No, they aren't. Mr Kapoor is from ..., and Mrs Kapoor ...
3 Is Mr Kingsley's name John?
4 Is Polly a dog?
5 Is Mr Hanson in a wheelchair?
6 Are Bill and Ben Sophie's pets?
7 Is Emily Sophie's sister?
8 Are Dan and Jo twins?
9 Is the Pretty Polly B&B in London?
10 Are Prunella and Sophie friends?

b) **Extra** *Make five new quiz questions like in a). Can your partner answer them?*

A: Is Mrs Shaw in Uganda?
B: No, she isn't. She's in New Zealand.

3 Can you see him? (Object pronouns)

Sophie and Ananda are watching a DVD: '7PK's weekends'. Complete what they say.

Sophie: Oh, look, there's ... *Ananda:* Yes, and there are ...	Jack, Dan and Jo, our garden, Emily, our two rabbits, you and me, our school, your mum, that girl from school, you, me	Can you see ... too?	me, you, him, her, it, us, you, them

Sophie: Oh, look, there's Jack! Can you see him too? – Ananda: Yes, and there are ...

4 Can you help me? (Object pronouns)

a) *Sophie and Toby have to lay the table for dinner.*
Complete the sentences with these object pronouns: ***me, it, them.***

1 I need help. Toby, can you help *me*?
2 Please take the juice to the living room and put ... on the table.
3 These glasses don't look very nice. Can you wash ..., please?
4 Oh no! We've got carrots again. I don't like ...
5 These are the good plates. Don't drop ...!
6 The cake looks very good. Can I try ...?
7 There's the chicken salad. Put ... on the table, please.
8 Sophie, I can't open the door. Can you open the door for..., please?

b) *Complete the sentences with object pronouns.*

Kim I know you like parties, Jim.
Jim Yes, I really like ...
Kim Well, my party is on Friday. Can you help ... to plan ...?
Jim Yes, OK. My cousin Laura is here on Friday.
Kim Oh, I know ... She can come too. Lots of people are coming. There's Tim –
Jim Oh, I like ...
Kim The party is in the park.
Jim Great. My mother can take ... there.
Kim Do you like pizza?
Jim Only with bananas on ... And banana sandwiches, please make lots of ... And banana juice. I have to have ...!
Kim I don't know why I invite ... to my parties!

5 WORDS Fourth word

a) *Finish the word groups on pieces of paper like this:*

1 evening – dinner
morning – ...
2 push – pull
open – ...
3 black – white
big – ...
4 come – go
buy – ...
5 collect – stamps
... – models
6 play – tennis
... – judo
7 sing – a song
... – a story
8 orange juice – drink
sandwich – ...

b) *Cut the pieces of paper into four. Mix them up and swap with a partner. Who can make the word groups again first? (Close your books!)*

6 STUDY SKILLS Notizen machen

a) *Partner B: Go to p. 115.*
Partner A: Read about what Emma wants for her birthday. Take notes so that you can tell your partner about her.

b) *Close your book. Use your notes to tell your partner about Emma's ideas for her birthday. Answer his or her questions if necessary.*

c) *Listen to your partner's story about Max's birthday party. You can ask him/her questions.*

Most 11-year-old girls want games, books or new clothes for their birthday.
Emma is different. On her 12th birthday, she wants money from her birthday guests - lots of money. But not for presents - she wants it for the zoo.
'I don't need a lot of presents ,' Emma says. 'I want the money for the zoo because I love animals. The snakes are my favourites. They're great!'

7 What's in the fridge? (some and any)

It's shopping day at the Carter-Brown house. Complete the dialogues. Use some and any.

1 Mrs C-B: Have we got enough drinks, Sophie?
Sophie: We've got *some lemonade and some orange juice*, but we haven't got *any milk*.
Mrs C-B: Is there ... apple juice?
Sophie: No, ...
2 Mrs C-B: What about for dinner, Sophie?
Sophie: We've got ..., but we haven't ...
Mrs C-B: Are ...
Sophie: ...
3 Mrs C-B: And breakfast stuff?
Sophie: ...
Mrs C-B: Is ...?
Sophie: ...

	✓	✗
1. drinks	lemonade orange juice	milk apple juice
2. dinner	chicken cheese sausages	fish
3. breakfast	muesli eggs	cornflakes marmalade

8 Happy birthday! (some and any)

Partner B: Go to p. 116.
Partner A: Look at the picture. Tell your partner about it. Ask questions about his/her picture.

I've got Have you got I haven't got	some any	bananas • biscuits • books • cakes • CDs • chicken • crisps • fruit salad • lemonade • orange juice • presents • sausages • soap • socks • sweets	in my picture. in your picture?

A: I've got some crisps in my picture. Have you got any in your picture?
B: Yes, I have. And I've got some books. What about you?
A: No, I haven't got any books. I've got some ...

9 It's 10 o'clock on Saturday (Present progressive: positive statements)

a) *Complete the sentences with the correct form of be.*

1 It's 10 o'clock on Saturday and the twins *are* buying a present for Sophie.
2 Their dad is at home. He ... cleaning the house.
3 Now it's 1 o'clock. Mr Shaw ... making sandwiches and Jo ... feeding the cats.
4 'Dan, lunch is ready!' calls Mr Shaw. – 'I ... talking to Ananda, Dad. Just a minute.'
5 Now the twins and their dad ... eating the sandwiches.

b) *Complete the sentences with the correct form of be and the -ing form of the verb.*

1 It's 3.45. Mr Shaw ... (call) a friend.
2 'Hi, Indira. I ... (make) tea. Do you want some?'
3 'Thanks Mike, but I ... (write) e-mails now.'
4 It's 4.00. 'I've got a nice cake too. I ... (put) it on the table now.'
5 'Sorry, Mike, but now I ... (get) things ready for our jumble sale.'
6 At 4.15 Mr Shaw is on the phone again. 'Indira? I ... (put) some nice music in the CD player.'
7 'OK, OK. I ... (come)!'

10 Can you help me, please? (Present progressive: positive statements)

Why can't the kids help this teacher at Cotham School? Make sentences. Be careful with the spelling.

1 *Ananda* ____ wait for Mr Kingsley
Sorry, I'm waiting for Mr Kingsley.
2 *Dan and Jo* ____ make a poster for our Geography lesson
3 *Sophie* ____ write a story
4 *Jack* ____ go to the film club
5 *Emily* ____ work in the computer room
6 *Dilip* ____ help Emily

Can you help the teacher? No? Why not?

11 Bill and Ben are playing (Present progressive: positive and negative statements)

It's 11 o'clock on Saturday 26th March. Say what the pets and people are and aren't doing.

1 *Bill and Ben are playing in the park. They aren't eating fish.*

1 ~~eat fish~~

2 play ~~hockey~~

3 ~~watch~~ TV

4 play ~~the piano~~

5 ~~read~~

6 play ~~tennis~~

7 clean ~~the~~ kitchen

8 make ~~sandwiches~~

12 I think Sophie is ... (Present progressive)

Make groups. Which group can find the most right answers?

a) *Look at the pictures. Talk about what you think the people are doing. Then write it down.*

A: I think Sophie is eating in picture 1.
B: No, I don't think she's eating.
I think she's ...
C: I think B is right. Let's write 'Sophie is ...'

b) *Report to the other groups.*
Group A: We think Sophie is ...
Group B: We think that's right. / No, we think she's ...

c) *Who's right? Check on p. 117.*

1

2

3

4

5

6

7

8

13 Questions and answers (Present progressive: questions)

a) *Jack and Jo are talking on the phone. Complete their dialogue.*

1 'Hi, Jack. ... you ... (write) your essay?'
'No, ...'
'Hi Jack. Are you writing your essay?'
'No, I'm not.'
2 'Oh, ... you ... (read) a book?'
'Yes, ...'
3 'And ... your dad ... (play) basketball?
'No, ...'
4 'So, ... your mum and dad ... (watch) TV?
'No, ... '
5 'Well, ... your mum ... (make) dinner?'
'Yes, ...'
6 '... we ... (talk) too much?'
'No, *we* aren't, but *you* ... (talk) too much: Goodbye, Jo!'

b) **Extra** *Dilip is listening to CDs. He can't hear what Ananda is saying. Write his questions. Use* **what** *or* **where**.

1 Ananda: Mum is calling.
Dilip: *Sorry, what is Mum doing?*
2 Ananda: She is calling. She's working in the shop.
Dilip: *Sorry, ... is she working?*
3 Ananda: In the shop. Dad is cleaning the windows.
Dilip: *... is Dad cleaning?*
4 Ananda: He's cleaning the shop windows. And I'm reading a magazine.
Dilip: *Sorry, ... are you reading?*
5 Ananda: A magazine. But it's difficult with your music. I'm going out.
Dilip: *Sorry, ... are you going?*
Ananda: OUT! Goodbye!

14 LISTENING The Hokey Cokey

a) *At English parties people often dance the Hokey Cokey. Before you try it, check: do you know these words?*

circle • arm • shake • leg • jump • turn around • hold hands • bend • knee • stretch

If not, look in the Dictionary on pp. 179–191.

b) *Now listen and dance.*

15 PRONUNCIATION [əʊ] or [ɒ]

a) *Listen to some yellow words [əʊ] and some orange words [ɒ] on the CD. When you hear a yellow word, hold up a yellow pen; when you hear an orange word, hold up an orange pen. Now close your eyes and do it again.*

b) *Say the words. Which is the odd word out?*

1 got – joke – lots	*3* shop – box – phone	*5* not – toast – boat
2 sock – most – close	*4* bowl – drop – throw	*6* photo – road – top

Listen and check.

c) **Extra** *Listen to Sophie and Ananda. Then learn the dialogue and practise with a partner.*

16 GETTING BY IN ENGLISH Would you like ... ?

John, a student from Bristol, is staying with Marcel's family in Germany. Today he's going to the fair with Marcel and his grandmother. Grandma can't speak English, so Marcel has to help her and John. Complete his sentences.

The ghost train

The fair

Oma — Frag John, ob er Hunger hat.
Marcel — John, are you ...?
John — Yes, I am!
Marcel — Ja, hat er.
Oma — Frag John, ob er Hähnchen oder Pizza essen möchte.
Marcel — Would you like some ... or some ...?
John — No, I'd like some chips, please.
Marcel — Er möchte ...
Oma — Und was möchte er trinken?
Marcel — What ...?
John — A cola, please.
Oma — Mag John die Musik?
Marcel — Do you ...?
John — No, not really.
Marcel — ...
Oma — Was möchte er denn machen?
Marcel — What would ...?
John — What's that ride there?
Marcel — It's a *Geisterbahn* ... er, a ...
John — Great. I'd like to go on that!
Marcel — Oma, er möchte ...
Oma — Toll. Sage ihm, ich fahre auch mit.
Marcel — Grandma ...

Sophie's party – a play

Look at the pictures of Sophie's party. Who are the guests? What are they doing?

Scene 1: twenty six tree thirty four
Saturday, 26th March, 3.34 pm. Sophie and her mum are waiting for the party guests in the living room. Prunella is there too.

Sophie — They aren't coming, Mum.
Mum — Don't worry, Sophie. Good guests always come five minutes late!
Sophie — Really?
Mum — Really!
Prunella — To audience The doorbell!
Mum — See? There's somebody now.

At the front door

Sophie — Hello, Dan. Hello, Jo. Come in.
Dan — Hi, Sophie!
Jo — And happy birthday! We've got a present for you – here!
Sophie — Thank you. Thanks a lot.
Dan — You're welcome.
Prunella — What's the present? What is it? Oh, the doorbell again.
Sophie — Oh, sorry, there's the doorbell again.

Back at the front door

Sophie — Hello, Jack. Come in.
Jack — Hi, Sophie. Happy birthday! This present is from Ananda and me.
Sophie — Thank you. But where *is* Ananda?
Jack — She's following Mr Green.
Sophie — Wow! Tell me everything later.

Scene 2:
Now all the guests are there. Sophie is opening Dan and Jo's present.

Sophie — A necklace! Wow, it's great. Thanks, Dan, thanks, Jo.
Jo — Now open Jack and Ananda's present.
Dan — Look, there's a box inside.
Jo — With holes.
Dan — Maybe it's a pet. A hamster?
Jo — Or a snake?
Dan — Or a tortoise?
Sophie — It's a mouse! Fantastic!

Jack — And your mum says it's OK, you can have a mouse.
Sophie — Oh, it's so sweet! Thank you, Jack!
Prunella — To audience And Emily is afraid of mice, so that's great too! – Oh good, here's the birthday cake! Let's sing ...
All — Happy birthday to you, happy birthday to you, happy birthday, dear Sophie, happy birthday to you!

Scene 3:
After tea it's time for some party games.

Prunella — Look, they're playing 'Pass the parcel' now. The music is playing and they're passing a parcel round ... Oops! No more music. Jack has got the parcel.
Jo — Open it, Jack! Hurry up!
Jack — OK, OK. Ah, here's a piece of paper.
Ananda — What's on it?
Jack — 'Sing a song.'

Prunella Ouch: Jack can't sing! Ah, good, now the music is playing again ... Oh, no more music! And who has got the parcel?

Dan Hurry up, Jo!

Jo I *am* hurrying! It's another note: 'Choose a partner and walk arm in arm.' ... Sophie?

Prunella How sweet! Jo and Sophie are walking arm in arm. Oh, now the parcel is going round again ... and ... no more music!

Dan Is it another note, Ananda?

Jo Hurry up Ananda, we're all waiting!

Ananda It's the prize! A really cool pen!

Scene 4:
The party games are over – but now Prunella is playing games.

Prunella Mmm, Dan's crisps are good!

Dan Hey, Jo, don't eat from my plate!

Jo What are you talking about?!

Prunella Hee, hee, hee! Now let's pull Ananda's hair.

Ananda Ouch! Who was that?

Jack Who was what?

Sophie Stop that, Prunella! Go away! This party is for real people.

Prunella Hee, hee, hee!

Dan Are you talking to me, Sophie?

Sophie To you? No, I'm talking to ... oh, here's my sister.

Emily Hi, Baby Soph! How's the party? Any orange juice for me?

Jo Baby Soph! Is that your nickname, Sophie? I like it! Baby Soph, Baby Soph ... uuurrrgghh ...

Suddenly there's a piece of cake in Jo's mouth.

Emily Ha, ha, ha! That's a big piece of cake! Aaaah!

And now there's a mouse on Emily's head.

Emily Take it away! Take it away!

Ananda What's happening here? How can a little mouse get from a box to ...?

Sophie Ananda, come and tell me all about Mr Green.

Working with the text

1 Extra Right or wrong?

Are these sentences from the play right or wrong? Correct the wrong sentences.

1. 'Hee, hee, hee! Now let's pull Emily's hair.'
2. 'Choose a partner and dance the Hokey Cokey.'
3. 'Oh, sorry, there's my mobile again.'
4. 'It's a mouse! Fantastic!'
5. 'This party is for poltergeists.'
6. 'It's the prize! A really nice book!'

2 Scenes

a) *Read 'Sophie's party' in groups. Give each scene a title. Compare titles with other groups.*

A: Scene 1 – our title is 'Where are the guests?'.
B: Our title is 'The ...'.

b) *Write another scene for 'Sophie's party'. Think of a title, for example* 'Outside the house', 'Ananda the detective', ...
Read your new scene to the class. Choose the best scene.

c) *Act out the play.*

▸ WB 18 (p. 56), Activity page 3 **Checkpoint 3** ▸ WB (p. 57)

Extra Party doorstoppers

You need ...

brown or white bread, butter, chutney

a board, knives, salt and pepper, cocktail sticks

lettuce, tomatoes, cucumber, avocados

chicken, ham, salami

cheese

How to do it

1 Put butter on three pieces of bread.

2 Put ingredients on one piece of bread. Put a second piece of bread on top. Add more ingredients and the third piece of bread.

3 Cut your doorstopper like this.

You can make ...

an Italian doorstopper – with tomato, mozzarella cheese and lettuce.

an Indian doorstopper – with cucumber, chicken and chutney.

1 How to make ...

Listen to the CD and read the recipe.

2 A recipe

Think of your own doorstoppers and write a recipe. Draw pictures for it. You can put it in your DOSSIER.

School: not just lessons

I can …

… talk about school.

a) *Collect all your ideas on school in a mind map. Look back at Welcome, Unit 1 and the other units for help with words and phrases.*

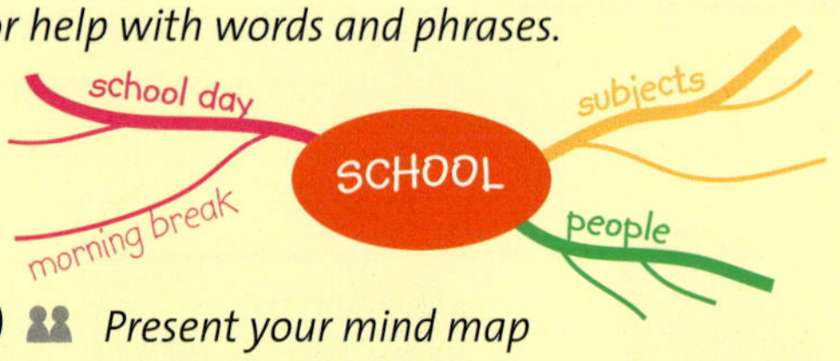

b) *Present your mind map to a partner. Add new ideas to your mind map.*

…

1 School activities

a) *Look at the notices. What activities have Cotham students got at school? (Remember pp. 52–53 too.) What activities have you got at your school? Fill in a copy of the chart.*

Cotham	My school
Camera Club	…

b) *Compare your chart with a partner's.*

2 Ananda and Dilip

a) *Listen and try to answer these questions:*

- *Which notices are Dilip and Ananda talking about?*
- *Which clubs are Ananda, Jack, Sophie, Dan and Jo in?*
- *What have they got to do with the Spring Show?*

b) *Listen again and check your answers. Then add new ideas, words or phrases to your mind map.*

3 Extra ACTIVITY A new school club

a) *What new club would you like at your school? What information can go on the club web site?*
The name of the club / What it does / Who can be in it / When and where it meets / …
You can add pictures.

b) *All groups put their information on the wall. Read about all the clubs. Which one do you want to go to? Why?*

► P 1 (p. 90) • WB 1–2 (p. 58)

YEAR 7 ASSEMBLY
is in the New Dance Studio
this week only!

Why?
The Spring Show rehearsals are in the Assembly Hall.

MOBILE PHONES
Please remember:
Students *may* bring mobile phones to school.
They *may NOT* use them in lessons.

SPORTS RESULT

Year 7 Hockey
2nd May
Cotham 1 Bath 2

Year 7 Football
2nd May
Portway 1 Cotham 3

Judo (Team A)
2nd place at the Bristol Judo Championships

Rehearsals for the Spring Show

Photos by the Camera Club

Remember! Spring Show: 6th May

The Junior Choir is singing and getting ready for the Spring Show.

The Dance Club is rehearsing with the Drama Club!

The Art Club is painting a pirate ship for Wednesday's show.

The Computer Club is making the programmes. They have to be ready on 6th May!

The Junior Band is practising for the big day.

1 The Spring Show – a poster

What has the poster got to do with Ananda, Jack, Sophie, Dan and Jo?

– Look at the poster for one minute. Then close your book and ask your partner two questions about it. Answer his/her questions.

– What musicals do you know? Have you got a favourite?

2 After the rehearsal: at Sophie's

Prunella — You're late, Sophie. Where were you?
Sophie — I was at the dress rehearsal.
Prunella — How was it?
Sophie — It was OK. We were all very nervous, because the show is tomorrow.
Prunella — And was the Music teacher happy?
Sophie — Miss White? Yes, I think she was.
Prunella — And, were you good?
Sophie — Well, I wasn't bad. My group was in the big pirate scene at the end.
Prunella — Pirates? Wow! Oh, the show sounds so good, and I can't go.
Sophie — I'm sorry. Poor Prunella.

3 GAME Where were you?

Throw a ball to somebody and say a time. He/She asks questions to find out where you were.
A: At 4 o'clock last Saturday.
B: Were you at home?/at judo lessons?/...
A: No, I wasn't. / Yes, I was.
The student with the ball goes on.

Looking at language

*In **2** Prunella and Sophie are talking about the past. What pronouns do you use with **was** and **were**? Fill in a copy of the chart.*

was	were
...	you
...	...

► GF 17–18: Simple past: was/were (pp. 141–142) • P 2–4 (pp. 90–91) • WB 3–5 (pp. 59–60)

4 After the rehearsal: at Jack's

Jack was home at 6 o'clock. 'Hi, Mum. Hi, Dad – I'm home!' he shouted.
'I'm in here, Jack,' his dad answered from the kitchen. 'How was your rehearsal?'
'We were fantastic, Dad! Yesterday we were terrible! But today the band played two songs without a mistake.'
'That's great. Mum and I can't wait to see this show. We talked about it last night.'
'Where *is* Mum?' Jack asked.
'Upstairs, I think. She was here a minute ago.'

Jack stopped at Mr Green's room. There were people in there. Jack listened.
'Look at this!' It was Mr Green.
Then there was another voice. It was very quiet. It was a woman's voice, but who was it?
The woman talked again. 'I see you're using plastic explosives now.'
Then Jack realized that the woman was his mother.
Jack walked to the stairs. 'Plastic explosives! I have to tell the SHoCK Team. But ... my mother – a part of this?!'

5 Who was it?

Complete the sentences.

1 ... shouted. *Jack shouted.*
2 ... asked about the rehearsal.
3 ... asked about his mum.
4 ... listened at Mr Green's door.
5 ... talked about plastic explosives.

Looking at language

a) *When was it? Find the words and phrases in the first part of* **4**. *at 6 o'clock, yesterday ...*

b) *Make a chart with these verbs and their simple past forms from* **4**.
shout • answer • play • talk • ask • listen • walk

c) *Find the two other verbs in the simple past in the second part of* **4**.
How are the spellings different?

6 Now you

Use the time phrases and the verbs and write what you did. Then talk to a partner.

A: Yesterday evening I played cards. What about you?
B: I called my grandma. At the weekend I ...

yesterday evening • last Wednesday • two weeks ago • on my last birthday • ...

helped • listened to • played • talked to • watched • ...

► *GF 19a: Regular verbs (p. 142) • P 5–8 (pp. 91–92) • WB 6–9 (pp. 61–62)*

7 Pirate King

a) *Listen to the CD. Put the pirates' jobs in the right order.*

b) *Listen again. Do the pirates' jobs. Sing the chorus with the Cotham students:*

All — For I am a Pirate King!
And it is, it is a glorious thing
To be a Pirate King!
For I am a Pirate King!

Girls — You are!

Boys — Hurrah for the Pirate King!

A

B

C

D

8 Dan's diary

Tuesday, 5th May

After school we had our dress rehearsal for the Spring Show. It was good. The pirate scene was fantastic – our ship looked really great. Jo had his patch on his right eye at first and on his left eye at the end.
He sang the pirate song all the way home! He thinks he has got a great voice. He hasn't – I know!!!

Came home late, had dinner, did my homework. It's time for bed. I'm really tired!
SHoCK Team: Jack phoned. He said Green is planning something with plastic explosives! Jack is afraid that his mother is helping him.

Wednesday, 6th May

SHoCK Team: We went to school early today to meet the SHoCK Team. Ananda and Sophie don't think Mrs Hanson is a spy, but Jack, Jo and I aren't so sure. Sophie saw Green in a supermarket yesterday. He was alone.

The Spring Show is this evening. I hope it's good – but Jo is a pirate, so ...

\> *What does Dan say about the Spring Show dress rehearsal?*
– What does he say about his brother's voice?
– Who thinks Jack's mum is a spy? Who doesn't't?

Looking at language

*Find these simple past forms in **8**. What are the infinitives?*

came • did • had • said • sang • saw • went

Now make a chart with the infinitives and the simple past forms.

Infinitive	Simple past
come	came
...	did
...	...

▸ GF 19b: Irregular verbs (p. 142) • P 9–10 (pp. 92–93) • WB 10–11 (pp. 62–63)

9 After the Spring Show

a) *Listen to the CD. Who liked the show and who didn't?*
b) *What other things can you remember about the Spring Show? Take notes. Compare with a partner.*
c) *Now check in a group.*

10 An article for the school magazine

Five weeks after the Spring Show, Ananda had this report in the school magazine.

The Computer Club by Ananda Kapoor (7PK)

It was a good year for the computer club. The school is still talking about the Spring Show – well, we were a part of that. We didn't go up on stage, of course: we designed the programmes. We made a CD cover too. We didn't have a lot of time, but we were happy with it. The highlight of our year was our internet project. We linked up with a school in Hanover, Bristol's twin town in Germany. We found out that German schools are very different! For example: there's no school uniform in Germany and school starts at 8 o'clock. I didn't know that. We often write to our German e-friends and swap information.

To all school clubs!
How was your year? Did you do anything special?
Did you go on a trip? Where did you go?
What did you do there? What did you see?
Tell us about it. Write a report for our next magazine!

11 German schools, English schools

a) *How is your school different from Cotham School? Make a chart like this:*

My school	Cotham School
School starts at ...	School starts at ...
...	...

Find four more different things.
You can use your mind map from p. 84.

b) *Talk to your partner about your chart. Can you add to your charts?*

DOSSIER ***My diary***

Write your diary for a day last week.
It can be a real day, a funny day, a ...

12 GAME

Make teams of four. Two teams play together.
Team A: *Call a number from the box.*
Team B: *Make sentences with the verb.*
You have 30 seconds.

1 didn't call	5 didn't talk
2 didn't come	6 didn't walk
3 didn't have	7 didn't want
4 didn't hear	8 didn't write

Team A: Number 5!
Team B: We didn't talk in class today.
The man in black didn't talk to Jack.

The team with the most correct sentences wins.

► *GF 20: Negative statements (p. 143) • P 11–14 (pp. 93–94) • WB 12–13 (pp. 63–64)*

► *GF 21: Questions (p. 143) • P 15–17 (pp. 94–95) • WB 14–15 (p. 64)*

1 REVISION The SHoCK Team – a flow chart (Simple present)

a) *Copy the flow chart into your exercise book. Complete it with verbs from the box.*

be (3x) • follow (2x) • get off • get on • give • have got • plan • run • see • start • talk • tell • think • walk • watch • wear

Jack's family *has got* a B&B, the Pretty Polly B&B. There ... a new guest there, Mr Green.

He always ... sunglasses, and he never ... to the other guests. Jack ... Mr Green ... a spy or a bank robber.

One day there ... a scary man at Mr Green's door.

When Jack ... the man in black, he ... away.

Jack ... his friends about it, and they ... a team of detectives, the SHoCK Team.

They ... to ... Mr Green. One Saturday Ananda ... Mr Green to the station.

A woman ... the train from London and ... Mr Green a little parcel. Then she ... a train to London.

Mr Green ... out of the station and Ananda ... him.

b) *Add to the flow chart when you read more about the SHoCK Team. Start on p. 87.*

2 Mr Kingsley's e-mail (was/were: positive and negative statements)

a) *Fill in* **was** *(4x),* **were** *(5x),* **wasn't** *(4x) or* **weren't** *(1x).*

Subject: My day

Hi Jim,
Thanks for your e-mail. I ... here yesterday so I'm writing now.
Today is over! I'm so happy! There ... a lot of work at school. First there ... seven lessons, then there ... the dress rehearsal for the show tomorrow. We ... all very nervous, but the rehearsal ... good. My drama group ... very good. Their costumes ... great, but there ... enough, so there ... two boys in jeans! The pirates ... really scary. We've got a nice new music teacher, but she ... very happy! The choir ... very good, I'm afraid. But the band ... too bad.
Hmm, maybe she hasn't got any plans for after the show tomorrow. Maybe she

b) *Write an e-mail (three or four sentences) to a friend about yesterday.* *Yesterday was ...*

3 Were you at home? (was/were: questions and short answers)

Use the chart and ask your partner questions. He/She answers with short answers.

Was Were	you your mother your father your friends your grandparents your pet ...	at home at school at work in the garden at the shops at the football match ...	yesterday? at the weekend? ...?

A: *Was your mother in the garden yesterday?*
B: *Yes, she was. / No, she wasn't. / I don't know. / I can't remember.*

4 Mr Kingsley's school days (was/were: wh-questions)

a) *Form 7PK is asking Mr Kingsley about his school days. Write down their questions with* **what**, **when**, **where**, **who** *or* **how** + **was/were**. *Match the questions to the answers.*

1 ... your old school?
2 ... your favourite subject?
3 ... your best friends?
4 ... old ... you on your first day?
5 ... long ... you at that school?

a) It was English, of course!
b) I was eleven.
c) It was in Bristol too.
d) They were two boys – Mike and Winston.
e) I was there from ... Mmm, no, I don't want to tell you that!

b) **Extra** *In groups, ask one of your teachers the questions. Where did they go to school? Was English their favourite subject? Tell the class.*

5 WORDS School clubs

a) *What can you do in the Cotham school clubs? Think of as many pairs of verbs and nouns as you can.*

verb	noun
sing	songs/in the choir
learn	dances/in the dance club
play	the clarinet/in the band/...
paint	...
...	

b) *Check a partner's list. Can you add any more pairs to your list?*

c) *Make groups of six.*

Each person gets three pieces of paper and writes a verb and a noun from his/her list on each. Put the pieces of paper in a box. In turns, take out a piece of paper and mime the activity. Can the group guess what the person is doing and which club he/she is in?

A: You're shouting.
B: No, I'm not shouting.
C: You're singing! You're in the choir.
B: Right. Your turn.

6 School a hundred years ago (Simple past: regular verbs in positive statements)

a) *Fill in the simple past forms of the verbs.*

A hundred years ago children usually ... (start) school early in the morning. They ... (walk) to school, and after school they often ... (help) their parents in the house or garden. Lessons ... (look) very different. The teachers ... (talk) all the time and the children ... (listen) to them. They never ... (work) in groups, ... (talk) to their partners or ... (play) games in the lessons.

b) *Write about your first year at school. Use words and phrases from a) or from the chart.*

my teacher	often		questions.
I	never	answer • ask • help • laugh •	groups.
we	sometimes	listen to • play • shout (at) •	mum.
my school	always	talk (to) • watch • work • ...	music.
...	...		...

In my first year at school I often answered questions. My teacher never laughed. We ...

7 After school (Simple past: regular verbs in positive statements)

Partner B: Look at p. 116.
Partner A: Tell your partner what Jo did after school last week. Ask him/her about Dan.

A: On Monday Jo played football. What about Dan?
B: He ... On Tuesday Dan ... What about Jo?

On one day the twins did the same thing after school. When was it?

	Jo	Dan
Monday	play football	?
Tuesday	start his Maths project	?
Wednesday	work on his Maths project	?
Thursday	call his mum	?
Friday	listen to sport on the radio	?

8 PRONUNCIATION Past forms

blue verbs · (-*ed* [d]/[t] = no extra syllable)
Liz **liked** lists. Pat **played** the piano.

red verbs · (-*ed* [ɪd] = extra syllable)
Harry **hated** homework. Sheila **shouted** 'Shush'!

a) *Listen. Hold up a blue pen for the blue verbs and a red pen for the red verbs.*

b) **Extra** *How many verbs can you remember from a)? Make lists, then compare your lists with a partner. Listen again and check.*

blue verbs	red verbs
watched	*started ...*

c) *Read the poem out loud to your partner. Then listen to the poem and check your pronunciation together: is it [-ɪd], [-d] or [-t] at the end? Then read the poem out loud again.*

I climbed a tree and looked for Lee.
I wanted to play, I waited all day.
Lee shouted, 'You clown!
Why don't you come down?'
I loved that tree but I hated Lee.

9 Dan's report (Simple past: positive statements)

Dan watched Mr Green yesterday. Fill in the simple past forms of the verbs in his report.

SHoCK Team Report Card Name: *Dan Shaw*
19.35 Green (go) out. He (have got) a little parcel.
19.38 Outside the house he (look) left and right.
19.39 Then he (start) to walk to the end of the street.
19.42 Suddenly the man in black (come) out of a shop.
19.46 Green (see) him and (start) to run.
19.47 I (follow) Green.
19.52 Green (go) back to the B&B.
He (be) very nervous.
19.35: Green went out. He ...

10 LISTENING 'The elephants'

Here's a sketch from the Spring Show. There are six people on a train: three kids, a man, a woman and the ticket inspector.

***a)** Look at the title and the picture on the right. What do you think is happening?*

***b)** Listen to the sketch and put these sentences in the right order:*

1 The ticket inspector comes and tells the man he has to stop.
2 The friends are happy because they can sit.
3 The friends ask the man why he is doing that. He says he's scaring away elephants.
4 The woman says her elephant is very afraid.
5 A man starts to throw pieces of paper out of the window.

c) **Extra** *Your teacher can give you the sketch – then you can act it out. How can you make the train in your classroom? What other things do you need?*

11 WORDS An e-mail to Jay (Prepositions)

Complete Ananda's e-mail to her cousin Jay in New York.

Subject: Dress rehearsal

Dear Jay,
The dress rehearsal *for* (from/for) our Spring Show was great! All the children were very nervous. I'm not ... (in/on) the show, but I am ... (at/in) the Computer Club and we designed the programmes. The children practised every day ... (for/after) school. Then, ... (at/on) Tuesday, 5th May, the dress rehearsal started ... (on/at) 4 o'clock. Jo was one ... (of/from) the pirates. He had a patch ... (on/at) his right eye first, then ... (on/at) his left. Jack was very good ... (in/on) the band. We all listened ... (from/to) the music and watched the scenes ... (of/from) different musicals. ... (at/after) the end ... (for/of) the rehearsal we were all very happy. We're ready ... (at/for) the show tomorrow!
Do you have shows ... (at/in) your school ... (on/in) New York? Tell me ... (from/about) them.
Love, Ananda

12 Mr Shaw's list (Simple past: negative statements)

***a)** Mr Shaw wanted to do lots of things last weekend. Look at his list: say what he **didn't** do.*

Last weekend Mr Shaw didn't clean his bike.
He didn't ...

clean my bike
invite Indira to dinner ✓
check the boys' bikes ✓
call Grandma Thompson
help the boys with their homework
work in the garden
talk to the boys about the holidays
answer Catherine's e-mail
give the neighbours their book back
listen to my new CD ✓

***b)** Make a list of your usual weekend activities. Then tell a partner about last weekend. What did you do and what didn´t you do?*

At the weekend I often visit my grandma and go swimming.
Last weekend I visited my grandma but I didn't go swimming.

13 200 years ago they didn't watch TV (Simple past: negative statements)

The following sentences are wrong. Say what's wrong – use **didn't**.

1 200 years ago children watched TV in the evenings. (listen to stories)
200 years ago children didn't watch TV in the evenings. They listened to stories.
2 They went to school in cars. (walk to school)
3 Girls and boys went to school together. (go to different schools)
4 After dinner mums put plates in the dishwasher. (wash them in the sink)
5 Dads helped in the kitchen. (...)
6 Boys played computer games after school. (...)
7 Girls watched football matches. (...)

14 The Spring Show was great! (Simple past: mixed forms)

Complete the sentences. Use the simple past forms of the verbs in brackets.

1 The Spring Show *was* (be) last month.
2 After the show Dan ... (say), 'I ... (think) the pirate ship ... (look) great.'
3 But Jo ... (not like) the pirate ship.
4 The dance club ... (not dance) first. They ... (have to) wait till the end.
5 The Hansons ... (watch) the show.
6 'The band ... (not be) nervous,' Mrs Hanson ... (say) after the show. 'They ... (sound) good.'
7 'And the choir ... (be) great too,' ... (say) Mr Hanson.
8 At the end of the show there ... (be) a big pirate scene.
9 Everything ... (look) good. The students ... (not make) any mistakes.
10 The show ... (not be) just good, it ... (be) great!

15 Did the choir sing? (Simple past: questions)

Make questions with **did** *and match them to the answers.*

1 the choir: sing at the Spring Show
Did the choir sing at the Spring Show?
2 the students: play scenes from films too?
3 Jack: sing in the choir?
4 Jo: make any mistakes at the dress rehearsal?
5 the Computer Club: finish the programmes?
6 Dan: dance in the show?
7 Sophie's parents: think the show was terrible?

a) No, he didn't. But he helped to paint the pirate ship.
b) No, they didn't. They thought it was fantastic.
c) Yes, they did. They played a scene from the film 'Billy Elliot'.
d) No, he didn't sing. He played in the band.
e) Yes, they did. They sang songs from different musicals.
f) Yes, they did. Ananda was very happy.
g) Yes, he did. He made a mistake with his patch.

16 A quiz (Simple past: questions)

a) *Make five teams. Each team chooses one unit from the book (Welcome – Unit 4) and writes five questions in the simple past about it. Your teacher tells you how much time you have.*

b) *Each team reads its questions. The other teams write their answers on a piece of paper. Each team corrects the answers to its quiz. The team with most correct answers wins.*

Unit 4 Quiz (Alex, Julia, Lukas, Vanessa)
1 Where did Mr Green go to meet the woman with the parcel?

Welcome Quiz (Andy, Lena, Maria, Martin)
1 Where did Sophie first see Prunella?
2 ...

17 GETTING BY IN ENGLISH The school show

a) *How can you say these things in English? (You can find the answers on these pages.)*

1 Wie war's? (p. 86)
2 Ich war nicht schlecht. (p. 86)
3 Gestern waren wir schrecklich. (p. 87)
4 Deine Mutter und ich können es kaum erwarten, die Show zu sehen. (p. 87)
5 Wir sind heute früh zur Schule gegangen. (p. 88)
6 Er war allein. (p. 88)

b) *Prepare the dialogue with a partner. Then act it out.*

A: Frag B, wie sein/ihr Wochenende war.
B: Sag, dass es nicht schlecht war. Sag, dass du bei einer Show in der Schule warst und zwei Bands gesehen hast.
A: Frag, ob die Bands gut waren.
B: Sag, dass die erste Band schrecklich war.
A: Frag, ob die zweite Band auch schrecklich war.
B: Sag, dass sie toll war. Du kannst es kaum erwarten, ihre nächste Show zu sehen.
A: Frag, ob du dann mit B mitgehen kannst.
B: Sag ja, natürlich. Frag A, wie sein/ihr Wochenende war.
A: Sag, dass du am Samstag früh in die Stadt gegangen bist.
B: Frag, wo A am Sonntag war.
A: Sag, dass du zu einem Basketballspiel gegangen bist und dass du B's Bruder dort gesehen hast.
B: Frag, ob dein Bruder mit seiner Freundin da war.
A: Sag nein, er war allein.

STUDY SKILLS Unbekannte Wörter verstehen

Nachschlagen oder nicht?
Du kannst beim Lesen viel Zeit sparen, wenn du nicht jedes unbekannte Wort nachschlägst. Manchmal brauchst du das Wort zum Verständnis des Textes nicht. Und häufig kannst du die Bedeutung erschließen.

Wie?
Schau dir die Bilder an. Oft zeigen sie Dinge, die du im Text nicht verstehst. Manchmal kennst du ein ähnliches Wort – auf Deutsch oder auf Englisch. Und oft hilft der Zusammenhang, die Bedeutung zu erraten.

▸ *SF 6 (p. 124) • WB 16 (p. 65)*

A pirate story

It was in the Caribbean in the year 1719. The night was dark and windy. The ships were in the harbour, the sailors were in the tavern. They sat with their drinks and talked and laughed.

'And what ship are you from, friend?' said one young man to a sailor at his table,
'The *Silver Swordfish*,' answered the sailor.
'A great ship. Do many men sail on her?' asked the young man.
'Yes, 40 men.'
'Ah! 39 poor sailors on the ship and you here in the tavern!'
'No, no, boy, only two sailors are still on the ship,' said the sailor. 'The others are all here.'
'That's good, that's good,' said the young man.
'It is! Tell me, boy, what's your name?' asked the sailor.
'Bonny.'
'Well then, cheers, Mr Bonny!'
'Cheers!' said the young man. 'And goodbye.'

It was 2 o'clock in the morning. The harbour was dark. Two men ran to the *Silver Swordfish*: Mr Bonny and his captain, Jack Rackham. They had swords and pistols. In the shadows their men watched and waited.

Without a sound Captain Rackham and Mr Bonny climbed onto the ship.

'Who goes there?' called one of the sailors.
'A friend!' said Mr Bonny. 'But not *your* friend!' He took out his sword and killed the sailor.
'Who goes ... aaaaagh!' The second sailor was dead on the deck.
Captain Rackham called his men. They came out of the shadows and ran to the ship.
'We sail tonight, men!'

Captain Rackham and his men sailed for three days and three nights. On the fourth day the look-out saw a ship.
'Ship ahoy!' he shouted.
The pirates saw that it was a Spanish galleon.
'There's gold on that galleon,' said one of the pirates. 'And we want it!'

The *Silver Swordfish* rammed the galleon.

Mr Bonny started to take the gold back to the *Silver Swordfish*. Suddenly he saw a cabin boy.
'You!' he shouted. 'Help me with this gold!'
'Yes, sir,' said the boy. He was very scared.

At last all the gold was on the *Silver Swordfish*.
'You, boy!' said Mr Bonny to the cabin boy.
'What's your name?'
'Jonah,' said the boy.
'Jonah!' shouted Mr Bonny. 'Go and clean the captain's cabin. Now!'

The cabin boy did his work. Then he sat down in a dark corner. 'Just for a minute,' he said. But he was very tired and soon he was asleep.
When the captain and Mr Bonny came into the cabin, they didn't see the boy in the corner.
Later Jonah opened his eyes. At the table sat Captain Rackham and ... a beautiful woman.
But who was the woman?
'Ah, my pretty Ann Bonny!' the captain said.
'*Ann* Bonny!' shouted Jonah. Suddenly all was clear. 'But, but ... a woman on a ship is bad luck!'
Then the captain and Ann Bonny saw Jonah.
'Bad luck for you, boy!' Ann Bonny said. 'Our secret goes to the bottom of the sea ... with you!'

Boom ... boom ... boom. The sound of a drum mixed with the sound of the sea and the wind. All the men were on deck. The boy was on the plank. The captain pushed him with his sword.
'Walk, boy, walk!'
'Yeah. Walk the plank!' shouted the pirates.
The boy took a step. The captain pushed.
He took another step, and another ...
and then: down, down, down ...

THUD!

Jo opened his eyes. He was cold ... and on the floor of his room. Dan was asleep in the other bed.
'Hurrah for the Pirate King?' Jo said. 'I don't think so!'

Working with the text

1 New words

Here are some new words from the story. Did you
- *understand them from the pictures?*
- *understand them because they are like German words or other English words?*
- *understand them from the context?*
- *check them in the Dictionary?*

asleep • cabin • captain • gold • pistol • plank • rammed • sailor • scared • secret • silver • sword • tavern • windy

2 The story

a) *Look at these titles for different parts of the story. Where can you put them? Check with a partner.*

The gold • The tavern • Jonah in danger • The ship

'The tavern' goes on page ... before line ...

b) *Read the following sentences. Which heading do they go with? Write them in your exercise book in the right order.*

a) Bonny talked to a sailor in the tavern.
b) Bonny told Jonah to help with the gold.
c) Captain Rackham and Bonny climbed up onto the *Silver Swordfish*.
d) Jonah saw a beautiful woman.
e) Jonah was asleep in the captain's cabin.
f) Jonah was on the plank. The captain pushed him.
g) The sailor said there were only two men on the *Silver Swordfish*.
h) The *Silver Swordfish* rammed a Spanish galleon.
i) They killed two sailors.

c) **Extra** *Make a comic. Choose one or two headings from 2a)/b). Draw a picture for each sentence. Write speech bubbles for your pictures. Put your comic on the wall and read the other students' comics.*

► WB 17 (p. 66)
Checkpoint 5 ► WB (p. 67)

Extra Poems

The Poetry United Chant

WHAT DO WE WANT clap clap clap
WHAT DO WE LIKE clap clap clap
WHAT DO WE LOVE clap clap clap

GIVE US A P clap clap clap
GIVE US AN O clap clap clap
GIVE US AN E clap clap clap
GIVE US A T clap clap clap
GIVE US AN R clap clap clap
GIVE US A Y clap clap clap

GIVE US THE RHYTHM ... POETRY
WHAT WE WANT IS POETRY

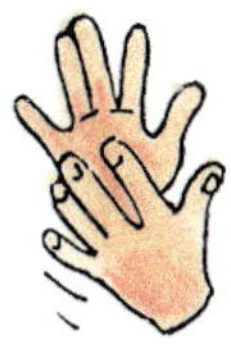

clap clap clap
clap clap clap
clap clap clap
YES!

Les Baynton

Halfway down

Halfway down the stairs
Is a stair
Where I sit.
There isn't any
Other stair
Quite like
It.
I'm not at the bottom.
I'm not at the top.
So this is the stair
Where
I always
Stop.

A.A. Milne

Rain

There are holes in the sky
Where the rain gets in,
But they're ever so small
That's why rain is thin.

Spike Milligan

Blue is the sea

Blue is the sea,
Green is the grass,
White are the clouds,
As they slowly pass.
Black are the crows,
Brown are the trees,
Red are the sails
Of a ship in the breeze.

Anonymous

1 Reading and listening to the poems

a) *Do 'The Poetry United Chant' in class.*

b) *Read the other poems quietly. Then listen to them on the CD. Now read them out loud.*

2 Enjoying the poem

Choose a), b), c) or d). Put your poem (or your favourite poem) in your DOSSIER. Or make a class poetry book.

a) *Write down your favourite poem. Draw a picture or take a photo to go with it.*

b) *Learn your favourite poem. Say it for the class or act it out.*

c) *Write down three words. Read them to your partner. He/She has to find rhyming words for them. Then find rhyming words for your partner's words. Together use all your words and write a poem.*

d) *Write a poem like 'Blue is the sea'. Write each line in the right colour. You can draw pictures too.*

Great places for kids

I can ...

... talk about where I live.
Collect ideas on the board.
...

I live in a flat/house. I like/don't like it because my bedroom/the garden/ ... is ...

It's near/a long way from my school/the city centre/...

There's a park/church/ shopping centre/... in our ... It's great/interesting/...

I live in ... It's a city/town/village.

... is a great place/boring for kids because ...

1 *Clifton Suspension Bridge: Walk or ride your bike over it.*

2 *Harbourside: Enjoy the old heart of Bristol.*

3 *Cabot Tower: Climb it and see Bristol.*

4 *The SS Great Britain: See a great old ship.*

5 *Aardman studios: Home of Bristol's favourite film stars*

6 *Explore-at-Bristol: Touch a tornado.*

1 Photos of Bristol

Look at photos 1–6. Which places would you like to visit? Why?

I'd like to go to Harbourside.
You can sit near the water/go on a boat trip/meet your friends/... there.

Yes, I'd like to go there too.

No, I wouldn't like to go there:
I don't like boats/museums/...

2 Form 7PK's project

Listen. Which photo does Mr Kingsley talk about? Which three questions do the students have to answer?

Is it easy to get there?

Is it open every day?

Is it interesting or fun for kids?

Is the price OK?

Is it only for kids?

How many places do the groups have to choose? Listen again and check.

► *P 1 (p. 106) • WB 1 (p. 68)*

1 Form 7PK's project begins

Form 7PK project:

Great places for kids

Placemat activity

1. Make a placemat like this on a big piece of paper:

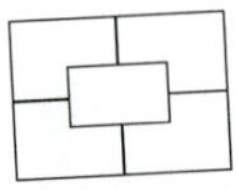

2. Each student must write three (or more) great places in one corner of the placemat. Use different colours! (3 minutes)
3. Talk about all the ideas in your group. Agree on the best three places. Write them in the middle of the placemat. (5 minutes)

Ananda, Jack, Jo and Sophie are in a group together. They've got their ideas in each corner of their placemat.

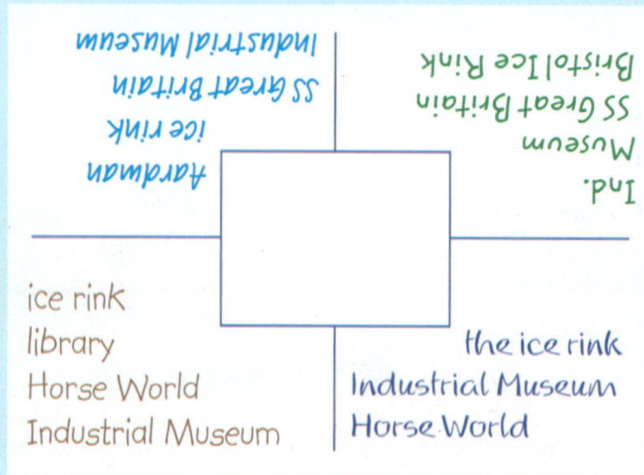

Now they have to agree on the best three ideas.

What two ideas have all the kids got?

2 The third place

Sophie	We've all got the Industrial Museum and the ice rink.
Jo	So what's our third place?
Sophie	What about Horse World?
Ananda	I don't think Horse World is a good idea. It's too far away. You need a car.
Jack	Yes, Ananda is right.
Jo	I think so too.
Sophie	OK. Then it's Aardman, the *SS Great Britain* or the library.
Jo	I don't think you can visit Aardman. I'm for the *SS Great Britain*.
Ananda	I'm against the Industrial Museum *and* the ship. Too much history.
Sophie	You're right. So let's take the library.
Jo	The library?
Jack	Yes, why not? It's a great place.
Ananda	And it's free. OK, Jo?
Jo	OK.
Sophie	Good. Now let's write our three places in the middle of the placemat.

Which three places do they choose? Why don't they want the other three places?

► *P 2–3 (p. 106) • WB 2 (p. 69)*

PROJECT Great places for kids (Part 1)

You can do a project like 7PK's.

Step 1 *Use a placemat like in **1**. Agree on three great places in your city/town/village. You can use these phrases.*

What about ... ?

I think ... is a good idea.

I think so too.

... is right.

I'm for ... because ...

I don't think ... is a good idea.

I'm against ... because ...

Let's take the ...

No, ... is wrong.

Step 2 *Find out more about your places. You can visit them; or collect brochures about them; or find information about them on the Internet.*

3 At the library

'It's really quiet,' Ananda whispered.
'That's why I like it,' Sophie whispered back.
'I come here because it's always so loud at home.'
'Hey, Jack,' Jo said. 'Isn't that Mr Green?'
'Oh, yes,' said Jack and started to walk towards Mr Green.
'What are you going to do?' Ananda asked him.
'I'm going to find out what he's reading!'
'Jack, he knows you,' Ananda said. 'And maybe he saw me at the station too. Soph...'
'I'm not going to do it!' said Sophie. 'I'm much too nervous. Jo, you go.'
So Jo went and looked. Then he came back to his friends. 'He's looking at plans,' he said.
'Plans of Clifton Suspension Bridge.'
'Oh no! He's going to ...' Jack stopped and looked at the others.
'What?' whispered Ananda. 'What's he going to do?'
'I think he's going to blow up the suspension bridge.'

Extra ▸ *GF 22: The going to-future (p. 144)* • *P 4–5 (p. 107)* • *WB 3 (p. 69)*

4 Now you

Talk to your partner about your plans:
What are you going to do this evening/on Saturday/...?
– I'm going to ... What about you?

5 At the Industrial Museum

'Let's take our photo over there, in front of that old car,' Jo said.
'No, here,' Jack said. 'This car is better.'
'All these cars look the same,' Sophie said.
'Let's take our photo with those buses over there. Look, that last bus is from Bristol.'
'Everything here is from Bristol, Sophie,' Jo said. 'You girls are ...'
'We girls are what, Jo?' Sophie asked. 'I hate it when people don't finish their sentences.'
'Yeah Sophie, and I hate it when ....'
'And I hate it when people argue,' Ananda said.
'Let's take the photo over there. Look, it's the world's first holiday caravan. Ready? OK, smile, please!'

▸ *GF 23: Word order (p. 145)* • *P 6–10 (pp. 108–109)* • *WB 4–8 (pp. 69–71)*

6 Sophie is the boss

Sophie Jo, Jack! Ananda is sticking the photos on now. What are you two doing?

Jo Well, at the moment we're writing notes for the presentation.

Sophie OK, but you should be careful. You boys always make a mess when you write.

Jo OK, Baby Soph. You're the boss!

Sophie Oh, no! Ananda! You're using too much glue now. I never use so much. Look, there's glue everywhere.

Ananda Sorry, boss. You're right – you're always right. So you stick a photo on your arm every day, I suppose. Or only on Fridays?

Looking at language

*Find and write down the sentences in **6** with the verbs stick, write and use.*

Simple present	Present progressive
... you stick a photo ...	Ananda is sticking the photos ...
...	...

Which verb form do you use with words like now, at the moment?

► GF 24: Simple present and present progressive (pp. 145–146) • P 11–12 (p. 108) • WB 9–12 (pp. 72–73)

7 The poster

Great places for kids in Bristol

Sophie Carter-Brown, Jack Hanson, Ananda Kapoor, Jo Shaw

Bristol Ice Rink

- ★ Lots of fun
  - Meet friends
  - Junior disco on Saturdays
- ★ In city centre: Frogmore Street
- ★ Not too expensive: £3.50 for students
- ★ Nice and cool in summer!

Bristol Industrial Museum

Remember Mr Kingsley's questions from p. 101? Use the poster and answer them for Bristol Ice Rink.

8 Presentation time

'Well, we've got time for one more presentation,' Mr Kingsley said. 'Let's take Jo, Sophie, Jack and Ananda.' The group went to the front of the classroom. Jack started. 'Our three places are the ice rink, the Industrial Museum and the library. Ananda is first.'
'OK, Jack,' Ananda said. 'I'd like to talk about the ice rink. We like it for lots of reasons ...'

9 The group's presentation

a) *Look at the presentation phrases. Try to write them down in the right order.*

1 Our three places are ...
2 Ananda is first.

b) *Now listen to the group's presentation and check. Who used the yellow phrases? Who used the orange phrases?*

c) *Listen again and take notes about what they say about the ice rink.*

d) *Choose your favourite place in Bristol. What is your class's favourite place?*

Our three places are ...

We like ... for lots of reasons.

Ananda is first.

Second ...

Have you got any questions?

And third, ...

That's the end of our presentation.

I'd like to talk about ...

Jo is next.

First, ...

► *WB 13–19 (p. 74)*

STUDY SKILLS Ergebnisse präsentieren

Vorbereitung *Notiert euch in Stichworten, was ihr sagen wollt. Spielt die Präsentation auf jeden Fall einmal ganz durch.*
Arbeitsteilung *Teilt euch beim Vortrag so auf, dass jede/r etwas sagt. Zum Beispiel so, dass eine/r durch die Präsentation führt und die anderen je einen der Orte präsentieren.*

► *SF 7 (p. 125)*

PROJECT Great places for kids (Part 2)

Finish your project.

Step 3 *Make a poster for your presentation. Use pictures and key words like in* **7**. *(Check with your teacher before you write on your poster.)*

Step 4 *Present your poster to the class (about 15 sentences). Use ideas from* **8** *and* **9**.

1 WORDS Are you a word champion?

a) *Put the words and phrases from the box in the right baskets. Some can go in two baskets. Your teacher tells you how much time you have.*

b) *Compare with a partner.*

A: I've got ... words in the basket 'At school'. How many have you got?

B: I've got ... I put 'library' in the basket 'At school'. Where did you put it?

badminton • basketball • birthday cake • bridge • church • clean your room • dance to music • do homework • do yoga • downstairs • drama lesson • flat • Geography • go swimming • go to bed • have a shower • have breakfast • hutch • invitation • kitchen • learn • lunch break • Maths • museum • open a present • party game • player • teacher • team • village • wardrobe • win

2 WORDS Word partners I

a) *Copy the words from the red box in red and the words from the blue box in blue on pieces of paper. Make word partners. Use each word once.* bank robber, bus ..., ...

bank • baseball • chocolate • drama • dress • exercise • glass • ice • lunch • mobile • orange • pet • shop • tennis

assistant • book • bowl • break • cake • club • juice • phone • racket • rehearsal • rink • robber • shop • team

b) **Extra** *Write a story with five of the word pairs from a). It can be funny/scary/...*

3 WORDS Word partners II

a) *Which words go with these verbs?*

take
have

away • breakfast • fun • notes • a train

get
do
make

dressed • home • homework • judo • a mess • a mistake • models • ready • up late

b) *Give your partner four word partners from a). He/She has to make sentences with them.*

c) *What nouns go with these verbs?*
watch – read – look at – play – write – ride – listen to   watch TV / a show / ...

d) **Extra** *Now write at least one sentence with each verb from c), for example:* After dinner I watch TV.

4 Extra Dan is going to … (going to-future)

Look at the pictures and say what the people are going to do.

1 Dan is going to play …
2 Jack is going to …
3 Mr Kapoor …
4 …

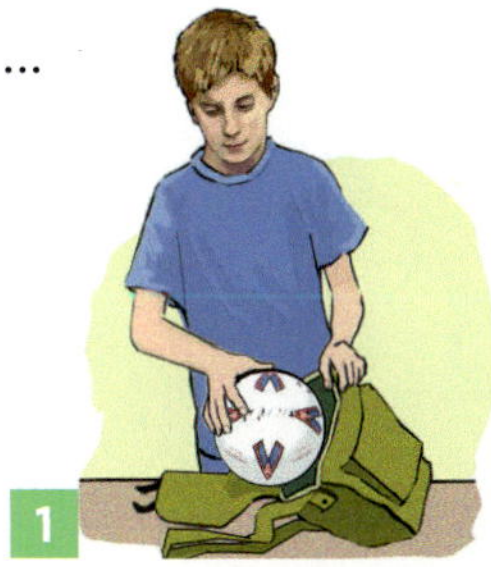
1

2

3

4

5

6

7

5 Extra Your plans (going to-future)

a) *Write down some funny plans for next week.*
Then talk to a partner about them.

A: On Monday I'm going to …
What are you going to do?
B: I'm going to … On Tuesday I'm … What are …?

Monday – sleep all day
Tuesday – dance with my dog
Wednesday – …

b) *Make appointments with three other partners.*
Tell them about your first partner's plans.

6 Remember? (Word order in subordinate clauses)

a) *Do you remember the stories in the book? Link the sentences with the word in brackets and write them in your exercise book. Be careful with the word order.*

1 Jo made a joke about Sophie's name. Mr Kingsley didn't like it. (when)
When Jo made a joke about Sophie's name, Mr Kingsley didn't like it.
2 The twins were both nervous. They went into the classroom. (before)
3 The twins' mum isn't in Bristol. She went to New Zealand. (because)
4 The SHoCK Team started. Mr Green was a guest at the Pretty Polly B&B. (when)
5 Sophie had to write an essay for homework. Prunella helped her. (when)
6 Prunella was sorry. Sophie didn't invite her to her party. (because)
7 Sophie found a mouse. She opened Jack and Ananda's present. (after)
8 Jonah knew Ann Bonny's secret. He had to walk the plank. (because)

b) *Now finish these sentences about yourself – remember the right word order.*

1 After I got home yesterday, …
2 I went to … last week because …
3 I said 'sorry' to … when …
4 Before I went to bed last night I …

7 Ananda and Dilip (this, that, these, those)

a) Write sentences with this is/these are.

1 ... my room.
2 ... my wardrobe.
3 ... my library books.
4 ... my new hockey shoes.
5 ... my cousins in this photo.
6 ... my favourite magazine.
7 ... my new CD player.

b) Write sentences with that's/those are.

1 ... my brother Dilip's room.
2 ... his boring comics.
3 ... his new mobile phone.
4 ... his shoes.
5 ... his favourite CDs.
6 ... his MP3 player. It's great.
7 ... his book about India.

8 PRONUNCIATION [ʃ], [tʃ] and [dʒ]

a) Listen. Which number is the boy? Which numbers are the monsters?

b) Put the words from the box in the right lists. Then listen and check.

armchair • bridge • church • English • finish • Geography • hutch • information • juice • orange • picture • question • shout • shopping • village • which • worksheet

[ʃ]	[tʃ]	[dʒ]
ship	*chip*	*job*
...	...	

c) Say one of the words in these pairs. Your partner then shows you the word.

1 ship – chip
2 share – chair
3 juice – choose
4 check – Jack
5 show – Jo
6 cheese – she's

Is he/she right? Check in the Dictionary.

9 REVISION Prunella's project (Simple present)

Prunella is working on her project, 'Great places for poltergeists'. Finish her sentences; use the simple present.

I ... (not/know) lots of places because I'm a poltergeist. I ... (live) in the Carter-Browns' house and ... (never/visit) other countries. But my uncle Henry ... (always/tell) me about fantastic places in different parts of the world. ... (you/know) Paris? Well, my uncle Henry ... (often/go) there. He ... (say) it's beautiful, but how ...(he/know)? He ... (not/have got) a head, so he can't see! My favourite place ... (be) my room. I ... (share) it with my friend Sophie. She ... (always/say) it ... (be) her room, but it ... (be) really our room.

10 REVISION What are they doing? (Present progressive)

Partner B: Look at p. 117.
Partner A: Look at the pictures and tell your partner what the people are doing. Then ask your partner what they're doing in his/her pictures. Two pictures are the same – find out which.

A: In my picture 1, Ananda is reading a book. What's she doing in your picture 1?
B: In my picture 1, she's ...

1 read

2 make

3 listen to

4 write

5 work

6 follow

7 look at

8 go to

11 Today is different (Simple present and present progressive)

Prunella usually plays tricks on Sophie's family, but at the moment she's trying to be nice. Fill in the verbs. Say what she usually/often/sometimes does and what she's doing now.

1. Prunella often drops (often/drop) cakes, but now she's making (make) a cake.
2. She (usually/take away) Sophie's clothes, but today she (wash) them.
3. She (sometimes/play) football in the living room, but she (clean) it now.
4. She (often/draw) pictures in Sophie's exercise book, but at the moment she (help) Sophie with her homework.
5. She (often/throw) plates, but she (wash) them right now.
6. She (sometimes/draw) on Mr Carter-Brown's car, but today she (clean) it.

12 Who's who? (Simple present and present progressive)

Complete the sentences with the simple present or the present progressive. Then say who the men in the picture are.

1. Mr Wiggle usually (wear) a white shirt, but today he (not wear) a white shirt.
2. Mr Woggle never (wear) red shoes, but he (like) red jeans.
3. Mr Waggle (love) red jeans, but he (not wear) them today.
4. Mr Waggle (wear) Mr Wiggle's white shirt today.
5. Mr Wiggle (think) green shoes are terrible. He never (wear) them.
6. Mr Woggle (not like) blue, but he (wear) blue today.

The Mr Green mystery

The story so far: Look at your flow chart from Unit 5 (p. 90). Update it. Compare your flow charts in class. Now read the story.

Jack opened the front door.
'Oh, hi Sophie! You're early!' he said.
'Hi, Jack! I'm sorry, I know the SHoCK Team meets at 6 o'clock, but ...'
'Oh, that's OK. Come in. It's nice to see you.'
'Hello, hello, hello!' called Polly from her cage in the kitchen.
'Hello, Polly,' answered Sophie.
'Let's go up to my room,' Jack said.
'Doorbell, doorbell!' Polly called.
'Sorry, Sophie.' Jack went and opened the door.
'Parcel for Mr Green.'
'Thank you.' Jack took the parcel in.
'I must put this parcel in Mr Green's room, Sophie,' he said.
He took the key from the kitchen.
'Are you sure he's out, Jack?' Sophie asked.
Jack knocked on Mr Green's door. No answer.
'OK, you go in,' said Sophie.
Jack opened the door. He went in and took the parcel to the table. And then he saw a piece of paper on the table. There was a number on it.
'Hmm,' Jack said, 'I know that number.' Then he remembered: 'It's Mum's phone number at work. Why has Mr Green got her number?'
Jack was worried now. He started to look at other things on the table.

What do you see on Mr Green's table?
Why do you think he's got these things?
Mr Green has got ...
Maybe he wants to/he's going to blow up/go to/call ...
Now read on. Were your ideas right?

Suddenly Sophie called: 'Jack! Somebody's coming!'
'Oh, no – it must be Mr Green!' Jack said and came out of the room. 'Let's wait on the stairs,' he whispered.
Then there was a voice in the hall. 'Hello, Michael,' it said. It wasn't Mr Green's voice. After a few seconds Jack and Sophie saw Mr Green – and the man in black.
'Who are you? How do you know my name?' Mr Green sounded scared.
'I know everything about you, Michael. We have to talk, you and me. Let's go into your room.'
'Yes, but ...'
'No "buts", Michael!'
The man in black pushed Mr Green into the room and closed the door.
'Call the police on your mobile, Sophie,' Jack whispered and ran to the door and listened.
'Turn on the computer,' the man in black said.
'Do you work for Howard?' Mr Green asked.
'Yes. And you know what he wants.'
'When I worked for him he took all my ideas,' Mr Green said. 'But he can't have this idea!'
'Can't? Howard hates it when people say "can't"!' the man said. 'I really don't want to hurt you, Michael, but ...'
Mr Green cried in pain: 'Aaagh!'
In the hall, Jack looked at the key in his hand – and locked Mr Green's door.
'What's that?' shouted the man in black. He ran to the door and tried to open it. 'Who's there? Open this door. Open it or ...'
Jack smiled and went back to Sophie.

Working with the text

1 Right or wrong?
Correct the wrong sentences.
1 Mr Green is scared.
2 The man in black's name is Howard.
3 Jack calls the police.
4 The man in black locks Mr Green's door.

2 What happens next?
Talk to a partner about these questions.
1 Does the man open the door and shout at Jack and Sophie?
2 Does the SHoCK Team come and help?

3 The end of the story
a) *Check these words in the Dictionary:*

invent • build • river • mountain • ground • save

b) *Now listen to the CD. Were your answers to* **2** *right or wrong?*

c) *Do you think the SHoCK Team did a good job? Why? Why not?*

d) **Extra** *Write the SHoCK Team's answer to Mr Green's question, 'What is the "SHoCK Team"?'*

► WB 16 (p. 75)

Checkpoint 6 ► WB (pp. 76–77)

Extra Merry Christmas

1 Christmas fun

a) *What Christmas words and phrases do you know? Write them down.*

b) *Now look at the Christmas cards. What other Christmas things and people can you see? Add them to your list. Compare your list with a partner.*

3 A Christmas puzzle

Find all the ten Christmas words in the Christmas box on the right and write them down.

Merry Christmas, Christmas Day, ...

4 SONG Jingle bells

Listen to 'Jingle bells'. Learn the song and sing it with your class. Or learn and sing another Christmas song.

5 ACTIVITY A Christmas card

Make your own Christmas card and send it to a friend.

D	V	T	H	J	L	P	N	U	D
C	A	R	D	T	F	A	S	H	A
X	O	E	U	N	H	A	P	P	Y
P	R	E	S	E	N	T	K	J	R
U	L	I	R	V	B	H	Q	L	H
D	C	A	K	E	M	E	R	R	Y
D	K	D	N	C	A	R	O	L	J
I	F	R	V	G	H	A	V	M	M
N	Y	H	Z	W	R	E	T	D	K
G	N	J	S	S	C	B	X	E	I

2 Now you

Talk about your family:

We don't have Christmas, but we have ... , and we eat ... and we ...

We have ... for Christmas dinner.

We don't write Christmas cards.

6 ACTIVITY Make a Christmas cracker

You need:

1 Make a hat.

2 Write a joke.

3 Cut the paper.

4 Put the hat, the joke and a small toy inside, roll up the cracker. Tie it.

▸ WB Activity page 4

Unit 1

1 WORDS What's different?

Look at the picture. Find out what's different in your partner's picture.

A: There's one apple in my picture.
B: Oh, there are two apples in my picture. They're green.
A: Yes, my apple is green too.
B: There are two plates in my picture.
A: Oh, there are …
…

11 WORDS The new timetable

a) *Answer your partner's questions.*

b) *Not all the subjects are in your timetable. Ask your partner what they are.*
B: What's lesson 4 on Monday?
A: Lesson 4 on Monday is Drama.

	Monday	Tuesday	Wednesday	Thursday	Friday
1	Maths	…	German	Geography	RE
2	Science	Geography	…	Maths	Drama
3	Science	…	English	English	Science
4	…	English	PE	…	PE
5	Music	PE	…	PE	…
6	…	Music	Drama	German	Maths

Unit 2

7 What they do every day (Simple present: positive statements)

a) *Look at the chart below. Find out about Jack.*
A: Jack gets up at … What about Ananda?
B: Ananda gets up at 7.30. She gets dressed at …

b) *What about you? Complete a copy of the chart. Then talk to your partner.*
A: I get up at … What about you?

c) **Extra** *Write about your partner's day.*

	Ananda	Jack	You	Your partner
get up	at 7.30	…	…	…
get dressed	at 7.40	…	…	…
have breakfast	at 7.45	…	…	…
clean teeth	at 8.00	…	…	…
come home from school	at 4.10	…	…	…
watch TV	at 7.30	…	…	…
go to bed	at 8.45	…	…	…

Unit 3

9 Sport in different countries (Simple present: wh-questions)

a) *Look at the people below. Which of these questions can you answer about them?*
Where ... come from?
What sport ... do?
When ... do sport?

b) *Answer your partner's questions. Then ask him or her questions about the missing information and write it in your exercise book.*
A: Where does Sanjay come from?
B: He comes from Delhi.
A: When does Sophie ...?
B: She ...

Unit 4

6 STUDY SKILLS Notizen machen

a) *Partner B: Read about Max's birthday party. Take notes so that you can tell your partner about it.*

b) *Close your book. Use your notes to tell your partner what Max and his friends are doing at their party. Answer his or her questions if necessary.*

c) *Listen to your partner's story about what Emma wants on her birthday. You can ask him/her questions.*

'Hi Max. Happy birthday! How's your party?'
'Thanks, Gran. It's great. My present from mum and dad is fantastic: my friends and I are going camping. Well, we're going camping in the garden. There are five of us. We're all boys, of course. We've got lots of food and drink – sausages, chips, cake and cola. My best friend Joe has got a CD/MP3 player with really great music. And a CD of ghost stories for tonight. We're playing "Billionaire" now. It's great fun.'

8 Happy birthday! (some and any)

Partner B: Look at the picture. Tell your partner about it. Ask questions about his/her picture.

I've got Have you got I haven't got	some any	bananas • biscuits • books • cakes • CDs • chicken • crisps • fruit salad • lemonade • orange juice • presents • sausages • soap • socks • sweets	in my picture. in your picture?

A: I've got some crisps in my picture. Have you got any in your picture?
B: Yes, I have. And I've got some books. What about you?
A: No, I haven't got any books. I've got some ...

Unit 5

7 After school (Simple past: regular verbs in positive statements)

Tell your partner what Dan did after school last week. Ask him/her about Jo.
A: On Monday Jo ... What about Dan?
B: He watched TV. On Tuesday Dan ... What about Jo?

On one day the twins did the same thing after school. When was it?

	Jo	Dan
Monday	?	watch TV
Tuesday	?	clean his dad's car
Wednesday	?	listen to music
Thursday	?	call his mum
Friday	?	play cards with Jack

Unit 6

10 REVISION What are they doing? (Present progressive)

Look at the pictures and tell your partner what the people are doing. Then ask your partner what they're doing in his/her pictures. Two pictures are the same – find out which.

A: In my picture 1, Ananda is reading a book. What's she doing in your picture?
B: In my picture 1, she's …

1 follow

2 sit

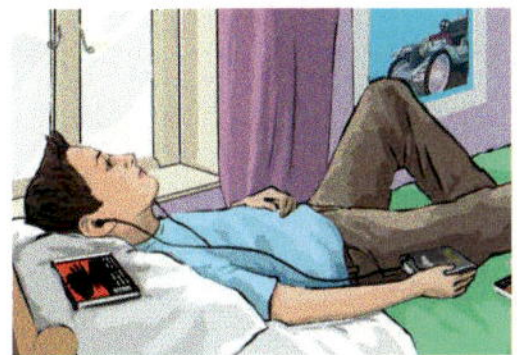
3 listen to

4 feed

5 work

6 take notes

7 ride

8 go to

Unit 4 (Lösung)

12 I think Sophie is …

Were you right? Here are the correct pictures.

1

2

3

4

5

6

7

8

SF 1 Wörter lernen – *Learning vocabulary* (Units 1–6)

Vokabeln kann man auf unterschiedliche Weise lernen. Hier sind ein paar Tipps. Probiere sie im Laufe des Schuljahres aus, dann weißt du, welche für dich besonders hilfreich sind.

Vokabeln lernen mit dem Vocabulary

Dein erster Weg führt dich zum Vocabulary (S. 148–178). Hier sind die neuen englischen Wörter und Wendungen aufgelistet, die du lernen musst. Das Vocabulary enthält viele Informationen. Auf S. 146 findest du Hinweise, wie es aufgebaut ist. Und so lernst du mit dem Vocabulary:

(to) **watch TV** [ti:'vi:]	fernsehen	TV = television ['telɪvɪʒn] **!** <u>im</u> Fernsehen = **<u>on</u>** TV: a good film **on TV**
after that	danach	First I feed the pets. **After that** I have my breakfast.

Schritt 1:
- Lies das englische Wort in der linken Spalte laut.
- Dann lies die deutsche Übersetzung in der mittleren Spalte.
- In der rechten Spalte findest du Tipps und Hilfen, z.B. einen Beispielsatz.
- Mach dies zunächst mit 7–10 Wörtern.

Schritt 2:
Jetzt teste dich, Zeile für Zeile:
- Decke die mittlere Spalte mit der deutschen Übersetzung ab. Sag die deutschen Wörter.
- Nun decke die linke und die rechte Spalte ab. Sag die englischen Wörter. Versuche auch immer noch die Beispielsätze aus der rechten Spalte zu nennen.

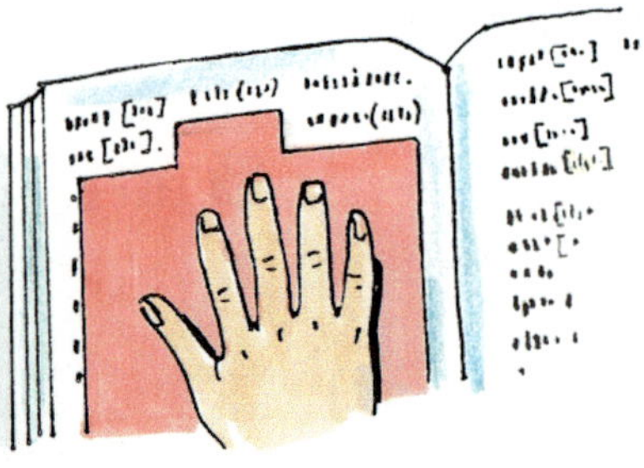

So kannst du dir eine Lernhilfe zum Abdecken der Spalten basteln:

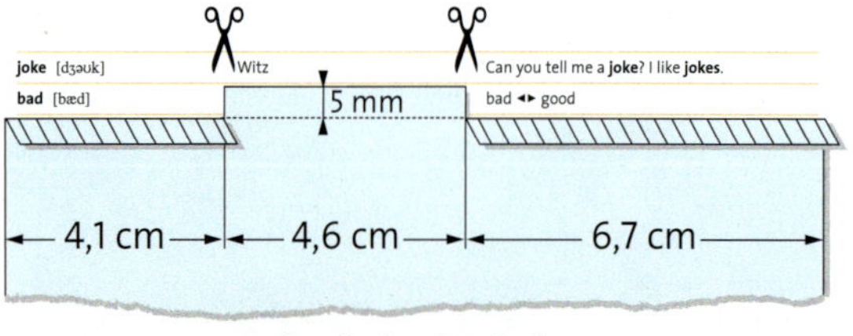

Englisch – Deutsch

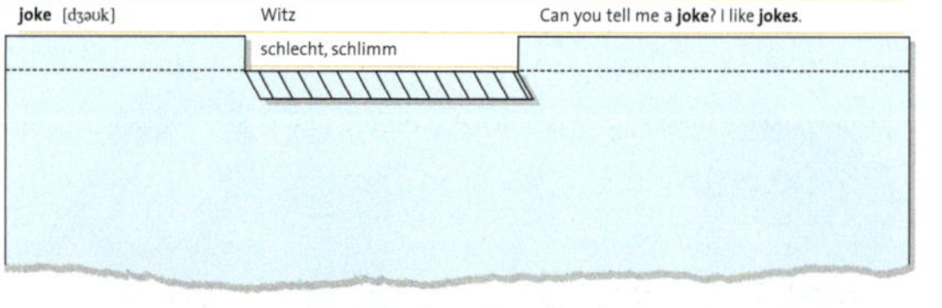

Deutsch – Englisch

Tipp
- Lerne portionsweise, immer 7–10 Wörter und Wendungen zusammen.
- Lerne Vokabeln regelmäßig, lieber jeden Tag 5–10 Minuten als einmal pro Woche 2 Stunden.
- Wiederhole die gelernten Vokabeln einmal in der Woche.
- Es macht mehr Spaß, wenn du Vokabeln mit jemandem zusammen lernst. Ihr könnt euch gegenseitig abfragen.

- Probier doch mal Aufgabe 8 auf S. 27.

Abschreiben erwünscht – Vokabeln aufschreiben

Viele Schüler lernen Vokabeln besonders gut, wenn sie sie aufschreiben.

▪ Vokabelheft mit drei Spalten
Leg ein Vokabelheft mit drei Spalten an.
- Schreibe das englische Wort in die linke Spalte, die deutsche Übersetzung in die mittlere Spalte und einen Beispielsatz (z.B. aus dem Vocabulary oder aus der Unit) in die rechte Spalte. Du kannst auch ein Bild malen.
  Achte darauf, dass du die Wörter richtig abschreibst.
- Lies die geschriebenen Wörter noch einmal laut.

▪ Elektronisches Vokabelverzeichnis
Es gibt Computerprogramme, die dich beim Üben und Wiederholen wie ein „Vokabeltrainer" unterstützen. Du kannst dazu dein *e-Workbook* und den *English Coach* benutzen.

▪ Networks
Du kannst neue Vokabeln ordnen und in Gruppen lernen – zum Beispiel mit einem Wörternetz (*network*).

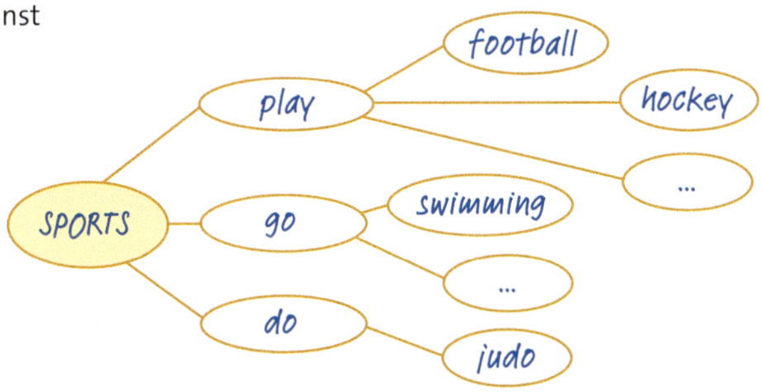

▪ Dein „Bilderbuch"
Vielleicht helfen dir kleine Skizzen, neue Vokabeln zu behalten.

Alles im Kasten – Vokabeln lernen mit Karteikarten

Manche können auch mit Karteikarten und einem Karteikasten prima Vokabeln lernen. Karteikarten lassen sich übrigens auch gut für *networks* oder Spiele mit Wörtern im Unterricht verwenden.
Nimm für den Karteikasten eine Pappschachtel und unterteile sie in fünf unterschiedlich große Fächer.

Vorderseite Rückseite

Schritt 1: Schreibe das englische Wort und einen Beispielsatz auf die Vorderseite einer Karteikarte und die deutsche Übersetzung auf die Rückseite. Dieses und weitere Kärtchen kommen in das erste, kleinste Fach.

Schritt 2: Wenn das erste Fach voll ist, nimm den ganzen Packen heraus und wiederhole die Wörter. Die Vokabeln, die du kannst, kommen in das nächste Fach. Die anderen kommen zurück in das erste Fach.

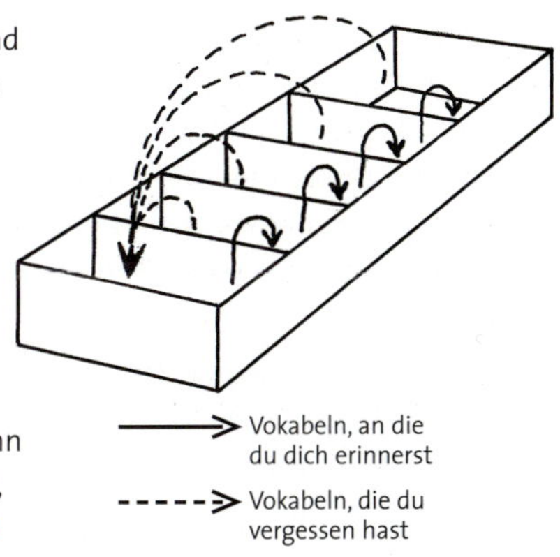

Schritt 3: Nach einiger Zeit ist auch das zweite Fach voll. Mach es wie mit dem ersten Fach: Die Vokabeln, die „sitzen", wandern weiter nach hinten in das nächste Fach. Vokabeln, die du wieder vergessen hast, kommen zurück ins erste Fach.

Schritt 4: So wandern die Karten Schritt für Schritt bis ins fünfte Fach. Wenn du diese Wörter nach einiger Zeit wiederholst und immer noch beherrschst, kannst du sie herausnehmen, denn **fünfmal gekonnt ist wirklich gekonnt!**

SF 2 **Stop – Check – Go** (Unit 1)

Hast du bei den Hausaufgaben viele Fehler gemacht? Hast du die neue Grammatik nicht verstanden? Schreibt ihr in nächster Zeit eine Englischarbeit? Dann solltest du STOP – CHECK – GO anwenden.

Stop
Mindestens einmal pro Unit, besser häufiger.

Check
Überprüfe, ob du den Stoff einer Unit verstanden hast. Wenn du nicht sicher bist, was zum Stoff einer Unit gehört, kannst du im Inhaltsverzeichnis nachschauen oder deine/n Lehrer/in fragen.
Für Unit 1 könntest du dich z.B. fragen:

- Vokabeln: Kann ich alle neuen Wörter schreiben und aussprechen? Weiß ich, was sie bedeuten? Kann ich Namen buchstabieren?
- Grammatik: Kenne ich die Formen von *be* und die Personalpronomen? Kann ich sagen, was ich und andere tun können und was nicht? Kann ich sagen, dass jemand etwas besitzt?
- Inhalt: Kann ich sagen, wie ich heiße und woher ich komme? Kann ich mich über Schulfächer unterhalten?

Zusammen mit einem Partner/einer Partnerin kannst du dir weitere Fragen zu Unit 1 überlegen. Am Ende jeder Unit wirst du zum Checkpoint im Workbook geschickt. Dort findest du Testaufgaben, mit denen du dich selbst prüfen kannst.

Go
Was kannst du besser machen? Frag deine/n Lehrer/in um Rat oder probiere die Vorschläge unten aus.

Tipp

Probleme mit den Vokabeln?
- Wenn du dir von manchen Wörtern die Bedeutung nicht merken kannst, schreibe sie auf Karteikarten oder male ein Bild dazu.
- Lass dich von jemandem abhören.
- Mach die *Words*-Übungen noch einmal. Du erinnerst dich z.B. nicht mehr an alle Schulfächer? Dann mach die Übung 10 auf S. 29 noch einmal.
- Schau dir das Skills File 1 auf S. 118/119 nochmal an.

Probleme mit der Grammatik?
- Lass dir Dinge, die du nicht verstanden hast, von deinen Mitschüler/innen erklären.
- Du bist z.B. unsicher, wie die Formen von *be* lauten? Schau dir das Grammar File dazu an (S. 128).
- Anschließend mach die Übungen zu *be* nochmal (S. 26–27).

Probleme mit dem Inhalt?
- Übe mit einem Partner/einer Partnerin kurze Dialoge zu den A-Sections der Unit.
- Mach die *Getting by in English*-Übung im Practice-Teil mit einem Partner/einer Partnerin.
- Benutze Hilfsmittel, z.B. die Listening-CD zum Schülerbuch oder das Workbook.

SF 3 Mindmaps (Unit 2)

Wozu dienen Mindmaps?

Mindmaps helfen dir beim Sammeln und Ordnen deiner Ideen. Sie können z.B. sehr hilfreich sein, wenn du etwas vortragen oder schreiben sollst.

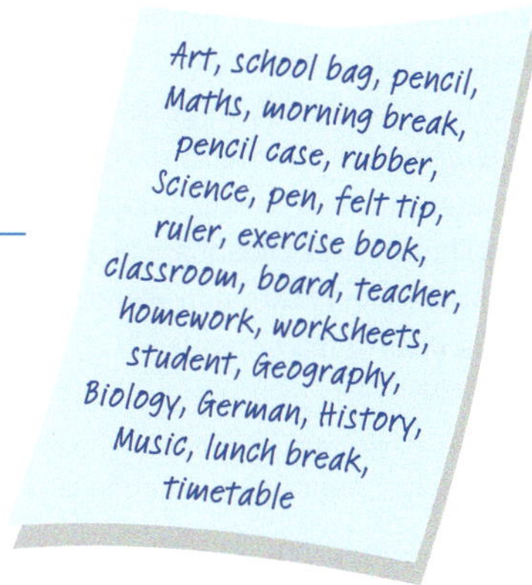

Wie lege ich eine Mindmap an?

Wie in diesem Beispiel zum Thema „Schule" kannst du als Erstes alles in einer Liste sammeln, was dir einfällt.

Was brauche ich?

- Ein leeres, unliniertes Blatt Papier, das du quer vor dich legst
- Stifte in verschiedenen Farben

Wie gehe ich am besten vor?

1. Schreib das Thema in die Mitte des Blattes und umrahme es mit einem Kreis oder einer Zeichnung.

2. Überlege dir, welche Oberbegriffe zu deiner Sammlung von Ideen passen. Am besten eignen sich dafür Nomen und Verben. Verwende unterschiedliche Farben. Jetzt hat deine Mindmap Hauptäste.

3. Ergänze jede Idee, die zu einem Oberbegriff passt, auf einem Nebenast.

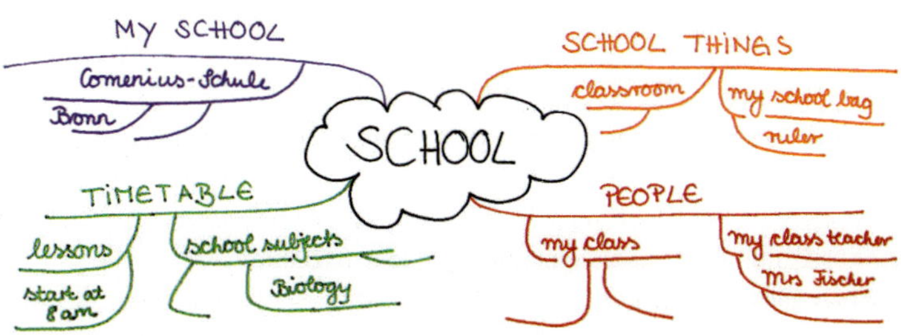

Du kannst statt Wörtern auch Zahlen oder Symbole eintragen und Bilder ergänzen.

Es gibt auch Computerprogramme, mit denen man Mindmaps erstellen kann.

- Alles verstanden? Dann probier doch mal Aufgabe 3 auf S. 42.

SF 4 Wörter nachschlagen – *Looking up words* (Unit 3)

Wozu ist das Dictionary gut?

Nimm an, du stolperst in einem Text über ein unbekanntes Wort; vielleicht hast du auch einfach vergessen, was es bedeutet. Oder du möchtest wissen, wie man ein Wort richtig ausspricht. Dann hilft dir das Dictionary (S. 179–191). Es enthält alle Wörter und Wendungen, die im Buch vorkommen.

Wie benutze ich das Dictionary?

1. Die blau gedruckten Stichwörter (z.B. **face, family**) sind alphabetisch angeordnet (also **f** vor **g**, **fa** vor **fe** und **fla** vor **flo**).
2. Beachte auch die Wörter, die schwarz hervorgehoben sind. Es sind:
   - zusammengesetzte Wörter (z.B. **family tree**)
   - abgeleitete Wörter (z.B. **finder** von **find**) oder
   - längere Ausdrücke (z.B. **the first day**).
3. Zusammengesetzte Wörter und längere Ausdrücke findest du oft unter mehr als einem Stichwort, z.B. **so far** unter **so** und unter **far**.
4. Aussprache und Betonung stehen in den eckigen Klammern. Du bist bei den Lautschriftzeichen unsicher? Dann schau dir S. 147 an.
5. Es ist wichtig, den ganzen Eintrag nach dem Stichwort zu lesen. Oft findest du zusätzliche Hinweise, z.B. auf
   - besondere Pluralformen
   - Änderungen der Schreibweise, z.B. Doppel-t bei **fit** – **fitting**.
6. Die Ziffern **1.**, **2.** usw. zeigen, dass das englische Stichwort mehrere Bedeutungen hat.

Was bedeuten die Abkürzungen und Symbole im Dictionary? – Schau nach auf S. 179.

face [feɪs] Gesicht 1 (22/155)
family ['fæməli] Familie Welc (12/151) • **family tree** (Familien-)Stammbaum 2 (41)
°**fancy-dress party** [ˌfænsi'dres] Kostümfest
fantastic [fæn'tæstɪk] fantastisch, toll 4 (81)
far [fɑː] weit (entfernt) 6 (102)
°**so far** bis jetzt, bis hierher

find [faɪnd] finden Welc (10) • **find out (about)** herausfinden (über) 3 (65) • **finder** Finder 5 (91)
finger ['fɪŋgə] Finger 4 (74/171)
finish ['fɪnɪʃ] beenden, zu Ende machen; enden 6 (103)
first [fɜːst] **1.** erste(r, s) Welc (14)
the first day der erste Tag Welc (14)
be first der/die Erste sein 6 (105)
2. zuerst, als Erstes 1 (20)
fish, *pl* **fish** [fɪʃ] Fisch 2 (37/159)
fit (-tt-) [fɪt] *(in der Größe)* passen 3 (54)
flat [flæt] Wohnung Welc (14)
floor [flɔː] Fußboden TOP 2 (51)
follow ['fɒləʊ] folgen; verfolgen 4 (71)
food [fuːd] **1.** Essen; Lebensmittel 1 (24); **2.** Futter 2 (39)

- Alles verstanden? Dann probier doch mal Aufgabe 10 auf S. 61.

SF 5 Notizen machen – *Taking notes* (Unit 4)

Worum geht es beim Notizen machen?

Manchmal liest oder hörst du etwas und willst es dir gut merken, z.B. um anderen davon zu erzählen. Da hilft es, wenn du dir in Stichworten *(key words)* Notizen machst.

Wie mache ich Notizen?

Am besten kannst du das an einem Beispiel sehen. Heike soll herausfinden, wie man in England Halloween feiert. Sie hat ihre englische Freundin Anne gefragt. Schau dir an, wie sie in Annes Antwort das Wichtige markiert und sich in Stichworten *(key words)* Notizen gemacht hat.

Dear Heike

Do I have a Halloween party? Yes, I do – every year. I invite some girls from the hockey team and from my class, but I don't invite any boys. It's a girls' party. This year I'm a vampire – that's me in the photo. Mum is a poltergeist. The party usually starts at seven o'clock. We play games like Poltergeist Party or Dance of the Vampires. Then we eat pizza and chocolate cake. My mum always tells a scary story at the end of the party. I like scary stories like 'Dracula'. Mum tells the best scary stories in the world!

Your friend
Anne

Anne: ✔ Halloween party – every year
invites some girls, ~~boys~~
Anne: vampire
party starts: at 7
play games, eat pizza + choc. cake
end of party: Mum tells scary story ☺

Tipp

- Verwende Ziffern (z.B. „7" statt „seven").
- Verwende Symbole und Abkürzungen, z.B. ✔ (für „Ja") und + (für „und") wie im Beispiel oben. Am besten erfindest du deine eigenen Symbole.
- Verwende „not" oder ✗ bei Verneinungen.

- Alles verstanden? Dann probier doch mal Aufgabe 6 auf S. 76.

SF 6 Unbekannte Wörter verstehen – *Understanding new words* (Unit 5)

Immer gleich im Wörterbuch nachschlagen?

Du liest einen englischen Text und kennst ein paar Wörter nicht? Schlage sie nicht gleich im Wörterbuch nach, denn das kostet Zeit und nimmt dir vielleicht den Spaß am Lesen. Häufig kannst du die Bedeutung dieser Wörter selbst herausfinden. Du wirst merken, dass du viel mehr verstehst, als du gedacht hast.

Was hilft mir, unbekannte Wörter zu verstehen?

1. Bilder sind eine große Hilfe. Oft zeigen sie die Dinge, die du in einem Text nicht verstehst. Schau dir das Bild rechts an und lies dann den folgenden Satz:

On the fourth day the look-out saw a ship.

Was könnte mit „look-out" gemeint sein?

2. Es gibt viele englische Wörter, die im Deutschen ähnlich geschrieben werden oder ähnlich klingen, so genannte „verwandte Wörter". Was bedeuten wohl die folgenden Wörter?

cabin • captain • deck • gold • kill • pistol • silver • Spanish • young

3. Manchmal stecken in unbekannten Wörtern bekannte Teile.

singer • **friend**ly • un**happy** • **end**less

4. Oft helfen dir auch die Wörter, die in der Nähe des unbekanntenWortes stehen. Kannst du im Beispiel unten aus dem Zusammenhang heraus verstehen, was mit „sail" gemeint ist?

'A great ship. Do many men sail on her?' asked the young man.

- Alles klar? Dann versuchs mal selbst: Was bedeutet **was asleep** im folgenden Satz? **He was very tired and soon he was asleep.**

SF 7 Ergebnisse präsentieren – *Giving a presentation* (Unit 6)

Information und Spannung

Du hast dich mit einem Thema beschäftigt und vieles herausgefunden, was du deiner Klasse jetzt vortragen willst. Wie schaffst du es, die Aufmerksamkeit deiner Mitschüler/innen zu fesseln und dabei selbst ganz ruhig zu bleiben? Die folgenden Hinweise helfen dir.

Wie mache ich eine gute Präsentation?

Vorbereitung

Schreib dir die wichtigsten Gedanken als Notizen auf (vgl. SF 5), z.B. auf nummerierte Karteikarten oder als Mindmap (vgl. SF 3).

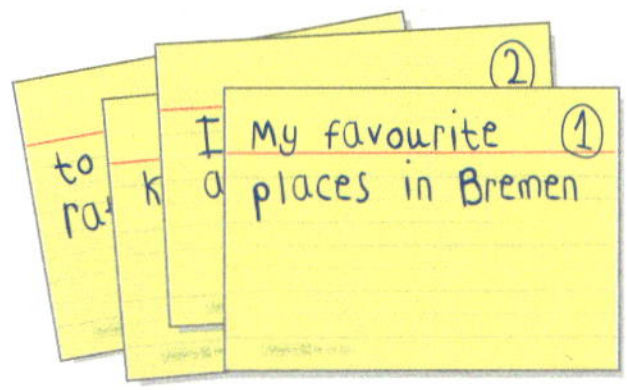

Bereite ein Poster (oder eine Folie) vor, wenn du deinen Vortrag interessanter gestalten willst. Deine Schrift sollte groß und für alle gut lesbar sein. Verwende keine Farben, die schwer zu lesen sind, wie z.B. Gelb.

Übe deine Präsentation allein, z.B. vor einem Spiegel. Das gibt dir Sicherheit. Sprich dabei laut und langsam.

Now I'd like to talk about pirates ...

Durchführung

Bevor du beginnst, hänge das Poster auf bzw. lege deine Folie auf den ausgeschalteten Projektor und schau noch einmal nach, ob deine Vortragskarten richtig sortiert sind.
Jetzt kannst du mit deiner Präsentation anfangen. Stelle dich vor deine Zuhörer und warte, bis es ruhig ist. Schau die Zuhörer an.

My presentation is about ...
First, I'd like to talk about ...
Second, ...

Erkläre zu Anfang, worüber du sprechen wirst. Lies nicht von deinen Karten ab, sondern sprich möglichst frei. Weise auf unbekannte Wörter und ihre Bedeutung hin.

Here's a new word. / Here are some new words.
... is ... in German.

Wenn du ein Poster oder eine Folie benutzt, zeige während des Vortrags auch darauf.

This picture/photo/... shows ...

Schluss

Wenn du alles vorgestellt hast, was du sagen wolltest, beende deine Präsentation. Frag deine Mitschüler/innen, ob sie noch Fragen haben.

That's the end of my presentation.
Have you got any questions?

Bedanke dich fürs Zuhören.

Thank you.

Mithilfe einer Grammatik (englisch: *grammar*) lernst du, wie eine Sprache funktioniert.
Im **Grammar File** (S. 126–146) findest du wichtige Regeln der englischen Sprache. Du kannst hier nachsehen, wenn

- du selbstständig etwas lernen oder wiederholen möchtest,
- du die Übungen aus dem P-Teil deines Englischbuchs oder aus dem *Workbook* machst,
- du dich auf einen Test oder eine Klassenarbeit vorbereiten willst.

Die **Abschnitte** 1–24 fassen zusammen, was du in den sechs Units über die englische Sprache gelernt hast.
In der **linken Spalte** findest du **Beispiele**, die dir zeigen, was richtig ist, und **Kästen mit Übersichten**, in denen das Wichtigste zusammengefasst ist.
In der **rechten Spalte** stehen **Erklärungen** und nützliche **Hinweise**.
Besonders wichtig sind die roten **Ausrufezeichen** (**!**). Sie zeigen, was im Deutschen anders ist, und machen auf Fehlerquellen aufmerksam.

Hinweise wie ▸ *Unit 1 (p. 20)* • *P 2–3 (pp. 25–26)* zeigen dir, zu welcher Unit und welcher Seite ein **Grammar File**-Abschnitt gehört und welche Übungen du dazu im P-Teil findest.

Am Ende eines Abschnitts stellt dir Polly oft eine kleine Aufgabe. Damit kannst du überprüfen, ob du alles richtig verstanden hast. Schreib die Lösungen in dein *exercise book*. Auf S. 146 kannst du deine Antworten überprüfen.

Grammatical terms (Grammatische Fachbegriffe)

adverb of frequency [ˌædvɜːb_əv ˈfriːkwənsi]	Häufigkeitsadverb
future [ˈfjuːtʃə]	Zukunft, Futur
imperative [ɪmˈperətɪv]	Imperativ (Befehlsform)
infinitive [ɪnˈfɪnətɪv]	Infinitiv (Grundform des Verbs)
irregular verb [ɪˌregjələ ˈvɜːb]	unregelmäßiges Verb
negative statement [ˌnegətɪv ˈsteɪtmənt]	verneinter Aussagesatz
noun [naʊn]	Nomen, Substantiv
object [ˈɒbdʒɪkt]	Objekt
object form [ˈɒbdʒɪkt fɔːm]	Objektform (der Personalpronomen)
past [pɑːst]	Vergangenheit
person [ˈpɜːsn]	Person
personal pronoun [ˌpɜːsənl ˈprəʊnaʊn]	Personalpronomen (persönliches Fürwort)
plural [ˈplʊərəl]	Plural, Mehrzahl
positive statement [ˌpɒzətɪv ˈsteɪtmənt]	bejahter Aussagesatz
possessive determiner [pəˌzesɪv dɪˈtɜːmɪnə]	Possessivbegleiter (besitzanzeigender Begleiter)
possessive form [pəˌzesɪv fɔːm]	*s*-Genitiv
present [ˈpreznt]	Gegenwart
present progressive [ˌpreznt prəˈgresɪv]	Verlaufsform der Gegenwart
pronoun [ˈprəʊnaʊn]	Pronomen, Fürwort
pronunciation [prəˌnʌnsiˈeɪʃn]	Aussprache
question [ˈkwestʃən]	Frage(satz)
question word [ˈkwestʃən wɜːd]	Fragewort
regular verb [ˌregjələ ˈvɜːb]	regelmäßiges Verb
short answer [ˌʃɔːt_ˈɑːnsə]	Kurzantwort
simple past [ˌsɪmpl ˈpɑːst]	einfache Form der Vergangenheit
simple present [ˌsɪmpl ˈpreznt]	einfache Form der Gegenwart
singular [ˈsɪŋgjələ]	Singular, Einzahl
spelling [ˈspelɪŋ]	Schreibweise, Rechtschreibung
subject [ˈsʌbdʒɪkt]	Subjekt
subject form [ˈsʌbdʒɪkt fɔːm]	Subjektform (der Personalpronomen)
subordinate clause [səˌbɔːdɪnət ˈklɔːz]	Nebensatz
verb [vɜːb]	Verb
word order [ˈwɜːd_ˌɔːdə]	Wortstellung
yes/no question	Entscheidungsfrage

Unit 1

GF 1 Personal pronouns Personalpronomen

Nomen: boy ▼ girl ▼ pencil ▼

Pronomen: ▲ he ▲ she ▲ it

Nomen stehen für Personen *(boy, girl)* und Dinge *(pencil)*, aber auch für Begriffe und Gefühle – also für Dinge, die du nicht sehen oder anfassen kannst, z.B *name* oder *luck* („Glück").

Auch **Pronomen (Fürwörter)** können für Personen, Dinge, Begriffe und Gefühle stehen.
Personalpronomen sind:
I, you, he, she, it, we, you, they.

Jack is eleven.
Jack is nice.
▼
He's nice.

Where's my pencil?
My pencil is red.
▼
It's red.

◄ Statt *Jack* und *my pencil* stehen hier die Personalpronomen *he* und *it*.

You are nice. = Du bist nett.
Ihr seid nett.
Sie sind nett.

Die deutschen Personalpronomen **du**, **ihr** und **Sie** heißen im Englischen alle ***you***.

Personalpronomen

Bei einer männlichen Person	– he
Bei einer weiblichen Person	– she
Bei einem Ding oder Begriff	– it
Bei einem Haustier	– he oder she
Bei einem Tier ohne Namen	– it
Bei mehreren Personen, Dingen, Tieren	– they

What colour is ...

... **the pencil?** – It's green. **der** Bleistift = Er ist grün.

... **the school bag?** – It's red. **die** Schultasche = Sie ist rot.

... **the ruler?** – It's brown. **das** Lineal = Es ist braun.

! Das Pronomen *it* steht für **alle** Dinge. (Deutsch: „er", „sie", „es")

► *Unit 1 (p. 20) • P 2–3 (pp. 25–26)*

Hast du alles verstanden? Dann kannst du jetzt die folgende Aufgabe lösen:
Suche die Personalpronomen. Wie viele sind es?

the • pencil • he • are • they • nice • you • your • I • we

Deine Antworten kannst du auf S. 146 überprüfen.

GF 2 The verb *(to) be* Das Verb *(to) be* („sein“)

a) Statements with *be*

Aussagen mit *be*

Wie du siehst, hat das Verb *be* in der Gegenwart *(present)* drei Formen: *am*, *are* und *is*.

Polly zeigt dir einige Lang- und Kurzformen von *be*.

***be* (present)**

Langformen: +	–	**Kurzformen:** +	–
I am	I am not	I'm	I'm not
you are	you are not	you're	you aren't
he/she/it is	he/she/it is not	he's/she's/it's	he/she/it isn't
we are	we are not	we're	we aren't
you are	you are not	you're	you aren't
they are	they are not	they're	they aren't

Beim Sprechen und in persönlichen Briefen werden meist die Kurzformen von *be* verwendet.

b) Questions with *be*

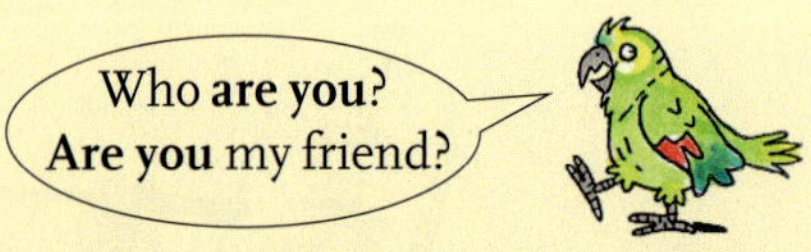

***be* (present)**

Fragen:

Am I ...?	Are we ...?
Are you ...?	Are you ...?
Is he/she/it ...?	Are they ...?

Fragen mit *be*

Du kannst eine Frage **mit** oder **ohne** Fragewort stellen:

Are you my friend? (ohne Fragewort)
Who are you? (mit Fragewort *who*)

Nach einem Fragewort wird *is* oft verkürzt:
Who's that?
Where's my book?
What's your name?

c) Short answers with *be*

Well, are you my friend? Are you my friend?
– No, I'm not ... uhhh ... yes, I am.

Kurzantworten mit *be*

Fragen ohne Fragewort werden nicht nur mit *Yes* oder *No* beantwortet, das wäre unhöflich. Du solltest eine **Kurzantwort** benutzen, z.B. *Yes, I am* oder *No, I'm not.*

***be* (present)**

Kurzantworten: +	–
Yes, I am.	No, I'm not.
Yes, you are.	No, you aren't.
Yes, he/she/it is.	No, he/she/it isn't.
Yes, we/you/they are.	No, we/you/they aren't.

! Nach *Yes* darfst du keine Kurzform verwenden.
Also nur
Yes, I am. / ***Yes, we are.***
usw.

▸ *Unit 1 (p. 21) • P 4–6 (pp. 26–27)*

Alles klar? Dann löse jetzt diese Aufgabe:
Wie könntest du auf die folgende Frage antworten? Welche Antworten sind üblich?

Are you eleven? – 1 Yes. • 2 Yes, I'm. • 3 Yes, I am. • 4 No. • 5 No, I'm not.

GF 3 *can*

a) Statements with *can* ('können')

Polly can talk, but she can't (cannot) sing.

Jo can play football.
Jo kann Fußball spielen.
Ananda can't play football.
Ananda kann nicht Fußball spielen.

Aussagen mit *can* („können")

Mit *can* und *can't* drückst du aus, was jemand tun kann oder nicht tun kann.

Wie du siehst, gibt es nur die Formen *can* und *can't* für *I/you/he/she/it/we/they*.

Die Langform von *can't* heißt *cannot*.

! Merke dir, dass das Verb direkt hinter *can* bzw. *can't* steht – anders als im Deutschen. Vergleiche die Beispiele links.

b) Questions with *can*

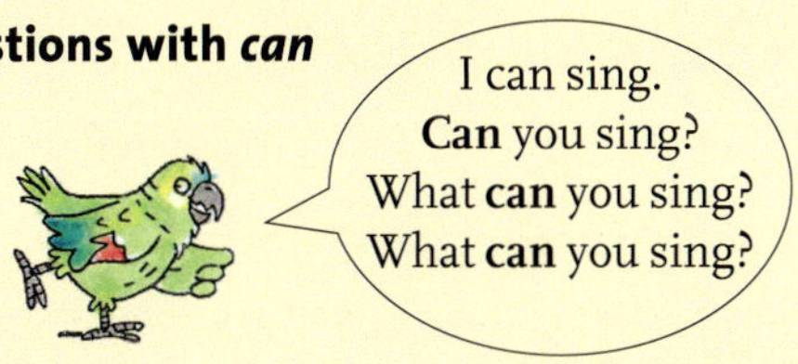

Fragen mit *can*

Fragen mit *can* bildest du so wie im Deutschen. Du kannst Fragen **mit** oder **ohne** Fragewort stellen:

Can you sing? (ohne Fragewort)
What can you sing? (mit Fragewort *what*)

c) Short answers with *can*

Can you do tricks? – **Yes, I can. / No, I can't.**
Can Polly sing? – **No, she can't.**

can und can't

Bei *can* und *can't* gibt es nur eine Form für alle Personen:
I, you, he/she/it, we, you, they can
I, you, he/she/it, we, you, they can't

▸ *Unit 1 (p. 22) • P 7 (p. 27)*

Kurzantworten mit *can*

◂ So bildest du Kurzantworten mit *can* und *can't*.

d) *can* ('dürfen')

Room 14 is empty. Can we go in?
Raum 14 ist leer. Dürfen wir hineingehen?
We can go in, but we can't write on the board.
Wir dürfen hineingehen, aber wir dürfen nicht an die Tafel schreiben.

can („dürfen")

Mit *can* und *can't* kannst du auch ausdrücken, was jemand tun darf oder nicht tun darf.

Extra

May we go in?
Dürfen wir hineingehen?
May I write on the board?
Darf ich an die Tafel schreiben?

Wenn du besonders höflich um Erlaubnis bitten möchtest, kannst du statt *can* auch *may* benutzen.

GF 4 **Imperatives** Befehle, Aufforderungen

Wie du siehst, ist die Befehlsform genauso wie der Infinitiv (die Grundform): *Walk*.
Bei einem verneinten Befehl steht *don't* davor: *Don't walk*. (Langform: *Do not walk*.)

Come in, please.
Komm/Kommt/Kommen Sie bitte herein.

◄ Im Englischen gibt es nur eine Befehlsform, egal mit wem du sprichst.

Write the words on the board, please.
Schreib die Wörter an die Tafel, bitte.
Polly, don't sing. And don't talk, please.
Polly, sing nicht. Und rede bitte nicht.

◄ Wenn du jemanden aufforderst, etwas zu tun, solltest du *please* verwenden. Das ist höflicher.

Befehlsformen

+ Sing.
– Don't sing.

► *Unit 1 (p. 23)* • *P 10 (p. 29)*

GF 5 **The verb *have got*** Das Verb *have got* („haben", „besitzen")

a) Statements with *have got*

Jack has got a parrot.
Jack hat einen Papagei.
Sophie hasn't got a parrot. She's got a dog.
Sophie hat keinen Papagei. Sie hat einen Hund.
Jo and Dan have got pets too.
Jo und Dan haben auch Haustiere.

Aussagen mit *have got*

Die Form *have got* gilt für *I, you, we* und *they*.

Bei *he/she/it* heißt die Form *has got*.

! – *She's got a dog.* = *She has got a dog.*
(nicht: *She ~~is got~~ a dog.*)
– *She's very nice.* = *She is very nice.*

have got

Langformen: +	–	Kurzformen: +	–
I have got	I have not got	I've got	I haven't got
you have got	you have not got	you've got	you haven't got
he/she/it has got	he/she/it has not got	he's/she's/it's got	he/she/it hasn't got
we have got	we have not got	we've got	we haven't got
you have got	you have not got	you've got	you haven't got
they have got	they have not got	they've got	they haven't got

b) Questions with *have got*

Have you got a pet?
Has Jack got a pet?

What have you got next?
When have we got Maths today?

have got

Fragen:

Have I got ...?	Have we got ...?
Have you got ...?	Have you got ...?
Has he/she/it got ...?	Have they got ...?

Fragen mit *have got*

! Wenn du eine Frage mit *have got* bildest, musst du das *got* an den richtigen Platz setzen: Es steht nach dem Subjekt (*you, Jack, we*).

c) Short answers with *have got*

Have we got Maths today? – **Yes, we have.** / **No, we haven't.**
Has Jack got a pet? – **Yes, he has.**
Has Sophie got a parrot? – **No, she hasn't.**
Have you got a pet? – **Yes, I have.** / **No, I haven't.**

▸ *Unit 1 (p. 24) • P 12–13 (p. 30)*

Kurzantworten mit *have got*

! 1 Bei der Kurzantwort fällt das *got* weg.
2 Nach *Yes* musst du immer die Langform verwenden.

Möchtest du jetzt wieder eine Aufgabe lösen? Welche Sätze sind richtig?

1 Have you got a dog? – Yes, we have.
2 Has he got a pet? – Yes, he has got.
3 Have you got Maths now? – Yes, we've.
4 Has Jack got PE today? – No, he hasn't.

Unit 2

GF 6 The plural of nouns Der Plural der Nomen

a parrot (Singular) 

two parrots (Plural) 

1 desks [desks] • lamps [læmps]
flats [flæts] • parrots ['pærəts]

2 beds [bedz] • bags [bægz]
girls [gɜːlz] • rooms [ruːmz]
boys [bɔɪz] • trees [triːz]
sisters ['sɪstəz]

Du bildest den Plural (die Mehrzahl) eines Nomens, indem du ***s*** an das Nomen anhängst:
Singular + *s* = Plural.

Bei der **Aussprache der Pluralendung** kommt es auf den letzten Laut des Singulars an:

◂ 1 [s] wie das Zischen der Schlange nach **stimmlosen Konsonanten** (Mitlauten), z.B. [k], [p], [t]

◂ 2 [z] wie das Summen der Biene nach **stimmhaften Konsonanten**, z.B. [d], [g], [l], [m], und nach **Vokalen** (Selbstlauten)

3 box**es** ['bɒks**ɪz**] • hous**es** ['haʊz**ɪz**]
hutch**es** ['hʌ**tʃɪz**] • cag**es** ['keɪ**dʒɪz**]

◀ **3** [ɪz] nach **Zischlauten**, z.B. [s], [z], [ʃ], [tʃ], [dʒ]
(Beachte, dass nach Zischlauten ***es*** oder ***s*** angehängt wird, je nach Schreibung des Singulars:
*box – box**es**, cage – cage**s**.*)

baby ▸ bab**ies** — family ▸ famil**ies**
activity ▸ activit**ies** — hobby ▸ hobb**ies**

! – ***y*** nach einem **Konsonanten** wird zu ***ies***.
(Aber ***y*** nach einem **Vokal** bleibt: ***boy*** → ***boys***.)

one **fish** ▸ two **fish**
mouse ▸ **mice**
tooth ▸ **teeth**

– Einige Nomen haben **unregelmäßige Pluralformen**.

▸ *Unit 2 (p. 38) • P 2 (p. 42)*

Jetzt kannst du wieder eine Aufgabe lösen.
*Wie bildest du die Pluralform dieser Wörter? Ordne die Wörter den Endungen **A** bis **D** zu, z.B. **1 A**.*

1 bag • 2 class • 3 child • 4 day • 5 park • 6 hutch
7 dictionary • 8 page • 9 family • 10 tooth

A: -s **B:** -es **C:** -ies
D: unregelmäßig

GF 7 The simple present Die einfache Form der Gegenwart

a) Positive statements

Bejahte Aussagesätze

◀ Jo und Dan reden hier über das, was sie regelmäßig tun (*every morning*, „jeden Morgen"). Ihre Sätze stehen im *simple present* (einfache Form der Gegenwart).

Dan and Jo **go** to school together.
Hamsters and rabbits **eat** carrots.

◀ Wie du siehst, haben Verben im *simple present* bei *I, you, we* und *they* keine Endung.

Toby **helps** Sophie with Harry, the hamster.
He **cleans** his cage.
Sophie **gives** Sheeba meat and water.
Sheeba **eats** in the kitchen.

◀ Aber bei der 3. Person Singular (*he/she/it*) wird ein ***s*** angefügt.

He, she, it – das „s" muss mit!

! Modale Hilfsverben *(can, may)* haben kein ***s*** bei *he/she/it*. Vergleiche:
*Toby/He **can help** Sophie.*
Aber: *Toby/He **helps** Sophie.*

Simple present

Bejahte Aussagesätze:

I/You	like	
He/She/It	likes	apples and bananas.
We/You/They	like	

Simple present?
He, she, it?
YES, YES! An 's'!

▸ *Unit 2 (p. 39) • P 4 (p. 42), P 7 (p. 44)*

Versuche jetzt diese Aufgabe zu lösen:
Wo musst du ein **s** *hinzufügen?*

1 I like_ Maths.
2 Jo play_ football.
3 Ananda can_ play_ hockey.
4 Rabbits eat_ carrots.
5 Ben can_ climb_ trees.
6 Sophie feed_ the pets.

b) 3rd person singular: pronunciation and spelling

3. Person Singular: Aussprache und Schreibweise

Wie beim Plural der Nomen (S. 131/132, GF 6) gibt es ein paar Besonderheiten. Lies dir alle Beispiele laut vor. Achte auf das Schlangen-[s] und das Bienen-[z].

1 Sheeba **likes** meat. [-ks]
She **sleeps** in a basket. [-ps]
Jack **writes** great essays. [-ts]

◂ **1** [s] nach **stimmlosen Konsonanten**, z.B. [k], [p], [t]

2 Toby **cleans** the cage. [-nz]
Jack **tells** his friends about Polly. [-lz]
Mrs Shaw **lives** in New Zealand. [-vz]
Ananda **plays** hockey. [-eɪz]

◂ **2** [z] nach **stimmhaften Konsonanten**, z.B. [n], [l], [v], und nach **Vokalen**

3 Dan **uses** a blue pencil. [-zɪz]
Prunella opens and **closes** things. [-zɪz]
She **pushes** Sophie's bed. [-ʃɪz]
After his homework Jack **watches** TV. [-tʃɪz]

◂ **3** [ɪz] nach **Zischlauten**, z.B. [s], [z], [ʃ], [tʃ], [dʒ]
(Beachte, dass nach Zischlauten ***es*** oder ***s*** angehängt wird, je nach Schreibung des Infinitivs: *push – push**es**, use – use**s**.*)

Ananda **copies** sentences from the board.
Toby **tries** to help Sophie.

! – ***y*** nach einem **Konsonanten** wird zu ***ies***:
copy → *copies*, ***try*** → *tries*.
(Aber ***y*** nach einem **Vokal** bleibt: ***play*** → ***plays***.)

Sophie **goes** to Cotham School in Bristol now.
She **does** her homework in her room. [dʌz]
Prunella **says**, 'Sophie, get up!' [sez]

– Die Verben *go*, *do* und *say* sind unregelmäßig:
go + es → goes
do + es → does (*I do* [duː] – *she does* [dʌz])
say + s → says (*I say* [seɪ] – *she says* [sez]).

▸ *Unit 2 (p. 39) • P 5–6 (p. 43)*

Wenn du überprüfen möchtest, ob du alles verstanden hast, versuche diese Aufgabe zu lösen:
Bei welchen Verben musst du bei he/she/it **-es** *anhängen?*

sleep • push • write • do • watch • pull • go • play

c) Negative statements

I don't need your help with the essay, Prunella.
You don't like me, Sophie.
We don't write essays every day.
Our teachers don't give homework every day.

Verneinte Aussagesätze

Bei *I, you, we* und *they* verneinst du eine Aussage im *simple present* mit ***don't* + Infinitiv** (Grundform).
Die Langform von *don't* heißt *do not*.

Prunella doesn't sleep.
Ananda doesn't like the Drama teacher.
Toby doesn't do judo on Saturdays.
Dan doesn't make his bed every morning.

Bei *he/she/it* benutzt du jedoch ***doesn't* + Infinitiv**.
Die Langform von *doesn't* heißt *does not*.

! Das ***s*** der 3. Person Singular steckt jetzt im *doe**s**n't*.
Also nicht: *She doesn't sleeps* ~~s~~.

Simple present

Verneinte Aussagesätze:

I	don't	like	
You	don't	like	
He/She/It	doesn't	like	apples and bananas.
We	don't	like	
You	don't	like	
They	don't	like	

Polly says,
Please don't guess.
In *doesn't* + verb
there's just one 's'!

▸ *Unit 2 (p. 40)* • *P 10–11 (p. 45)*

Jetzt kannst du wieder eine Aufgabe lösen:
Wie heißen die verneinten Formen?

1 We play hockey.
2 Toby does judo.
3 Parrots eat meat.
4 Sophie cleans the cage.

GF 8 Possessive determiners Possessivbegleiter

This is **my** room.

No, this is **my** room, Sophie.

Your room, Prunella? Well, then it's **our** room. OK?

Wörter wie „mein", „dein", „unser" sind **Possessivbegleiter** (besitzanzeigende Begleiter).
Sie stehen vor einem Nomen (hier: *room*) und zeigen an, wem etwas gehört.

◂ Prunella und Sophie zeigen dir einige Formen:
my, your und *our room*.

Possessivbegleiter

my	room	*mein Zimmer*	our	room	*unser Zimmer*
your	room	*dein/Ihr Zimmer*	your	room	*euer/Ihr Zimmer*
his	room	*sein Zimmer*	their	room	*ihr Zimmer*
her	room	*ihr Zimmer*			
its	room	*sein/ihr Zimmer*			

Your sister isn't nice, Sophie. But **you're** nice.
That's Jo. Dan is his brother. **He's** nice too.
Dan has got a cat. Its name is Bill. **It's** black.
Sophie and Emily are sisters. Their name is Carter-Brown. **They're** new in Bristol.

! Einige Possessivbegleiter kann man leicht mit Kurzformen von *be* verwechseln.
Schau dir die Beispiele links genau an.

Possessivbegleiter und Kurzformen von *be*

your	*dein/e, euer/eure, Ihr/e*	–	**you're**	(you are)
his [hɪz]	*sein/e*	–	**he's** [hiːz]	(he is)
its	*sein/e, ihr/e*	–	**it's**	(it is)
their	*ihr/e* (Plural)	–	**they're**	(they are)

► *Unit 2 (p. 41) • P 14 (p. 46)*

Und hier wieder eine kleine Aufgabe:
Welches sind die Possessivbegleiter?

my • you're • his • their • he's • our • it's • her • they're • your • its

GF 9 The possessive form Der *s*-Genitiv

Wenn du sagen willst, dass etwas jemandem gehört (oder zu jemandem gehört), benutzt du den ***s*-Genitiv**.

Englisch: **Jack**'s room
Deutsch: **Jacks** Zimmer

! Anders als im Deutschen wird im Englischen das ***s*** mit einem Apostroph angehängt.

Singular: The **dog**'s basket is in the kitchen.
Der Korb des Hundes ...
Our **teacher**'s name is Mr Kingsley.

◄ Im Singular wird ***'s*** an das Nomen angehängt.
Für die Aussprache gelten dieselben Regeln wie für das Plural-***s*** (siehe Seiten 131/132, GF 6).

Plural: The **Kapoors**' flat is over the shop.
The **twins**' mum is in New Zealand.

◄ Wenn die Pluralform auf ***s*** endet, hängst du nur einen Apostroph an das Nomen.

This is **Jo and Dan**'s family tree.
Dies ist **Jos** und **Dans** Familienstammbaum.

◄ Bei zwei Personen hängst du nur einmal ***'s*** an, und zwar an das zweite Nomen.

Der *s*-Genitiv

Singular: Nomen + 's (the **dog**'s basket)
Plural: Pluralform des Nomens + ' (the **rabbits**' hutch)

► *Unit 2 (p. 41) • P 15 (p. 47)*

Alles klar? Dann löse jetzt diese Aufgabe:
*Wie viele Personen oder Tiere sind es? Sind es **ein** oder **mehrere** Brüder, Kaninchen, Papageien, ...?*

1 **my brother**'s room
2 **my brothers**' room
3 **the rabbits**' hutch
4 **the parrot**'s cage
5 **the twins**' teacher
6 **Jo**'s CDs

Unit 3

GF 10 The simple present Die einfache Form der Gegenwart

a) Yes/No questions

Entscheidungsfragen

Entscheidungsfragen sind Fragen, auf die man mit „Ja" oder „Nein" antworten kann.

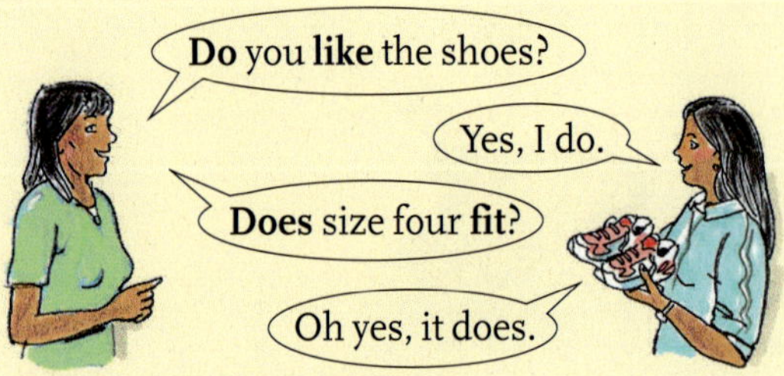

◄ Fragen im *simple present* bildet man mit ***do*** oder ***does***:
- ***do*** bei *I, you, we* und *they*,
- ***does*** bei *he/she/it* (3. Person Singular).

Do you **like** the colour, Ananda?
Do the shoes **look** OK, Mum?
Do we **need** help?

Die Wortstellung ist wie beim Aussagesatz:
*We **need** help.* (Aussagesatz)
*Do we **need** help?* (Fragesatz)

Does Ananda **want** the hockey shoes?
Does she **like** the T-shirt too?
Does it **fit**?

! Das ***s*** der 3. Person Singular steckt jetzt im *Does*.
Das Verb steht ohne Endung:

*Size four **fits**.* (Aussagesatz)
Aber: ***Does** size four **fit**?* (Fragesatz)
Nicht: *Does it ~~fits~~?*

Simple present

Entscheidungsfragen:

Do	I	like ...?	Do	we	like ...?
Do	you	like ...?	Do	you	like ...?
Does	he/she/it	like ...?	Do	they	like ...?

Polly says,
Please don't guess.
In questions with *Does*
there's just one 's'!

► *Unit 3 (p. 54) • P 4–5 (p. 59)*

Versuche jetzt diese Aufgabe zu lösen: Stelle Fragen. Frage nach den Personen in Klammern.

1 Jack makes models. (Sophie?) *Does Sophie ...?*
2 Dan and Jo go swimming. (Ananda and Dilip?)
3 Jack and Sophie like music. (Emily?)

b) Short answers

Kurzantworten

Do you **get up** early? – **Yes, I** do. / **No, I** don't.
Does Jack **hate** sport? – **Yes, he** does.
Does Ananda **play** football? – **No, she** doesn't.
Do we **need** a pen? – **Yes, we** do. / **No, we** don't.
Do the shoes **fit**? – **Yes, they** do.

Entscheidungsfragen werden nicht nur mit *Yes* oder *No* beantwortet, sondern mit einer Kurzantwort:
- bei der Antwort *Yes* mit *do* oder *does*,
- bei der Antwort *No* mit *don't* oder *doesn't*.

► *Unit 3 (p. 54) • P 6–8 (pp. 59–60)*

Dazu wieder eine Aufgabe:
Welche Kurzantwort ist richtig?

Does Jack like football? – 1 No, he don't. • 2 No, she doesn't. • 3 No, he doesn't.

c) Questions with question words

When do you **play** tennis, Prunella?
And **where do** you **play**?

How does Uncle Henry **play** without a head?
And **why does** he **take** my racket?

▸ *Unit 3 (p. 55) • P 9 (p. 60)*

Fragen mit Fragewörtern

Fragen mit Fragewörtern *(When, Where, What, How, Why)* bildest du wie Entscheidungsfragen (siehe Seite 136, GF 10 a).
Das Fragewort steht am Anfang, vor *do* oder *does*:

	Do	*you*	***play*** *tennis?*	(Entscheidungsfrage)
When	***do***	*you*	***play*** *tennis?*	(Fragen mit Fragewort)
How	***does***	*he*	***play*** *tennis?*	

Wieder eine kleine Aufgabe?
Wie heißen die Sätze richtig? Bringe die Wörter in die richtige Reihenfolge.

1 does – When – come – Uncle Henry?
2 Prunella – play – Where – tennis – does?
3 you – do – do – What – in your free time?

GF 11 Adverbs of frequency: word order Häufigkeitsadverbien: Wortstellung

I never **sleep**.
I usually **go** in all the rooms at night.
I sometimes **play** tennis.

Jack always **writes** great stories.
Jack schreibt immer tolle Geschichten.

Prunella **can** often **help** Sophie.
Prunella kann Sophie oft helfen.

But Sophie **doesn't** always **need** her help.
Aber Sophie braucht ihre Hilfe nicht immer.

I'm usually nice to Sophie.
Emily **is** never nice to her.

▸ *Unit 3 (p. 56) • P 14 (p. 63)*

In Sätzen im *simple present* stehen oft Häufigkeitsadverbien *(always, usually, often, sometimes, never)*.
Sie drücken aus, wie regelmäßig etwas geschieht oder nicht geschieht.

◂ Häufigkeitsadverbien stehen gewöhnlich direkt **vor dem Vollverb** (z.B. *sleep, go, play*).

! Anders als im Deutschen stehen Häufigkeitsadverbien nie zwischen Verb und Objekt:

	Verb	**Objekt**			**Verb**		**Objekt**
Jo often	***plays***	***football*** .		*Jo*	***spielt***	*oft*	***Fußball*** .

Schau dir die Beispiele links genau an.

◂ Häufigkeitsadverbien stehen **hinter** *am/are/is*.

Und wieder eine kleine Aufgabe:
Welches **always** *steht an der richtigen Stelle,* **1** *oder* **2***?*

Jay **always** (1) goes **always** (2) to basketball games.

GF 12 **The verb *(to) have to*** Das Verb *(to) have to* („müssen“)

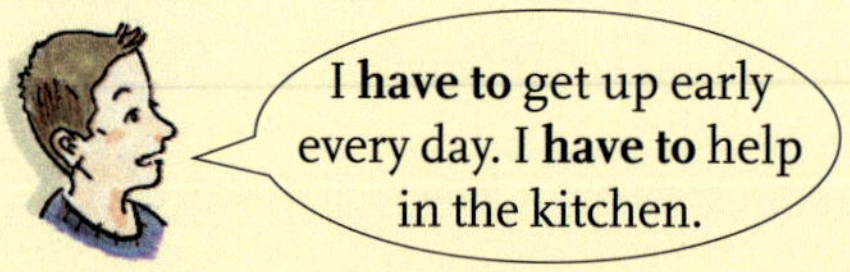

Wenn du ausdrücken willst, was du oder andere tun müssen, verwendest du *have to.*

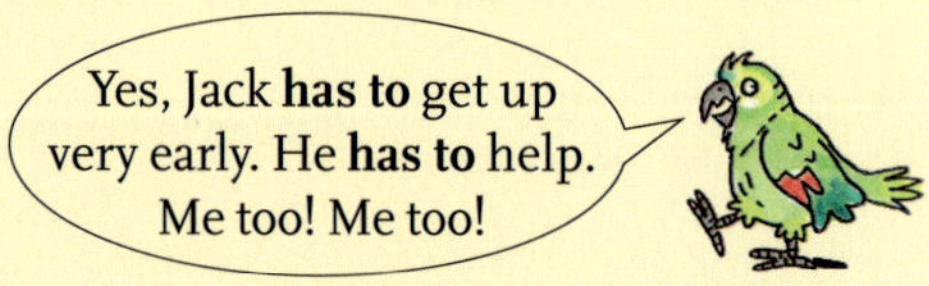

In der 3. Person Singular *(he/she/it)* heißt es *has to.*

! Das ***to*** nach ***have*** und ***has*** muss immer dabeistehen.

Jack's parents have to **make** breakfast for the guests. But they don't have to **make** lunch.
Jacks Eltern müssen das Frühstück ... machen. Aber sie müssen nicht das Mittagessen machen.

Every evening Jack has to **lay** the table.
But he doesn't have to **go** to yoga.

Do you have to **help** a lot, Jack? – **Yes, I** do.
And does Polly have to **work**? – **No, she** doesn't!

Why do Mum and Dad have to **go** out?

◄ Wie du siehst, werden verneinte Sätze, Fragen und Kurzantworten mit Hilfe von *do/does* gebildet – wie bei anderen Verben auch.
Schau dir die Beispiele links genau an.

(to) have to

+		–		?	
I/you	have to	I/you	don't have to	Do I/you	have to ...?
he/she/it	has to	he/she/it	doesn't have to	Does he/she/it	have to ...?
we/you/they	have to	we/you/they	don't have to	Do we/you/they	have to ...?

► *Unit 3 (p. 57) • P 16–17 (pp. 63–64)*

Bringe die Wörter in die richtige Reihenfolge:

1 help – Jack – his mum – has to.
2 doesn't – He – have to – clean – the rooms.
3 he – make – Does – breakfast – have to?

Unit 4

GF 13 **Personal pronouns: object forms** Personalpronomen: Objektformen

I can't do this homework. You can help me.
You don't know me, but I know you.
There's Jack. **He**'s nice. Can you see him?
Ananda? **She**'s nice. We all like her.
It's my birthday cake. Do you like it?
We go swimming on Fridays. Come with us.
Dan and Jo, **you** like fruit. So this is for you.
The twins? **They** aren't here. I can't see them.

◄ Bei den Personalpronomen unterscheiden wir die **Subjektformen** *(I, he, ...)* und die **Objektformen** *(me, him, ...).*

Anders als im Deutschen gibt es für jede Person nur eine Objektform:

- *You can help me.* — *Du kannst **mir** helfen.*
- *You can ask me.* — *Du kannst **mich** fragen.*

I like her.	Ich mag **sie**.	*(Sophie, meine Lehrerin, ...)*
I like it.	Ich mag **sie**.	*(meine Schule, die Stadt, ...)*
I like them.	Ich mag **sie**.	*(meine Eltern, die Stiefel, ...)*

▸ *Unit 4 (p. 70)* • *P 3–4 (pp. 75–76)*

! Die deutsche Objektform „sie“ kann auf Englisch *her, it* oder *them* heißen.

Hier wieder eine kleine Aufgabe:
Welches sind die Objektpronomen?

she • him • we • her • us • I • them • me

GF 14 *some* and *any* *some* und *any*

We've got **some** crisps and **some** cheese.

Wir haben einige Kartoffelchips und etwas Käse.

◂ *some* steht vor allem in bejahten Aussagesätzen. Es kann „einige“ oder „etwas“ heißen.

But we haven't got **any** orange juice. Have we got **any** biscuits?

Aber wir haben keinen Orangensaft. Haben wir Kekse?

◂ In verneinten Aussagesätzen und in Fragen steht meist *any*.

! Im Deutschen kann man fragen „Haben wir Kekse?“, aber im Englischen wird meist *any* eingefügt: *Have we got any biscuits?*

Yes, of course we've got **some** – with chocolate on.

Ja, natürlich haben wir welche mit Schokolade.

Angebot: Would you like **some** biscuits?
Möchtest du ein paar Kekse?

Bitte: Can I have **some** juice, please?
Kann ich (etwas) Saft haben, bitte?

▸ *Unit 4 (p. 71)* • *P 7–8 (p. 77)*

! Wenn du mit einer Frage etwas anbietest oder um etwas bittest, verwendest du *some*.

Sieh dir die Zeichnungen an:
Wo brauchst du some, *wo brauchst du* any?

Toby has got ..., but he hasn't got ...

GF 15 The simple present and the present progressive
Die einfache Form der Gegenwart und die Verlaufsform der Gegenwart

simple present I **help** in the kitchen **every day**.

present progressive I'm **helping** in the kitchen **right now**.

▸ *Unit 4 (p. 72)*

Wie du weißt, kannst du mit dem ***simple present*** über die Gegenwart sprechen, z.B. wenn du sagen willst, was jemand jeden Tag tut. (Siehe Seite 132–134, GF 7.)

Wenn du allerdings sagen möchtest, dass jemand **gerade in diesem Moment** etwas tut, musst du das ***present progressive*** (die Verlaufsform der Gegenwart) verwenden.
Eine Verlaufsform gibt es im Deutschen nicht.
Aber manchmal sagt man „Ich bin gerade dabei, fernzusehen" (= *I'm watching TV*).

GF 16 The present progressive Die Verlaufsform der Gegenwart

a) Positive and negative statements

Sophie is helping in the kitchen.
Sophie hilft (gerade) in der Küche.
Emily isn't helping.
Emily hilft (gerade) nicht.
Mr Carter-Brown and Toby are watching TV.
Mr Carter-Brown und Toby schauen (gerade) fern.

Sophie You're making a mess, Prunella.
Prunella I'm not making a mess, Sophie.
I'm getting things ready for the party.
Sophie But you're dropping mum's plates ...

Present progressive

+		–	
I'm	working	I'm not	working
you're		you aren't	
he's/she's/it's		he isn't/she isn't/it isn't	
we're		we aren't	
you're		you aren't	
they're		they aren't	

▸ *Unit 4 (p. 72) • P 9–12 (pp. 78–79)*

Bejahte und verneinte Aussagesätze

Das *present progressive* wird mit *am/are/is* + *-ing*-Form des Verbs gebildet:
Sophie ***is helping***. *Emily* ***isn't helping***.

Du bildest die *-ing*-Form, indem du *ing* an den Infinitiv anhängst: ***help*** + ***ing*** = ***helping***.

! Merke aber:
1 Ein stummes ***e*** fällt weg:
make → making, give → giving.
2 Nach einem einzelnen, betonten Vokal (a, e, i, o, u) wird der Konsonant (p, t, g, m, n, ...) verdoppelt:
drop → dropping, get → getting, run → running.

Jetzt kannst du wieder eine Aufgabe lösen:
Wie bildest du die -ing-Formen dieser Verben?
*Ordne die Verben den Buchstaben **A** bis **C** zu, z.B. **1 A**.*

1 clean • 2 come • 3 eat • 4 run • 5 make • 6 sit

A: help → helping
B: ride → riding
C: swim → swimming

b) Questions and short answers

Are you working, Dad?
– Yes, I am. / No, I'm not.
Is Sophie's mum making a salad?
– Yes, she is. / No, she isn't.
Are Dan and Jo running in the park?
– Yes, they are./ No, they aren't.
What are you doing? – I'm reading.
Where's Jack going? – To the park.

▸ *Unit 4 (p. 74)* • *P 13 (p. 79)*

Fragen und Kurzantworten

In Fragen sind Subjekt *(you, Sophie's mum)* und *am/are/is* vertauscht.

Die Kurzantworten sind genauso wie beim Verb *be* (vgl. S. 128, GF 2 c).

Ein Fragewort *(what? where?)* steht wie im Deutschen am Anfang der Frage.

Kannst du auch diese Aufgabe lösen?
Bringe die Wörter in die richtige Reihenfolge:

1 Sophie's dad – is – What – watching on TV?
2 What's – doing – Mr Green?

Unit 5

GF 17 The simple past Die einfache Form der Vergangenheit

Before the rehearsal the students were nervous.

Last week Ananda followed Mr Green to the station.
Letzte Woche ist Ananda Mr Green zum Bahnhof gefolgt. / Letzte Woche folgte Ananda Mr Green ...

▸ *Unit 5 (p. 86)*

Mit dem *simple past* kannst du über Vergangenes berichten – z.B. wenn du eine Geschichte erzählst.

Mit Zeitangaben wie *last week, yesterday, three days ago* kannst du sagen, **wann** etwas geschehen ist oder **wann** jemand etwas getan hat.

GF 18 The simple past of the verb *(to) be*
Die einfache Form der Vergangenheit des Verbs *(to) be*

Where were you after the dress rehearsal?

▸ *Unit 5 (p. 86)* • *P 2–4 (pp. 90–91)*

Beim *simple past* von *be* gibt es nur zwei Formen:
I, he/she/it *was*
you, we, they *were*.

◂ Die verneinten Formen heißen ***wasn't*** und ***weren't***.

◂ Die Frage bildest du mit ***Was I ... / Were you...?*** usw.

◂ Die Kurzantworten heißen ***Yes, I was. / No, you weren't.*** usw.

Fragewörter stehen wie immer am Satzanfang.

Und wieder eine kleine Aufgabe:
Welche Kurzantwort ist richtig?

Was Sophie in the pirate scene at the end? –
1 No, she was. 2 Yes, she were.
3 Yes, she was. 4 Yes, she wasn't.

GF 19 The simple past: positive statements

Die einfache Form der Vergangenheit: bejahte Aussagesätze

a) Regular verbs

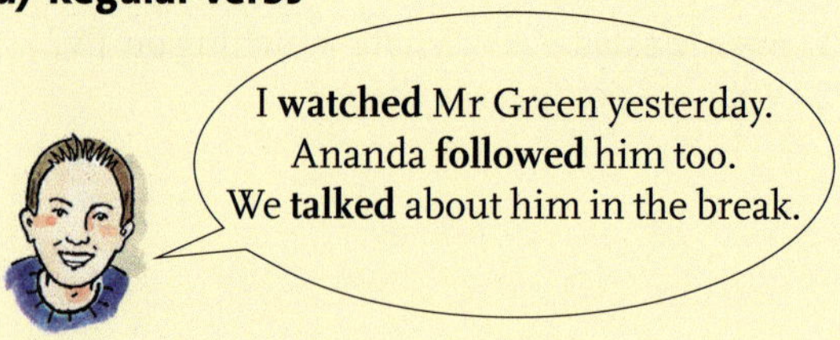

Regelmäßige Verben

Bei regelmäßigen Verben bildest du das *simple past* durch Anhängen von ***ed*** an den Infinitiv:
watch → *watched* [wɒtʃt],
follow → *followed* ['fɒləʊd],
talk → *talked* [tɔːkt].

Es gibt für **alle** Personen nur eine Form.

1 Ananda phoned Jack on his mobile.
2 Jack stopped and listened at Mr Green's door.
3 He tried to hear the woman's voice.
4 He wanted to see who the woman was. She sounded like his mother.

▸ *Unit 5 (p. 87) • P 6–8 (pp. 91–92)*

! Merke aber:

1 Ein stummes ***e*** fällt weg: *phone* → *phoned*.
2 Einige Konsonanten werden verdoppelt: *stop* → *stopped*, *plan* → *planned* (vergleiche hierzu Seite 140, GF 16 a).
3 ***y*** nach einem Konsonanten wird zu ***ied***: ***try*** → *tried*, ***hurry*** → *hurried*.
4 Nach ***t*** und ***d*** wird die ***ed***-Endung [ɪd] ausgesprochen: *wanted* ['wɒntɪd], *sounded* ['saʊndɪd].

b) Irregular verbs

Lots of people went to the Spring Show.
(Infinitiv: **go**)
The Hansons came home late after the show.
(Infinitiv: **come**)
Mr Hanson said, 'The show was great!'
(Infinitiv: **say**)

After the show they had dinner very late.
(Infinitiv: **have**)
One of the pirates had a parrot.
(Infinitiv: **have got**)

▸ *Unit 5 (p. 88) • P 9 (p. 92)*

Unregelmäßige Verben

Wie im Deutschen gibt es auch im Englischen eine Reihe von unregelmäßigen Verben. Jedes unregelmäßige Verb hat eine eigene Form für das *simple past*, die du einzeln lernen musst.

▸ *Liste unregelmäßiger Verben (p. 201)*

! *had* ist die *simple past*-Form von *have* und von *have got*.

Möchtest du jetzt wieder eine Aufgabe lösen?
Welche dieser Formen sind
simple past-*Formen?*

1 talked • 2 go • 3 had • 4 went
5 say • 6 were • 7 came • 8 tell
9 looked • 10 told

GF 20 The simple past: negative statements

Die einfache Form der Vergangenheit: verneinte Aussagesätze

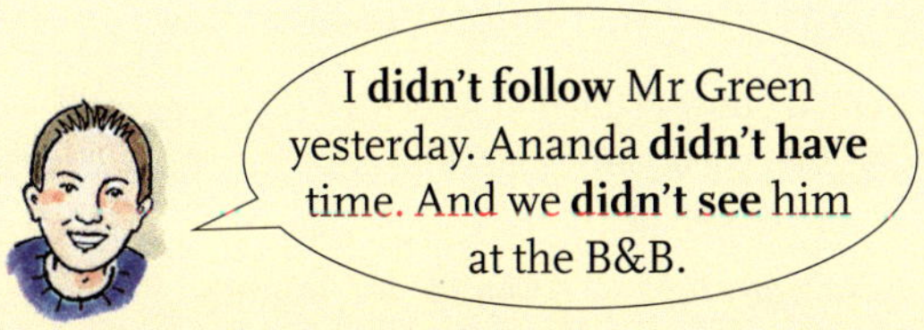

Eine Aussage im *simple past* verneinst du mit ***didn't*** + **Infinitiv**.
Dies gilt für alle Personen und für regelmäßige und unregelmäßige Verben.

Verneinte Aussagesätze

Vergleiche:

Simple present	I don't **play** the clarinet.	Jo doesn't **play** the clarinet.
Simple past	I didn't **play** the clarinet.	Jo didn't **play** the clarinet.

▸ *Unit 5 (p. 89) • P 12–14 (pp. 93–94)*

GF 21 The simple past: questions and short answers

Die einfache Form der Vergangenheit: Fragen und Kurzantworten

Did your dad **go** to the Spring Show, Jo?
– **Yes, he** did. / **No, he** didn't.

Did your parents **like** the show, Jack?
– **Yes, they** did. / **No, they** didn't.

What did all the teachers **say**?
When did the show **finish**?

Fragen im *simple past* bildest du mit ***did***:
Did he go?
(Nicht: *Did he ~~went~~?*)

Das Fragewort steht wie immer am Anfang.

Fragen

Vergleiche:

Simple present	Do you **play** the clarinet?	Does Jo **play** the clarinet?
Simple past	Did you **play** the clarinet?	Did Jo **play** the clarinet?

▸ *Unit 5 (p. 89) • P 15–16 (pp. 94–95)*

Und jetzt noch eine Aufgabe:
Frage nach den Personen in Klammern.

1 Jack's parents went to the show. (Mr Shaw?)
Did Mr Shaw …?
2 The Carter-Browns liked the show. (The Hansons?)
3 Jo sang in the show. (Dan?)
4 Sophie danced in the pirate scene. (Ananda?)

Unit 6

GF 22 Extra The *going to*-future Das Futur mit *going to*

a) Positive and negative statements

I'm going to find out what Mr Green is reading.

Ich werde herausfinden, was Mr Green liest. / Ich will herausfinden, was Mr Green liest.

I think **he's going to blow up** the bridge.

Ich glaube, er hat vor, die Brücke zu sprengen.

I'm not going to do it!
Ich werde/will es nicht tun.

Sophie isn't going to help Jack. She's too nervous.
Sophie hat nicht vor, Jack zu helfen. ...

We aren't going to follow Mr Green tomorrow.
Wir werden Mr Green morgen nicht folgen. / Wir haben nicht vor, Mr Green morgen zu folgen.

Bejahte und verneinte Aussagesätze

Wenn du über Pläne und Absichten für die Zukunft sprechen willst, verwendest du das Futur mit ***going to***. So wird es gebildet:

be (am/are/is) +	***going to*** +	**Infinitiv**
I'm	*going to*	*find out* ...
He's	*going to*	*blow up* ...

! Merke dir, dass *I'm going to* hier nichts mit „gehen" zu tun hat. Im Deutschen heißt es „Ich werde", „Ich will", „Ich habe vor".

Bei der Verneinung verwendest du verneinte Formen von *be*:

I'm not
You aren't | *going to* + **Infinitiv**
He isn't
usw.

(Die Kurzformen von *be* findest du auf S. 128, GF 2 a.)

b) Questions and short answers

Is Ananda going to help Jack?
– Yes, she is. / No, she isn't.

Are the students going to visit Horse World?
– Yes, they are. / No, they aren't.

What's Mr Green going to do?
What are you going to do, Jack?
When are we going to give our presentation?

Fragen und Kurzantworten

In Fragen sind Subjekt *(Ananda, the students)* und *am/are/is* vertauscht.

Die Kurzantworten sind genauso wie beim Verb *be* (vgl. S. 128, GF 2 c).

Fragewörter *(what? when?)* stehen wie immer am Satzanfang.

Present progressive und *going to*-future

Vergleiche:

Dan Be quiet, please. I'm doing my homework. *(Dan macht gerade seine Hausaufgaben: present progressive)*

Jo I'm going to do my homework **tomorrow**. *(Jo hat vor, die Hausaufgaben morgen zu machen: going to-future)*

▸ *Unit 6 (p. 103) • P 4–5 (p. 107)*

Wie sagst du es auf Englisch? Verwende going to. *Sage, dass ...*

1 ... du vorhast, dein Fahrrad zu putzen. *I'm ...*
2 ... du dir morgen eine neue CD kaufen wirst.

GF 23 Word order in subordinate clauses Die Wortstellung in Nebensätzen

▸ *Unit 6 (p. 103) • P 6 (p. 107)*

Nebensätze beginnen meist mit Wörtern wie *because, when, that*:

... *because it's quiet.*
... *when it's quiet.*

! Anders als im Deutschen ist die Wortstellung im Nebensatz genauso wie im Hauptsatz, nämlich **Subjekt – Verb (– Objekt)**:

Hauptsatz			**Nebensatz**			
S	**V**	**O**		**S**	**V**	**O**
I	*like*	*the library*	*because*	*I*	*like*	*books.*
		...,	*weil*	*ich Bücher mag.*		

Wieder eine kleine Aufgabe: Welches ist der Nebensatz, **A** *oder* **B**?

1 Jack doesn't go to football matches (**A**) because he hates sport. (**B**)

2 When it's hot (**A**) the Bristol kids often go swimming. (**B**)

GF 24 The simple present and the present progressive in contrast
Die einfache Form und die Verlaufsform der Gegenwart im Vergleich

◂ Dan redet über das, was die Zwillinge und ihr Vater **regelmäßig** tun. Er verwendet die einfache Form der Gegenwart *(simple present)*.

Wörter wie ***often, usually, on Saturdays, every day*** zeigen dir, dass du die einfache Form verwenden musst.

◂ Jo redet über das, was sie **im Moment** tun oder nicht tun. Er verwendet die Verlaufsform der Gegenwart *(present progressive)*.

Das Wort ***now*** zeigt dir, dass du die Verlaufsform verwenden musst.

! Verben wie *know, want, need, like, hate, hear, see* werden normalerweise nicht im *present progressive* verwendet.

Simple present (einfache Form der Gegenwart)

1 Das ***simple present*** drückt aus, dass jemand etwas **wiederholt** tut:

Polly usually cleans her cage on Saturdays.

2 Das ***simple present*** wird auch verwendet, um **aufeinanderfolgende Handlungen** zu beschreiben, z.B. wenn man eine Geschichte erzählt (oft mit *First ..., then ..., after that ...*):

First Ananda follows Mr Green to the station, then she watches him. After that she calls Jack on her mobile.

▸ *Unit 6 (p. 104) • P 11–12 (p. 109)*

Present progressive (Verlaufsform der Gegenwart)

1 Das ***present progressive*** drückt aus, dass jemand **gerade im Moment** etwas tut:

Look, Polly is cleaning her cage now.

2 Das ***present progressive*** wird auch verwendet, um Handlungen zu beschreiben, die über einen längeren Zeitraum im Gange, also noch nicht abgeschlossen sind:

Jack and his friends are playing detectives. They're following and watching Mr Green.

Polly is cleaning her cage.

Und jetzt noch eine Aufgabe: Welche Sätze drücken aus, dass jemand gerade etwas tut?

1 Jo sometimes goes to bed late.
2 I'm doing my homework now.
3 Look, you're making a mess with the glue.
4 Mum usually goes shopping on Mondays.
5 Ananda is helping her mum and dad in the shop today.

Lösungen der Grammar-File-Aufgaben

p.127 he, they, you, I, we (5)
p.128 **3, 5**
p.131 **1, 4**
p.132 **1A, 2B, 3D, 4A, 5A, 6B, 7C, 8A, 9C, 10D**
p.133/1 **2, 6**
p.133/2 he/she/it push**es**, do**es**, watch**es**, go**es**
p.134 1 We **don't play** hockey.
2 Toby **doesn't do** judo.
3 Parrots **don't eat** meat.
4 Sophie **doesn't clean** the cage.
p.135/1 my, his, their, our, her, your, its
p.135/2 1 Singular (eine Person)
2 Plural (mehrere Personen)
3 Plural (mehrere Tiere)
4 Singular (ein Tier)
5 Plural (mehrere Personen)
6 Singular (eine Person)
p.136/1 1 **Does** Sophie **make** models?
2 **Do** Ananda and Dilip **go** swimming?
3 **Does** Emily **like** music?
p.136/2 3
p.137/1 1 When does Uncle Henry come?
2 Where does Prunella play tennis?
3 What do you do in your free time?
p.137/2 1 (Jay always goes to basketball games.)
p.138 1 Jack has to help his mum.
2 He doesn't have to clean the rooms.
3 Does he have to make breakfast?
p.139/1 him, her, us, them, me
p.139/2 Toby has got **some** biscuits, but he hasn't got **any** orange juice.
p.140 **1A, 2B, 3A, 4C, 5B, 6C**
p.141 1 What is Sophie's dad watching on TV?
2 What's Mr Green doing?
p.142/1 3
p.142/2 **1, 3, 4, 6, 7, 9, 10**
p.143 1 Did Mr Shaw go to the show?
2 Did the Hansons like the show?
3 Did Dan sing in the show?
4 Did Ananda dance in the pirate scene?
p.144 1 I'm going to clean my bike.
2 I'm going to buy a CD tomorrow.
p.145 **1B, 2A**
p.146 **2, 3, 5**

English sounds (Englische Laute)

Die Lautschrift in den eckigen Klammern zeigt dir, wie ein Wort ausgesprochen und betont wird.
In der folgenden Übersicht findest du alle Lautzeichen.

Vokale (Selbstlaute)

[iː]	**g**ree**n**	[eɪ]	sk**a**t**e**
[i]	happ**y**	[aɪ]	t**i**m**e**
[ɪ]	**i**n	[ɔɪ]	b**oy**
[e]	y**e**s	[əʊ]	**o**ld
[æ]	bl**a**ck	[aʊ]	n**ow**
[ɑː]	p**ar**k	[ɪə]	h**ere**
[ɒ]	s**o**ng	[eə]	wh**ere**
[ɔː]	m**or**ning	[ʊə]	t**our**
[uː]	bl**ue**		
[ʊ]	b**oo**k		
[ʌ]	m**u**m		
[ɜː]	T-sh**ir**t		
[ə]	**a** partn**er**		

Konsonanten (Mitlaute)

[b]	**b**ox	[f]	**f**ull
[p]	**p**lay	[v]	**v**ery
[d]	**d**a**d**	[s]	**s**i**s**ter
[t]	**t**en	[z]	plea**s**e
[g]	**g**ood	[ʃ]	**sh**op
[k]	**c**at	[ʒ]	televi**s**ion
[m]	**m**u**m**	[tʃ]	tea**ch**er
[n]	**n**o	[dʒ]	**G**ermany
[ŋ]	si**ng**	[θ]	**th**anks
[l]	he**ll**o	[ð]	**th**is
[r]	**r**ed	[h]	**h**e
[w]	**w**e		
[j]	**y**ou		

Tipp

Am besten kannst du dir die Aussprache der einzelnen Lautzeichen einprägen, wenn du dir zu jedem Zeichen ein einfaches Wort merkst – das [iː] ist der **green**-Laut, das [eɪ] ist der **skate**-Laut usw.

Betonung

['] und [ˌ] sind **Betonungszeichen**.
Sie stehen immer vor der betonten Silbe.

['] zeigt die Hauptbetonung,
[ˌ] zeigt die Nebenbetonung.

Beispiel:
mobile phone [ˌməʊbaɪl ˈfəʊn]
Hauptbetonung auf **phone**,
Nebenbetonung auf der ersten Silbe: **mobile**

Der „Bindebogen"

Der **Bindebogen** [‿] zeigt an, dass zwei Wörter beim Sprechen aneinandergebunden und wie ein Wort gesprochen werden.

Beispiele:
What colour is ...? [ˌwɒt ˈkʌlər‿ɪz]
Mum and Dad [ˌmʌm‿ən ˈdæd]
This is ... [ˈðɪs‿ɪz]

The English alphabet (Das englische Alphabet)

a	[eɪ]	**h**	[eɪtʃ]	**o**	[əʊ]	**v**	[viː]
b	[biː]	**i**	[aɪ]	**p**	[piː]	**w**	[ˈdʌbljuː]
c	[siː]	**j**	[dʒeɪ]	**q**	[kjuː]	**x**	[eks]
d	[diː]	**k**	[keɪ]	**r**	[ɑː]	**y**	[waɪ]
e	[iː]	**l**	[el]	**s**	[es]	**z**	[zed]
f	[ef]	**m**	[em]	**t**	[tiː]		
g	[dʒiː]	**n**	[en]	**u**	[juː]		

Diese Wörterverzeichnisse findest du in deinem Englischbuch:

- Das **Vocabulary** (Vokabelverzeichnis – S. 148–178) enthält alle Wörter und Wendungen, die du lernen musst. Sie stehen in der Reihenfolge, in der sie in den Units vorkommen.
- Das **Dictionary** besteht aus zwei alphabetischen Wörterlisten zum Nachschlagen:
  Englisch – Deutsch: S. 179–191
  Deutsch – Englisch: S. 192–201.

So ist das Vocabulary aufgebaut:

- Hier siehst du, wo die Wörter vorkommen.
  p. 21/A 3 = Seite 21, Abschnitt 3
  p. 27/P 7 = Seite 27, Übung 7
- Die Lautschrift zeigt dir, wie ein Wort ausgesprochen und betont wird. (→ Englische Laute: S. 147)
- Eingerückte Wörter lernst du am besten zusammen mit dem vorausgehenden Wort, weil die beiden zusammengehören.
- Diese Kästen solltest du dir besonders gut ansehen.
- In diesen Kästen werden wichtige Wörter und Wendungen zu den Themen der Unit zusammengestellt.

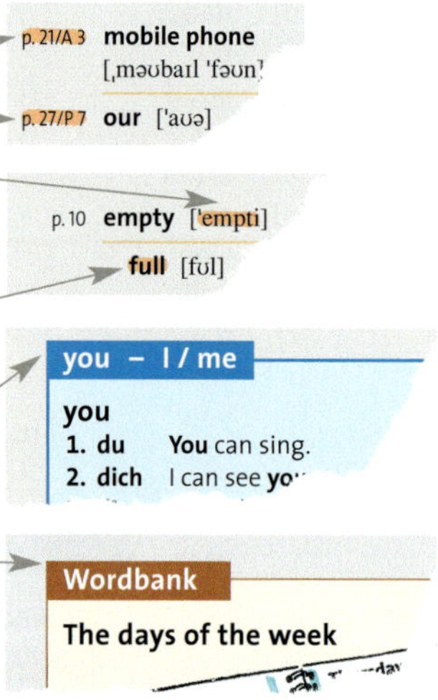
p. 21/A 3 **mobile phone** [ˌməʊbaɪl ˈfəʊn]
p. 27/P 7 **our** [ˈaʊə]
p. 10 **empty** [ˈempti]
full [fʊl]
you – I / me
you
1. du **You** can sing.
2. dich I can see **yo**...
Wordbank
The days of the week

Tipps zum Wörterlernen findest du im Skills File auf den Seiten 118 und 119.

Abkürzungen / Symbole

p. = page (Seite)
pp. = pages (Seiten)

sing = *singular* (Einzahl)
pl = *plural* (Mehrzahl)
no pl = *no plural*

jn. = jemanden
jm. = jemandem

◂▸ ist das „Gegenteil"-Zeichen. Beispiel: **full ◂▸ empty** (**full** ist das Gegenteil von **empty**)

! Hier stehen Hinweise auf Besonderheiten, bei denen man leicht Fehler machen kann.

'Hello' and 'Welcome'

Wordbank

pp. 6–8 **What about you?**

Hi, I'm Tatjana.	Hallo, ich bin Tatjana.	**I've got a brother and a sister.**	Ich habe einen Bruder und eine Schwester.
What's your name?	Wie heißt du?	**We live in Frankfurt, in ... Street.**	Wir wohnen in Frankfurt, in der ...straße.
– Hello. My name is ...	– Hallo. Ich heiße ... / Mein Name ist ...	**My favourite colour is ...**	Meine Lieblingsfarbe ist ...
Where are you from?	Wo kommst du her?	**I like apples.**	Ich mag Äpfel.
– I'm from ...	– Ich komme aus ... / Ich bin aus ...	**I don't like bananas.**	Ich mag keine Bananen. / Ich mag Bananen nicht.
My mum and dad are from ...	Meine Mutter und mein Vater kommen aus ...	**Can you sing a song in English?**	Kannst du ein Lied auf Englisch singen?
How old are you?	Wie alt bist du?	**– Yes, I can. / No, I can't.**	– Ja, kann ich. / Nein, kann ich nicht.
– I'm ... years old.	– Ich bin ... Jahre alt.		

p. 6	**pretty** [ˈprɪti]	hübsch	
	What about you? [ˌwɒt_əˌbaʊt ˈjuː]	Und du? / Was ist mit dir?	I'm from Bristol in England. **What about you?**
p. 8	**Welcome (to Bristol).** [ˈwelkəm]	Willkommen (in Bristol).	
	I can talk to ... [tɔːk]	ich kann mit ... reden / ich kann mich mit ... unterhalten	
	my partner [ˈpɑːtnə]	mein Partner / meine Partnerin	

Aussprache

Wie ein englisches Wort ausgesprochen wird, zeigt dir die **Lautschrift**. Sie steht in eckigen Klammern:

- **welcome** ['welkəm]
- **talk** [tɔːk]
- **partner** ['pɑːtnə]

Zwei Dinge kannst du an diesen Beispielen sehen:
Erstens werden englische Wörter oft anders ausgesprochen, als man denkt.
Zweitens enthält die Lautschrift auch ein paar „komische" Zeichen wie [ə], [ɔː] oder [ɑː]:
[ə] ist ein schwaches „e" wie am Ende von „bitt**e**".
[ɔː] kennst du aus dem Wort „baseb**a**ll".
[ɑː] ist ein langes „a" wie in „Kr**a**m".

→ Übersicht über die englischen Laute und Lautschriftzeichen: S. 147

this is ['ðɪs_ɪz]	dies ist	[ð] gibt es im Deutschen nicht. Der Laut klingt etwa so, als ob jemand die weichen „s"-Laute in „**S**en**s**e" lispelt.
he's [hiːz]	er ist	= he is [z] ist ein weiches „s" wie in „le**s**en".
she's [ʃiːz]	sie ist	= she is [ʃ] klingt wie das „sch" in „**sch**ön".
from Bristol **too** [tuː]	auch aus Bristol	! **too** steht am Ende des Satzes.
new [njuː]	neu	new ◄► old
with [wɪð]	mit	
his [hɪz]	sein, seine	
twin brother ['twɪn brʌðə]	Zwillingsbruder	Dan is Jo's **twin brother**. Dan and Jo are **twins**. [ʌ] klingt ähnlich wie das kurze „a" in „K**a**mm".
they're [ðeə] = **they are** [ðeɪ_ɑː]	sie sind	This is Jo.  This is Dan. **They're** twins.
I can talk about ... [ə'baʊt]	ich kann über ... reden	[aʊ] klingt wie das „au" in „bl**au**".
page [peɪdʒ]	(Buch-, Heft-)Seite	Abkürzung: **p.** 5 = **page** 5 • **pp.** 5–7 = **pages** 5–7 *French:* la page

Wordbank

p. 9 Viele dieser Wörter kennst du bestimmt schon oder du kannst deren Bedeutung leicht erraten.

boys

girls

trees

numbers

He is happy. **She is not happy.**

Listen to the band!

We can play football.

a boat **water**

a skateboard

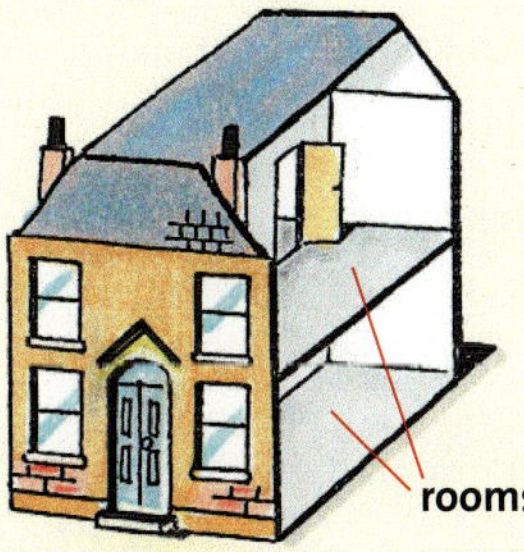
rooms
a big house

it's [ɪts]	er/sie/es ist	= it is

	a great place [ə greɪt 'pleɪs]	ein großartiger Ort/Platz, ein toller Ort/Platz	
	I can see a ... [siː]	ich kann ein/eine ... sehen	[s] ist ein hartes, scharfes „s" wie in „la**ss**en".
	photo ['fəʊtəʊ]	Foto	! **auf** dem Foto = **in** the photo
	kite [kaɪt]	Drachen	[aɪ] klingt wie das „ei" in „Kl**ei**d".
p. 10	**Park Road** [ˌpɑːk 'rəʊd]	Parkstraße	

a **kite**

Betonung

['] und [ˌ] sind Betonungszeichen.
Sie stehen immer vor der betonten Silbe.

['] zeigt die Hauptbetonung,
[ˌ] zeigt die Nebenbetonung.

Betonungszeichen helfen, die Wörter richtig zu betonen:
– Im Deutschen heißt es ***Park**straße*.
– Im Englischen sagt man *Park **Road*** [ˌpɑːk 'rəʊd]
(Hauptbetonung auf dem Wort „road").

when [wen]	wenn	Are you happy **when** the house is empty?
empty ['empti]	leer	
full [fʊl]	voll	full ◄► empty
I close ... [kləʊz]	ich schließe ... / ich mache ... zu	
thing [θɪŋ]	Ding, Sache	
I open ... ['əʊpən]	ich öffne ... / ich mache ... auf	open ◄► close
I push ... [pʊʃ]	ich drücke ... / ich schiebe ... / ich stoße ...	
I pull ... [pʊl]	ich ziehe ...	push ◄► pull
I drop ... [drɒp]	ich lasse ... fallen	[ɒ] klingt wie das „o" in „B**o**ck" oder „d**o**ch".
then [ðen]	dann, danach	
I laugh [lɑːf]	ich lache	

you – I / me

you

1. du	**You** can sing.	=	**Du** kannst singen.
2. dich	I can see **you**.	=	Ich kann **dich** sehen.
3. dir	I can play with **you**.	=	Ich kann mit **dir** spielen.

I / me

1. ich	**I** can sing.	=	**Ich** kann singen.
2. mich	Can you see **me**?	=	Kannst du **mich** sehen?
3. mir	Play with **me**.	=	Spiel mit **mir**.

	you look [lʊk]	du schaust / du guckst	
	but [bət, bʌt]	aber	Sophie is a girl, **but** Jack is a boy.
	You can't find me. [faɪnd]	Du kannst mich nicht finden.	
	That's me. [ˌðæts 'miː]	Das bin ich.	
p. 11	**I think** [θɪŋk]	ich glaube / ich meine / ich denke	[θ] gibt es im Deutschen nicht. Der Laut klingt etwa so, als ob jemand den harten „s"-Laut in „be**ss**er" lispelt. [ŋ] ist wie „ng" in „Di**ng**" oder das „n" in „pi**n**k".
	That's right. [ˌðæts 'raɪt]	Das ist richtig. / Das stimmt.	
	very nice [ˌveri 'naɪs]	sehr schön, sehr nett	! Das englische „v" wird wie in „Vampir" und „Vase" gesprochen – nicht wie in „Vater"!
	You can take the baby. [teɪk]	Du kannst das Baby nehmen.	

You can help me. [help]	Du kannst mir helfen.	
in here [ɪn 'hɪə]	hier drinnen	
Who are you? [huː]	Wer bist du?	
there [ðeə]	da, dort	
picture ['pɪktʃə]	Bild	! **auf** dem Bild = **in** the picture [tʃ] klingt wie „tsch" in „**tsch**üs".

Wordbank

p. 12

At school (In der Schule)

A family [1]

Mr[2] Scott, the father (dad) — **Mrs[3] Scott, the mother (mum)**

Sally Scott, Philip's sister — **Philip Scott, Sally's brother**

Their pets: Bob, the dog — **Bella, the cat**

Their friends: Jennifer Ray — **Robbie Carter**

The Scotts live in Bristol.
Die Scotts leben/wohnen in Bristol.

[1] a family – two families • [2] Mr ['mɪstə] • [3] Mrs ['mɪsɪz]

at 7 Hamilton Street [striːt]	in der Hamiltonstraße 7	
their father / their mother [ðeə]	ihr Vater / ihre Mutter	Dan and Jo and **their** father 
today [tə'deɪ]	heute	
the last day [ˌlɑːst 'deɪ]	der letzte Tag	
of the summer holidays [əv ðə ˌsʌmə 'hɒlədeɪz]	der Sommerferien	
Sorry, I'm late. ['sɒri], [leɪt]	Entschuldigung, dass ich zu spät bin/komme.	
shopping list ['ʃɒpɪŋ lɪst]	Einkaufsliste	
Let's look at the list. [lets]	Sehen wir uns die Liste an. / Lasst uns die Liste ansehen.	
you need ... [niːd]	du brauchst ... / du benötigst ...	
Me too. [tuː]	Ich auch.	I need a new school bag. – **Me too.**
pencil sharpener ['pensl ʃɑːpnə]	Bleistiftanspitzer	a **pencil sharpener** 
exercise book ['eksəsaɪz bʊk]	Schulheft, Übungsheft	

exercise ['eksəsaɪz]	Übung, Aufgabe	*French:* l'exercice *(m)*
for school [fə, fɔː]	für die Schule	I need a glue stick **for school**, Dad.
Let's go. [ˌlets 'gəʊ]	Auf geht's! (*wörtlich:* Lass uns gehen.)	
you two	ihr zwei	
I can say ... [seɪ]	ich kann ... sagen	

Wordbank

p. 13

What colour is ...? [ˌwɒt 'kʌlər‿ɪz]	Welche Farbe hat ...?	**What colour is** your pencil? – It's green. And **what colour is** your school bag? – It's red. *French:* la couleur

Aussprache

Der **Bindebogen** [‿] zeigt an, dass zwei Wörter beim Sprechen aneinandergebunden und wie ein Wort gesprochen werden.

What colour is ...? [ˌwɒt 'kʌlər‿ɪz]
Mum and Dad [ˌmʌm‿ən 'dæd]
This is ... ['ðɪs‿ɪz]

now [naʊ]	nun, jetzt	
plate [pleɪt]	Teller	a **plate** 
Oh well ... [əʊ 'wel]	Na ja ... / Na gut ...	

Wordbank

p. 14

The days of the week

It's Monday morning ...

flat [flæt]	Wohnung	
over the shop [ˌəʊvə ðə 'ʃɒp]	über dem Laden / über dem Geschäft	
Well, ... [wel]	Nun, ... / Also, ...	**Well,** is your new school nice?
uniform ['juːnɪfɔːm]	Uniform	*French:* l'uniforme *(m)*
tomorrow [tə'mɒrəʊ]	morgen	
the first day [fɜːst]	der erste Tag	[ɜː] kennst du aus dem Wort „T-Shirt".

at the new school	an/auf der neuen Schule	
Stop that! ['stɒp ðæt]	Hör auf damit! / Lass das!	
You can go to the shop. [gəʊ]	Du kannst zum Laden gehen.	
Why me? [waɪ]	Warum ich?	You can help your father now. – **Why me?**
poem ['pəʊɪm]	Gedicht	*French:* le poème
week [wi:k]	Woche	
p. 15 **newspaper** ['nju:speɪpə]	Zeitung	
I can have breakfast. [həv 'brekfəst]	Ich kann frühstücken.	
o [əʊ], **zero** ['zɪərəʊ]	null	! Wenn man seine Telefonnummer sagt, benutzt man **o** [əʊ]: 5 0 7 9 ... = five **o** seven nine ...
double ['dʌbl]	zweimal, doppelt, Doppel-	My phone number is 5 0 7 9 3 3 2. (five o seven nine **double** three two)
I can do tricks. [du: 'trɪks]	Ich kann (Zauber-)Kunststücke (machen).	
p. 16 **Bed and Breakfast (B&B)** [ˌbed_ən 'brekfəst]	Frühstückspension (*wörtlich:* Bett und Frühstück)	
parrot ['pærət]	Papagei	
They welcome you to ...	Sie heißen dich in ... willkommen	
wheelchair ['wi:ltʃeə]	Rollstuhl	[eə] kennst du aus dem Wort „**fair**".
at work [wɜ:k]	bei der Arbeit / am Arbeitsplatz	
Good luck (with ...)! [ˌgʊd 'lʌk]	Viel Glück (bei/mit ...)!	
Excuse me, ... [ɪk'skju:z mi:]	Entschuldigung, ... / Entschuldigen Sie, ...	*French:* Excusez-moi, ...

„Entschuldigung"

Excuse me, ...
sagt man, wenn man jemanden anspricht,
z.B. wenn man um etwas bittet:
Excuse me, what's the time, please?

Sorry, ...
sagt man, wenn man sich für etwas
entschuldigen möchte:
Sorry, I'm late.

trip [trɪp]	Reise; Ausflug	
back to Germany [ˌbæk tə 'dʒɜ:məni]	zurück nach Deutschland	[dʒ] kennst du aus „Job" und „Jeans".

Wordbank

p. 17 **What's the time?** (Wie spät ist es?)

It's eleven o'clock.

It's quarter past 11. (*oder:* **11.15**)

It's half past 11. (*oder:* **11.30**)

It's quarter to 12. (*oder:* **11.45**)

to  **past**

! 

Englisch: **half past 11**
Deutsch: **halb zwölf**

You're welcome.	Gern geschehen. / Nichts zu danken.

welcome

• Wenn du jemanden willkommen heißen willst:	**Welcome to** Germany!	**Willkommen in** Deutschland!
• Wenn sich jemand bei dir bedankt hat:	*A:* What's the time, please? *B:* Half past seven. *A:* Thank you. *B:* **You're welcome.**	*A:* Wie spät ist es, bitte? *B:* Halb acht. *A:* Danke. *B:* **Bitte, gern geschehen. / Nichts zu danken.**

! Nie: **Thank you. – ~~Please~~.** Sondern: **Thank you. – You're welcome.**

Unit 1: New school, new friends

Wordbank

p. 18

lots of ['lɒts‿əv]	eine Menge, viele, viel	
comic ['kɒmɪk]	Comic-Heft	I've got **lots of comics**.
there's [ðəz, ðeəz]	es ist (vorhanden); es gibt	= there is
there are ['ðər‿ə, 'ðeər‿ɑː]	es sind (vorhanden); es gibt	

There's ... / There are ...

Du kennst bereits **there** (= „da, dort"): **That's your room there.**

Mit **There's ...** und **There are ...** kannst du ausdrücken, ob etwas vorhanden ist oder nicht.
Im Deutschen sagt man meist „Es gibt ..." oder „Es ist/sind ...".

There's a football in my photo. But **there isn't a** skateboard in my photo.	Auf meinem Foto **ist ein** Fußball. Aber **es ist kein** Skateboard auf meinem Foto.
Are there skateboards in your photo? – Yes, **there are**. / No, **there aren't**.	**Gibt es** Skateboards auf deinem Foto? – Ja (, **gibt es**). / Nein (, **gibt es nicht**).
There are three books on the table.	**Es sind/Es liegen** drei Bücher auf dem Tisch.

! Nie: ~~It gives~~ ..., sondern immer: **There's ... / There are ...**

	marmalade ['mɑːməleɪd]	Orangenmarmelade	**!** Deutsch: Marmelade – Englisch: marmalade
p. 19	**in the morning**	am Morgen, morgens	
	word [wɜːd]	Wort	
	box [bɒks]	Kasten, Kästchen, Kiste	
	milk [mɪlk]	Milch	

	mobile phone [ˌməʊbaɪl 'fəʊn]	Mobiltelefon, Handy	! Deutsch: **Handy** Englisch: **mobile phone** oder **mobile**
p. 20/A 1	**before** [bɪ'fɔː]	vor *(zeitlich)*	
	lessons ['lesnz]	Unterricht	
	lesson ['lesn]	(Unterrichts-)Stunde	*French:* la leçon
	student ['stjuːdənt]	Schüler/in; Student/in	! Betonung auf der 1. Silbe: **student** ['stjuːdənt]
	nervous ['nɜːvəs]	nervös, aufgeregt	! Betonung auf der 1. Silbe: **nervous** ['nɜːvəs]
	first [fɜːst]	zuerst, als Erstes	
	clever ['klevə]	klug, schlau	
	mad [mæd]	verrückt	
	Don't listen to Dan. [dəʊnt]	Hör nicht / Hört nicht auf Dan.	
	Come. [kʌm]	Komm. / Kommt.	
	Sit with me. [sɪt]	Setz dich / Setzt euch zu mir.	
p. 20/A 2	**wrong** [rɒŋ]	falsch, verkehrt	That's wrong. ◄► That's right.
	(It's) my turn. [tɜːn]	Ich bin dran / an der Reihe.	First it's **my turn**, then it's **your turn**.
p. 21/A 3	**our** ['aʊə]	unser, unsere	We're twins. **Our** names are Dan and Jo.
	her [hə, hɜː]	ihr, ihre	Ananda is from Bristol. **Her** dad is from Uganda.
	together [tə'geðə]	zusammen	
	I'm sorry.	Entschuldigung. / Tut mir leid.	

sorry

Mit **sorry** kannst du ...

• dich entschuldigen:	**Sorry**, I'm late.	**Entschuldigung**, dass ich zu spät komme.
• sagen, dass dir etwas leid tut:	My mum and dad aren't together. – Oh, **I'm sorry.**	Meine Mutter und mein Vater sind nicht zusammen. – Oh, **das tut mir leid**.
• nachfragen, wenn du etwas nicht richtig verstanden hast:	It's eleven o'clock. – **Sorry?**	Es ist elf Uhr. – **Wie bitte?**

	teacher ['tiːtʃə]	Lehrer/Lehrerin	Mr Keller is my English **teacher**.

Wordbank

p. 22

p. 22/A 6	**Meet Mr Kingsley.** [miːt]	Lerne Mr Kingsley kennen. / Triff Mr Kingsley.	
	form [fɔːm]	(Schul-)Klasse	Ananda is in **Form** 7PK.

	Tell me your names. [tel]	Sagt mir eure Namen.	**Tell** your teacher **about** your pets. (= Erzähle ... von ... / Berichte ... über ...)
	PE [ˌpiː‿'iː]	Sportunterricht, Turnen	
	enough [ɪ'nʌf]	genug	
	quiet ['kwaɪət]	leise, still, ruhig	
	joke [dʒəʊk]	Witz	Can you tell me a **joke**? I like **jokes**.
	bad [bæd]	schlecht, schlimm	bad ◄► good
	Can you remember that? [rɪ'membə]	Kannst du dir das merken?	
p. 22/A 8	**alphabet** ['ælfəbet]	Alphabet	! Betonung auf der 1. Silbe: **alphabet** ['ælfəbet]
	Throw a ball. [θrəʊ]	Wirf einen Ball.	
	Climb a tree. [klaɪm]	Klettere auf einen Baum.	Can cats **climb** trees? – Yes, they can. ! Das „b" wird nicht gesprochen: **climb** [klaɪm].
	Write ... [raɪt]	Schreibe ...	
	Do what I do. [duː]	Tue, was ich tue.	
p. 23/A 10	**timetable** ['taɪmteɪbl]	Stundenplan	
	Take out ... [ˌteɪk‿'aʊt]	Nehmt ... heraus	**Take out** your English books, please.
	Write down ... [ˌraɪt 'daʊn]	Schreibt ... auf	
	at 8.45 [ət, æt]	um 8.45	
	on Tuesday	am Dienstag	

on

The first lesson **on Tuesday** is English.	Die erste Stunde **am** Dienstag ist Englisch.
Write the words **on the board**, please.	Schreib die Wörter **an** die Tafel, bitte.
Write your names **on your exercise books**, please.	Schreibt eure Namen **auf** eure Hefte, bitte.
Your ruler is **on your chair**.	Dein Lineal liegt **auf** deinem Stuhl.
Look at the pictures **on page 24**.	Seht euch die Bilder **auf** Seite 24 an.

	with [wɪð]	bei	! **with** = **1.** mit – Look, there's Jo **with** his brother. **2.** bei – It's English **with** Mr Kingsley.

School subjects [1]

Art [ɑːt]	Kunst	**Maths** [mæθs]	Mathematik
Biology [baɪ'ɒlədʒi]	Biologie	**Music** ['mjuːzɪk]	Musik
Drama ['drɑːmə]	Schauspiel, darstellende Kunst	**PE** [2] [ˌpiː‿'iː]	Sportunterricht, Turnen
French [frentʃ]	Französisch	**RE** [3] [ˌɑːr‿'iː]	Religion, Religionsunterricht
Geography [dʒi'ɒgrəfi]	Geografie, Erdkunde	**Science** ['saɪəns]	Naturwissenschaft
German ['dʒɜːmən]	Deutsch		
History ['hɪstri]	Geschichte		

[1] ['sʌbdʒɪkts] Schulfächer [2] Physical Education [ˌfɪzɪkəl‿edʒu'keɪʃn] [3] Religious Education [rɪˌlɪdʒəs‿edʒu'keɪʃn]

	Spell ... [spel]	Buchstabiere ...	
	after ['ɑːftə]	nach *(zeitlich)*	after school ◄► before school
	break [breɪk]	Pause	Morning **break** is at 10.45 at Cotham School.
p. 23/A 11	**lunch** [lʌntʃ]	Mittagessen	**Lunch** is at 1.05.
p. 24/A 13	**food** [fuːd]	Essen; Lebensmittel	

Tipps zum Wörterlernen → S. 118–119 • Englische Laute → S. 147 • Alphabetische Wörterverzeichnisse → S. 179–191 / S. 192–201

	really ['rɪəli]	wirklich	
	I haven't got a chair. ['hævnt gɒt]	Ich habe keinen Stuhl.	I've got a sister, but **I haven't got a** brother.

at

Let's sit **at that table** there.	Setzen wir uns **an** den Tisch dort.
Look **at the board**, please.	Seht **an** die Tafel, bitte.
Let's look **at the list** now.	Sehen wir uns jetzt mal die Liste **an**.
The Shaws live **at 7 Hamilton Street**.	... **in** der Hamiltonstraße 7
Jo and Dan are **at school**, and Mrs Hanson is **at work**.	... **in** der Schule, ... **bei** der Arbeit
At 8.45 it's English with Mr Kingsley.	**Um** 8.45 ...

	bank robber ['bæŋk ˌrɒbə]	Bankräuber/in	
	all [ɔːl]	alle; alles	Sophie, Ananda, Jack – they're **all** in Form 7PK. We need pens, felt tips and pencils. That's **all**.
	like [laɪk]	wie	My pencil case is **like** your pencil case.
	him [hɪm]	ihn; ihm	! **him** = **1.** ihn – There's Jack. Can you see **him**? **2.** ihm – Let's help **him**.
	idea [aɪ'dɪə]	Idee, Einfall	[ɪə] klingt wie das „ier" in „**hier**".
	What have we got next? [nekst]	Was haben wir als Nächstes?	
p. 24/A 14	**boring** ['bɔːrɪŋ]	langweilig	
	class [klɑːs]	(Schul-)Klasse	I'm in **class** 5. *French:* la classe
	I hate ... [heɪt]	ich hasse, ich mag ... nicht	I like cats, but **I hate** dogs.
p. 25/P 1	**different (from)** ['dɪfrənt]	verschieden, unterschiedlich; anders (als)	! anders **als** = different **from**: Cats are **different from** dogs. Cats can climb. *French:* différent, e

Classroom English

p. 28/P 9	Can we +work with a partner?	Können wir mit einem Partner/einer Partnerin arbeiten?
	+What page are we on, please?	Auf welcher Seite sind wir, bitte?
	+What's for homework? ['həʊmwɜːk]	Was haben wir als Hausaufgabe auf?
	Sorry, +I haven't got my exercise book.	Entschuldigung, ich habe mein Heft nicht dabei.
	Can I help you with the +worksheets? ['wɜːkʃiːts]	Kann ich dir bei den Arbeitsblättern helfen?
	Write +sentences in your exercise book. ['sentənsɪz]	Schreibt Sätze in euer Heft.
	Can I open/close the +window, please? ['wɪndəʊ]	Kann ich bitte das Fenster öffnen/schließen?
	Can I go to the +toilet, please? ['tɔɪlət]	Darf ich zur Toilette gehen, bitte?

+ = new words

	or [ɔː]	oder	Is Sophie in Form 7PK **or** in Form 7BW?
p. 30/P 14	**sound** [saʊnd]	Laut	*French:* le son

How's the new school?

p. 32	**end** [end]	Ende	
	Hurry up. [ˌhʌri_'ʌp]	Beeil dich.	
	poor Sophie [pɔː, pʊə]	(die) arme Sophie	[ʊə] klingt wie das „ur" in „**Kur**".
	Come in. [ˌkʌm_'ɪn]	Komm rein/herein.	
	everything ['evriθɪŋ]	alles	

	tea [tiː]	Tee; *(auch:) leichte Nachmittags- oder Abendmahlzeit*	
	classmate ['klɑːsmeɪt]	Klassenkamerad/in, Mitschüler/in	
p. 33	How **was ...?** [wəz, wɒz]	Wie war ...?	How **was** the first day at your new school?
	world [wɜːld]	Welt	
	See you.	Bis bald. / Tschüs.	
	Go on. [ˌɡəʊ‿'ɒn]	Mach weiter. / Erzähl weiter.	
	a packet of mints [ə ˌpækɪt‿əv 'mɪnts]	ein Päckchen/eine Packung Pfefferminzbonbons	**!** Betonung auf der 1. Silbe: **packet** ['pækɪt]
	little ['lɪtl]	klein	
	Bye. [baɪ]	Tschüs!	Bye./Goodbye. ◄► Hi./Hello.
	more [mɔː]	mehr	
	Dilip likes ...	Dilip mag ...	I like tennis, and my brother **likes** football.
	her [hə, hɜː]	sie; ihr	**!** **her** = **1.** sie – There's Sophie. I can see **her**. **2.** ihr – Let's help **her**. **3.** ihr, ihre – There's Ananda and **her** dad. Where's **her** mum?
	He likes her **a lot.** [ə 'lɒt]	Er mag sie sehr.	

Topic 1: Make a birthday calendar

Wordbank

p. 35

The months[1] **of the year**

[1] [mʌnθs]

1 January ['dʒænjuəri]
2 February ['februəri]
3 March [mɑːtʃ]
4 April ['eɪprəl]
5 May [meɪ]

6 June [dʒuːn]
7 July [dʒu'laɪ]

8 August ['ɔːɡəst]
9 September [sep'tembə]
10 October [ɒk'təʊbə]
11 November [nəʊ'vembə]

12 December [dɪ'sembə]

Make a calendar. [ˌmeɪk‿ə 'kælɪndə]	Mache/Baue einen Kalender.	Let's **make a calendar** for our classroom. **!** Deutsch: Kalender – Englisch: calendar
birthday ['bɜːθdeɪ]	Geburtstag	**!** Deutsch: Ich **habe** im Mai Geburtstag. Englisch: My birthday **is** in May. (Nicht: ~~I've got birthday~~ ... / ~~I have birthday~~ ...)
when?	wann?	**!** **when** = **1.** wann; **2.** wenn

birthdays

My birthday **is** in May. **When's** your birthday?
– My birthday is in June. **On** 13th June.

Ich **habe** im Mai Geburtstag. **Wann hast** du Geburtstag?
– Ich habe im Juni Geburtstag. **Am** 13. Juni.

! Du schreibst: **on 13th June** – Du sagst: **on the thirteenth of June**

date [deɪt]	Datum	*French:* la date

Unit 2: A weekend at home

p. 36	**weekend** [ˌwi:k'end]	Wochenende	*French:* le weekend
	at home [ət 'həʊm]	daheim, zu Hause	

home

Dan is **at home**.	Dan ist **zu Hause**.
Jo, **come home**!	Jo, komm **nach Hause**!
Go home now.	Geh jetzt **nach Hause**.

Wordbank

[1][ʃelvz] • [2]['wɔ:drəʊb]

	I **share** a room **with ...** [ʃeə]	Ich teile mir ein Zimmer mit ...	
	people ['pi:pl]	Menschen, Leute	
	garden ['gɑ:dn]	Garten	! Deutsch: Gar**t**en – Englisch: gar**d**en
	desk [desk]	Schreibtisch	

p. 37 **Wordbank**

[1][maɪs] • [2][maʊs] • [3]['gɪni pɪg]

	hutch [hʌtʃ]	(Kaninchen-)Stall	
	basket ['bɑ:skɪt]	Korb	
	cage [keɪdʒ]	Käfig	
	budgie ['bʌdʒi]	Wellensittich	
	tortoise ['tɔ:təs]	Schildkröte	*French:* la tortue
p. 38	**I can act** the song [ækt]	ich kann das Lied aufführen	
p. 38/A 1	**afternoon** [ˌɑ:ftə'nu:n]	Nachmittag	
	plan [plæn]	Plan	
	essay (about, on) ['eseɪ]	Aufsatz (über)	Write an **essay about** Bristol.

The day: morning – afternoon – evening – night

morning ['mɔːnɪŋ]	Morgen, Vormittag	**evening** ['iːvnɪŋ]	Abend
afternoon [ˌɑːftə'nuːn]	Nachmittag	**night** [naɪt]	Nacht, später Abend

in the morning	morgens, am Morgen	**on Friday morning**	freitagmorgens, am Freitagmorgen
in the afternoon	nachmittags, am Nachmittag	**on Friday afternoon**	freitagnachmittags, am Freitagnachmittag
in the evening	abends, am Abend	**on Friday evening**	freitagabends, am Freitagabend
! **at night**	nachts, in der Nacht	**on Friday night**	freitagnachts, Freitagnacht
at the weekend	am Wochenende		

life [laɪf], *pl* **lives** [laɪvz]	Leben	! **life** in Bristol [laɪf] – **das Leben** in Bristol We **live** in ... [lɪv] – Wir **leben/wohnen** in ...
easy ['iːzi]	leicht, einfach	
difficult ['dɪfɪkəlt]	schwierig, schwer	*French:* difficile
I **get up** at ... [ˌget‿'ʌp]	ich stehe um ... auf	
(to)* **get up**	aufstehen	
every ['evri]	jeder, jede, jedes	I get up at 6.45 **every** morning.
I **clean my teeth.** [kliːn], [tiːθ]	Ich putze mir die Zähne.	**Clean your teeth**, Jack. Dan, can you **clean** the bathroom, please?
tooth [tuːθ], *pl* **teeth** [tiːθ]	Zahn	one **tooth**  lots of **teeth** 
(to) **sleep** [sliːp]	schlafen	
I **wash my hands.** [wɒʃ]	Ich wasche mir die Hände.	**Wash your hands**, Jack. Dan, can you **wash** the car, please?
bus [bʌs]	Bus	a **bus**  *French:* le bus
(to) **read** [riːd]	lesen	
p. 39/A 2 (to) **get dressed** [ˌget 'drest]	sich anziehen	First I clean my teeth, then I **get dressed**.
(to) **tidy** ['taɪdi]	aufräumen	At the weekends I **tidy** my room.
(to) **give** [gɪv]	geben	
(to) **feed** [fiːd]	füttern	
meat [miːt]	Fleisch	Dogs eat **meat**.
(to) **drink** [drɪŋk]	trinken	
bowl [bəʊl]	Schüssel; *hier:* Fressnapf	a **bowl**   a goldfish **bowl**
everywhere ['evriweə]	überall	Oh no, now there's water **everywhere**.
carrot ['kærət]	Möhre, Karotte	! Betonung auf der 1. Silbe: **carrot** ['kærət]
sometimes ['sʌmtaɪmz]	manchmal	
(to) **try to do** [traɪ]	versuchen, zu tun	Let's **try to play** my new game. (*or:* Let's **try and play** my new game.)
(to) **put** [pʊt]	legen, stellen, *(etwas wohin)* tun	**Put** all the photos in the box. 

*Mit dem vorangestellten **(to)** kennzeichnen wir den Infinitiv (die Grundform) des Verbs.

here – there – where

	Ort		Richtung	
here	**Here**'s Dan.	**hier**	Come **here**, Jo.	**hierher**
there	**There**'s the ball.	**da, dort**	Paul Road is nice. Let's go **there**.	**dahin, dorthin**
where	**Where**'s Sheeba?	**wo?**	**Where** can we put the basket?	**wohin?**

	after that	danach	First I feed the pets. **After that** I have my breakfast.
	food [fuːd]	Futter	! **food** = **1.** Essen, Lebensmittel; **2.** Futter
	(to) **watch** [wɒtʃ]	beobachten, sich etwas ansehen; zusehen	
	(to) **watch TV** [tiːˈviː]	fernsehen	TV = television [ˈtelɪvɪʒn] ! <u>**im**</u> Fernsehen = <u>**on**</u> TV: a good film **on TV**

(to) look – (to) see – (to) watch

Look. Can you **see** Sheeba? – Yes, I can **see** her.	**Schau./Guck mal**. Kannst du Sheeba **sehen**? – ...
Toby **watches** Sophie.	Toby **beobachtet** Sophie. / Toby **schaut** Sophie **zu**.
Don't **watch TV** now, Dan. You've got a lot of homework.	**Sieh** jetzt nicht **fern**, Dan. ...

p. 39/A 3	**all day / all the time**	den ganzen Tag (lang) / die ganze Zeit	
p. 40/A 5	**Thanks.** [θæŋks]	Danke.	= Thank you.
	help	Hilfe	! **help** = **1.** helfen; **2.** Hilfe
	of course [əv ˈkɔːs]	natürlich, selbstverständlich	Is Prunella a Poltergeist? – Yes, **of course** she is.
	Here you are. [ˌhɪə juː‿ˈɑː]	Bitte sehr. / Hier bitte.	

„bitte“

– in Bitten und Aufforderungen:	**please**	→ What's the time, **please**? / Open the window, **please**.
– wenn du jemandem etwas gibst:	**Here you are.**	→ Can you give me that pen, please? – **Here you are.**
– wenn sich jemand bei dir bedankt:	**You're welcome.**	→ Thank you. – **You're welcome.**
– wenn du etwas nicht richtig verstanden hast („**Wie bitte?**“):	**Sorry?**	→ Where are the twins? – **Sorry?**

	This is **all wrong.**	Das ist ganz falsch.	Can I see your homework? – Oh no, it's **all wrong**.
	(to) **argue** [ˈɑːgjuː]	sich streiten, sich zanken	Sophie sometimes **argues** with her sister.
	(to) **do judo** [ˈdʒuːdəʊ]	Judo machen	
	early [ˈɜːli]	früh	early ◄► late
	till [tɪl]	bis *(zeitlich)*	On Sundays I sleep **till** 11 o'clock.
p. 40/A 6	**letter** [ˈletə]	Buchstabe	lots of **letters** *French:* la lettre
p. 41/A 7	**grandma** [ˈgrænmɑː]	Oma	= grandmother
	grandpa [ˈgrænpɑː]	Opa	= grandfather
	grandparents [ˈgrænpeərənts]	Großeltern	*French:* les grands-parents

	parents ['peərənts]	Eltern	*French:* les parents
	at the top (of) [tɒp]	oben, am oberen Ende, an der Spitze (von)	
	because [bɪ'kɒz]	weil	Why are you late for school, Emily? – I'm late **because** the bus was late.
	dead [ded]	tot	
	child [tʃaɪld], *pl* **children** ['tʃɪldrən]	Kind	one **child** ! [tʃaɪld]  three **children** ! ['tʃɪldrən] 
	son [sʌn]	Sohn	
	daughter ['dɔːtə]	Tochter	
	uncle ['ʌŋkl]	Onkel	*French:* l'oncle *(m)*
	aunt [ɑːnt]	Tante	
	married (to) ['mærɪd]	verheiratet (mit)	! verheiratet **mit** = married **to**
	cousin ['kʌzn]	Cousin, Cousine	*French:* le cousin, la cousine
	so [səʊ]	also; deshalb, daher	Polly is a parrot, **so** she lives in a cage.
	grandchild ['græntʃaɪld], *pl* **grandchildren** ['-tʃɪldrən]	Enkel/in	
	single ['sɪŋgl]	ledig, alleinstehend	not married
	divorced [dɪ'vɔːst]	geschieden	divorced ◂▸ married *French:* divorcé(e)
	without [wɪ'ðaʊt]	ohne	without ◂▸ with
	just [dʒʌst]	(einfach) nur, bloß	Don't **just** sit there. Come and help me.
	man [mæn], *pl* **men** [men]	Mann	
	woman ['wʊmən], *pl* **women** ['wɪmɪn]	Frau	
p. 45/P 11	(to) **remember** [rɪ'membə]	sich erinnern (an)	! Kannst du dich **an ihren Namen erinnern**? = Can you **remember her name**?
	quiz [kwɪz], *pl* **quizzes** ['kwɪzɪz]	Quiz, Ratespiel	
p. 47/P 16	**guest** [gest]	Gast	

A day in the life of ...

p. 48	**by** [baɪ]	von	'A day in my life' – an essay **by** Jack Hanson.
	(to) **have a shower** ['ʃaʊə]	(sich) duschen	I get up at 7.15, then I **have a shower**.
	shower	Dusche	
	(to) **get things ready** ['redi]	Dinge fertig machen, Dinge vorbereiten	In the evening I **get my things ready** for school.
	ready	bereit, fertig	Are you **ready**? Can we go? Dan, Jo! Breakfast is **ready**.
	again [ə'gen]	wieder; noch einmal	Look, there's that little dog **again**. Can you say that **again**, please?
	(to) **do homework**	die Hausaufgabe(n) machen, die Schularbeiten machen	**Do** your **homework** first. Then you can play. ! **Hausaufgaben sind** langweilig. = **Homework is** boring. *(kein Plural)*
	interesting ['ɪntrəstɪŋ]	interessant	! Betonung auf der 1. Silbe: **interesting** ['ɪntrəstɪŋ]

other ['ʌðə]	andere(r, s)	Jo is at home. The **other** children are at school.
country ['kʌntri]	Land	Germany is a big **country**.
spy [spaɪ]	Spion/in	
(to) **wear** [weə]	tragen, anhaben *(Kleidung)*	Can I **wear** your blue T-shirt, Dan? – Yes, OK.
sunglasses ['sʌnglɑːsɪz]	(eine) Sonnenbrille	! **glasses** und **sunglasses** sind Pluralwörter: I need my **glasses**. Where **are they**? Ich brauche meine **Brille**. Wo **ist sie**?
glasses ['glɑːsɪz]	(eine) Brille	
us [əs, ʌs]	uns	We're here. Can you see **us**?
(to) **fit** [fɪt]	passen	The T-shirt is too big. It doesn't **fit**.
story ['stɔːri]	Geschichte, Erzählung	*French:* l'histoire *(f)*

Der Plural von Wörtern auf „-y"

-y nach **Konsonant** wird im Plural zu **-ies**:

one	countr**y**	famil**y**	hobb**y**	sp**y**	stor**y**
lots of	countr**ies**	famil**ies**	hobb**ies**	sp**ies**	stor**ies**

-y nach **Vokal** bleibt:

one	bo**y**	da**y**	essa**y**
lots of	bo**ys**	da**ys**	essa**ys**

(to) **hear** [hɪə]	hören	! (to) **hear** = hören (können) (to) **listen (to)** = zuhören, horchen **Listen**. Can you **hear** the dogs in the park?
alarm clock [ə'lɑːm klɒk]	Wecker	

Topic 2: A tour of the house

p. 50	**tour (of the house)** [tʊə]	Rundgang, Tour (durchs Haus)	! ein **Rundgang durch** Bristol = a **tour of** Bristol
	(to) **look different/great/old**	anders/toll/alt aussehen	Sophie has got a new school bag. It **looks great**.
	a lot [ə 'lɒt]	viel	
	(to) **happen (to)** ['hæpən]	geschehen, passieren (mit)	A lot can **happen** in a story.
	upstairs [ˌʌp'steəz]	oben; nach oben	
	downstairs [ˌdaʊn'steəz]	unten; nach unten	
	stairs *(pl)* [steəz]	Treppe; Treppenstufen	

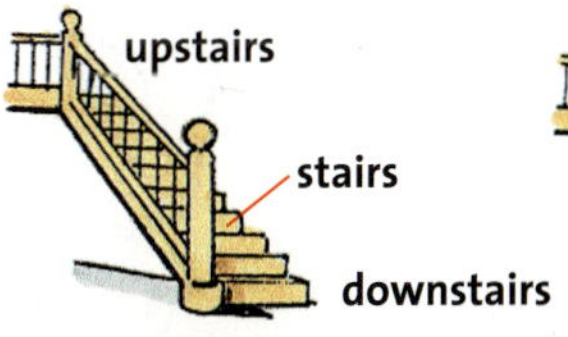

	sofa ['səʊfə]	Sofa	
	armchair ['ɑːmtʃeə]	Sessel	
	bath [bɑːθ]	Badewanne	
	dining room ['daɪnɪŋ ruːm]	Esszimmer	
	fridge [frɪdʒ]	Kühlschrank	
	cooker ['kʊkə]	Herd	
	dishwasher ['dɪʃwɒʃə]	Geschirrspülmaschine	
	sink [sɪŋk]	Spüle, Spülbecken	
	cupboard ['kʌbəd]	Schrank	
p. 51	**strange** [streɪndʒ]	seltsam, sonderbar	*French:* étrange
	comfortable ['kʌmftəbl]	bequem	That sofa looks very **comfortable**.

a **sofa**

an **armchair**

a **sink**

a **dishwasher**

a **fridge**

a **cooker**

a **cupboard**

floor [flɔː]	Fußboden	Jo, put your books on the desk, not on the **floor**.
cold [kəʊld]	kalt	
hot [hɒt]	heiß	hot ◄► cold
over there [ˌəʊvə 'ðeə]	da drüben, dort drüben	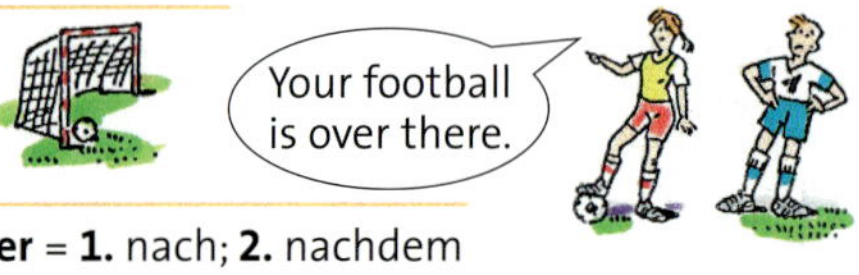
after ['ɑːftə]	nachdem	**!** **after** = **1.** nach; **2.** nachdem
before [bɪ'fɔː]	bevor	**!** **before** = **1.** vor; **2.** bevor
(to) **do the dishes** ['dɪʃɪz]	das Geschirr abwaschen	
them [ðəm, ðem]	sie; ihnen	Look, the twins. Can you see **them**? Let's help **them**.
hour ['aʊə]	Stunde	*French:* l'heure *(f)*
clean [kliːn]	sauber	**!** **clean** = **1.** *(verb)* sauber machen, putzen; **2.** *(adjective)* sauber
dream [driːm]	Traum	
warm [wɔːm]	warm	
funny ['fʌni]	witzig, komisch	

Unit 3: Sports and hobbies

Wordbank

p. 52

My hobbies (Meine Hobbys)

On Mondays I go swimming.

On Tuesdays I play football.

On Wednesdays I ride my bike.

On Thursdays I play hockey.

On Fridays I play computer games.

And you?

sport [spɔːt]	Sport; Sportart	I like **sport**. What are your favourite **sports**?

Sports

American football [əˌmerɪkən 'fʊtbɔːl]	Football
badminton ['bædmɪntən]	Badminton, Federball
baseball ['beɪsbɔːl]	Baseball
basketball ['bɑːskɪtbɔːl]	Basketball
dancing ['dɑːnsɪŋ]	Tanzen
football ['fʊtbɔːl]	Fußball
hockey ['hɒki]	Hockey
judo ['dʒuːdəʊ]	Judo
riding ['raɪdɪŋ]	Reiten, Reitsport
swimming ['swɪmɪŋ]	Schwimmen
table tennis ['teɪbl tenɪs]	Tischtennis
tennis ['tenɪs]	Tennis
volleyball ['vɒlibɔːl]	Volleyball

! Verschiedene Sportarten – verschiedene Verben: You **play** football, badminton, hockey, … .
You **do** judo. / You **do** sport. („Sport treiben")
You **go** riding, swimming, … .

free time [ˌfriː 'taɪm]	Freizeit, freie Zeit	
free [friː]	frei	
p. 53 **dancing lessons** ['dɑːnsɪŋ lesnz]	Tanzstunden, Tanzunterricht	
(to) **dance** [dɑːns]	tanzen	*French:* danser
guitar [gɪ'tɑː]	Gitarre	! Mike **spielt Gitarre**. = Mike **plays the guitar**.
model ['mɒdl]	Modell *(-flugzeug, -schiff usw.)*	! Betonung auf der 1. Silbe: **model** ['mɒdl]
(to) **go riding** ['raɪdɪŋ]	reiten gehen	
(to) **ride** [raɪd]	reiten	! (to) **ride** = reiten – (to) **ride a bike** = Rad fahren
stamp [stæmp]	Briefmarke	
card [kɑːd]	(Spiel-, Post-)Karte	
(to) **collect** [kə'lekt]	sammeln	People **collect** stamps, cards, posters, comics, ...
I **like swimming/dancing/...**	ich schwimme/tanze/... gern	I **like swimming**. And you? – I **don't like swimming**, but I **like riding**.

Wordbank

p. 54/A 1

assistant / shop assistant [ə'sɪstənt]	Verkäufer, Verkäuferin	! Betonung auf der 2. Silbe: **assistant** [ə'sɪstənt]
Good afternoon.	Guten Tag. *(nachmittags)*	! **Guten Tag.** = **Hello. / Good morning. / Good afternoon.** (Nicht: ~~Good day.~~)
size [saɪz]	Größe	
(to) **try on** [ˌtraɪ_'ɒn]	anprobieren *(Kleidung)*	Can I **try on** your new dress? – Not now. You can **try** it **on** tomorrow.
these [ðiːz]	diese, die (hier)	
..., you know. [nəʊ]	..., wissen Sie. / ..., weißt du.	He's really good at football, **you know**.
(to) **know**	wissen	Do you **know** where Jack is? – He's at school. ! Aussprache: (to) **know** [nəʊ] – **now** [naʊ]
(to) **want** [wɒnt]	(haben) wollen	I don't **want** these shoes. I **want** the red boots.
(to) **buy** [baɪ]	kaufen	Can we **buy** the red boots, please?
(to) **sell** [sel]	verkaufen	(to) sell ◄► (to) buy

p. 54/A 2	**clothes** *(pl)* [kləʊðz, kləʊz]	Kleidung, Kleidungsstücke	All my **clothes** are black.
	stuff [stʌf]	Zeug, Kram	What's that red **stuff** on your shirt? Ketchup?
	(to) **choose** [tʃuːz]	(sich) aussuchen, (aus)wählen	We have to **choose** a name for our new dog. *French:* choisir
p. 55/A 3	**project (about, on)** ['prɒdʒekt]	Projekt (über, zu)	**!** Betonung auf der 1. Silbe: **pro**ject ['prɒdʒekt] *French:* le projet
	(to) **ask** [ɑːsk]	fragen	
	piano [pi'ænəʊ]	Klavier, Piano	**!** Sie **spielt Klavier**. = She **plays the piano**.
	alone [ə'ləʊn]	allein	Does Prunella play tennis **alone**? – No, she plays with Uncle Henry.
	head [hed]	Kopf	
	always ['ɔːlweɪz]	immer	Prunella **always** plays tennis with her uncle.
	(to) **win** [wɪn]	gewinnen	And she always **wins**!
	neighbour ['neɪbə]	Nachbar, Nachbarin	
	anyway ['eniweɪ]	sowieso	I don't like that shirt. And it doesn't fit **anyway**.
p. 55/A 5	(to) **skate** [skeɪt]	Inliner/Skateboard fahren	I like **skating**. We always go **skating** on Sundays.
	skates [skeɪts]	Inliner	
p. 56/A 6	**often** ['ɒfn]	oft, häufig	I **often** ride my bike to school.
	Dear Jay **...** [dɪə]	Lieber Jay, ...	
	quick [kwɪk]	schnell	
	some [səm, sʌm]	einige, ein paar	There are **some** apples for you in the kitchen.
	question ['kwestʃn]	Frage	You ask lots of **questions**. **!** Fragen stellen = (to) ask questions *French:* la question
	(to) **answer** ['ɑːnsə]	antworten; beantworten	
	answer (to) ['ɑːnsə]	Antwort (auf)	Here's a quick **answer to** your question.
	match [mætʃ]	Spiel, Wettkampf	Football **matches** are often on Saturdays.
	Love ... [lʌv]	Liebe Grüße, ... *(Briefschluss)*	
	(to) **love** [lʌv]	lieben, sehr mögen	
	the next morning/day [nekst]	am nächsten Morgen/Tag	
	never ['nevə]	nie, niemals	never ◂▸ always
	usually ['juːʒuəli]	meistens, gewöhnlich, normalerweise	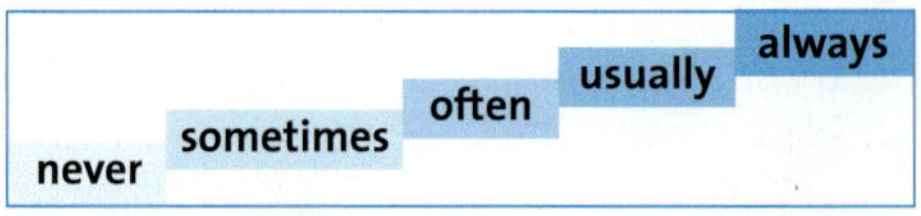
	(to) **walk** [wɔːk]	(zu Fuß) gehen	I never ride my bike to school. I always **walk**.
	Say hi to Dilip **for me.**	Grüß Dilip von mir.	
p. 57/A 9	(to) **have to** do ['hæv tə, 'hæf tə]	tun müssen	I can't help you with your homework, I **have to** feed the rabbits.
	at least [ət 'liːst]	zumindest, wenigstens	These shoes aren't cool, but **at least** they fit.
	most people [məʊst]	die meisten Leute	**Most** children like hamsters and rabbits. **!** **die meisten** Kinder = **most** children

	(to) **understand** [ˌʌndəˈstænd]	verstehen, begreifen	In English, please. I don't **understand** German.
	(to) **lay the table** [leɪ]	den Tisch decken	I always **lay the table** for breakfast on Sundays.
	dinner [ˈdɪnə]	Abendessen, Abendbrot	*French:* le dîner
p. 57/A 10	**right now** [raɪt ˈnaʊ]	jetzt sofort; jetzt gerade	I need your help **right now**. Sorry, I can't help you **right now**.
	(to) **teach** [tiːtʃ]	unterrichten, lehren	Mr Kingsley is a teacher. He **teaches** English.
	(to) **learn** [lɜːn]	lernen	
	(to) **shout** [ʃaʊt]	schreien, rufen	Some teachers **shout** a lot. Don't **shout at** me. (= Schrei mich nicht an.)
p. 57/A 11	**busy** [ˈbɪzi]	beschäftigt	Can you help me? Or are you **busy**?
p. 58/P 2	**snake** [sneɪk]	Schlange	
p. 60/P 8	(to) **know** [nəʊ]	kennen	! (to) **know** = **1.** wissen; **2.** kennen
	appointment [əˈpɔɪntmənt]	Termin, Verabredung	
	(to) **meet** [miːt]	sich treffen	! (to) **meet**: **1.** Can **we meet** at 8 o'clock? (Können **wir uns** ... **treffen**?) **2.** Can **you meet us** after school? (Kannst **du uns** ... **treffen**?)
p. 61/P 10	**under** [ˈʌndə]	unter	Oh, there's my book – **under** the desk.
	meaning [ˈmiːnɪŋ]	Bedeutung	
p. 61/P 11	**person** [ˈpɜːsn]	Person	*French:* la personne
p. 62/P 13	**on the radio** [ˈreɪdiəʊ]	im Radio	*French:* à la radio
p. 63/P 14	**news** *(no pl)* [njuːz]	Nachrichten	! Hier <u>sind</u> die Nachrichten. = Here <u>is</u> the news.
p. 63/P 15	(to) **link** [lɪŋk]	verbinden, verknüpfen	Can you **link** the words and the pictures?
p. 63/P 16	**car** [kɑː]	Auto	a **car** 

The SHoCK Team

p. 65	**the only** guest [ˈəʊnli]	der einzige Gast	Dan and Jo are **the only** twins in 7PK.
	suddenly [ˈsʌdnli]	plötzlich, auf einmal	**Suddenly** everything was quiet.
	noise [nɔɪz]	Geräusch; Lärm	Listen! There's a **noise** at the window. What's all that **noise**? I can't do my homework.
	down [daʊn]	hinunter, herunter, nach unten	
	up [ʌp]	hinauf, herauf, nach oben	up ◄► down
	outside the room [ˌaʊtˈsaɪd]	vor dem Zimmer; außerhalb des Zimmers	Sophie's rabbits live **outside** the house – in a hutch in the garden.
	outside	draußen	Where's Sheeba? – She's **outside**, in the garden.
	scary [ˈskeəri]	unheimlich; gruselig	
	(to) **run** [rʌn]	laufen, rennen	
	away [əˈweɪ]	weg, fort	Go **away**, Prunella. I have to do my homework.
	(to) **call** [kɔːl]	rufen; anrufen; nennen	Please **call** your dog. It's in our garden. **Call** me tomorrow. Here's my phone number. Her name is Elizabeth, but we **call** her Liz.

left – right

Do you write with your **left** hand or your **right** hand?	Schreibst du mit der **linken** oder mit der **rechten** Hand?
Jack looks **left** and **right**, but he can't see the man.	Jack schaut **nach links** und **nach rechts**, aber ...
On the left, you can see Morris, my cat.	**Links/Auf der linken Seite** ...
My dog Alice is **on the right**.	... **rechts/auf der rechten Seite**.

police *(pl)* [pə'li:s]	Polizei	❗ **police** ist immer Plural: Where <u>**are**</u> the **police**? We have to call <u>**them**</u>. (Wo ist die Polizei? Wir müssen sie rufen.)
into ... ['ɪntə, 'ɪntʊ] **out of ...** ['aʊt‿əv]	in ... (hinein) aus ... (heraus/hinaus)	 **into** the house **out of** the house
door [dɔ:]	Tür	
maybe ['meɪbi]	vielleicht	**Maybe** Mr Green is a bank robber?
visitor ['vɪzɪtə]	Besucher/in, Gast	*French:* le visiteur, la visiteuse
(to) **phone** [fəʊn]	anrufen	❗ **phone** = **1.** *(noun)* Telefon; **2.** *(verb)* anrufen
(to) **agree (with)** [ə'gri:]	*(jm.)* zustimmen	❗ Ich **stimme** <u>**dir**</u> **zu**. = I **agree** <u>**with you**</u>.
This is about Mr Green.	Es geht um Mr Green.	**This is about** the SHoCK Team, not about Jack.
(to) **mean** [mi:n]	meinen, sagen wollen	❗ • What do you **mean**, a spy? = Was **willst** du damit **sagen**, ein Spion? • What do you **think**: is he a spy? = Was **meinst (glaubst)** du: Ist er ein Spion?
(to) **find out (about)** [ˌfaɪnd‿'aʊt]	herausfinden (über)	
detective [dɪ'tektɪv]	Detektiv, Detektivin	
p. 66 **a piece of paper** [əˌpi:s‿əv 'peɪpə]	ein Stück Papier	**a piece of paper** 
group [gru:p]	Gruppe	
(to) **show** [ʃəʊ]	zeigen	Can you **show** me your new computer?
(to) **add (to)** [æd]	hinzufügen, ergänzen, addieren (zu)	**Add** blue **to** yellow and you've got green.
(to) **start** [stɑ:t]	starten, anfangen, beginnen (mit)	
watch [wɒtʃ]	Armbanduhr	❗ **watch** = **1.** *(verb)* beobachten, sich ansehen **2.** *(noun)* Armbanduhr
clock [klɒk]	(Wand-, Stand-, Turm-)Uhr	 **watches**  **clocks**
(to) **wait (for)** [weɪt]	warten (auf)	Don't **wait for** Prunella – she's always late.

Topic 3: An English jumble sale

p. 67	**jumble sale** ['dʒʌmbl seɪl]	Wohltätigkeitsbasar	
	money ['mʌni]	Geld	
	pound (£) [paʊnd]	Pfund *(britische Währung)*	
	pence (p) *(pl)* [pens]	Pence *(Mehrzahl von „penny")*	10**p** [piː] = 10 **pence**
	penny ['peni]	*kleinste britische Münze*	1**p** [piː] = 1 **penny**
	euro (€) ['jʊərəʊ]	Euro	
	cent (c) [sent]	Cent	
	What about ...?	Wie wär's mit ...?	
	too much [tuː 'mʌtʃ]	zu viel	! **too** = **1.** auch – The flat is big, and the garden is big **too**. („auch groß") **2.** zu – The house is **too** big. („zu groß")
	How much is/are ...? [ˌhaʊ 'mʌtʃ]	Was kostet/kosten ...? / Wie viel kostet/kosten ...?	**How much is** the felt tip? And **how much are** the pencils?
	It's £1.	Er/Sie/Es kostet 1 Pfund.	The felt tip **is** £1.75, and the pencils **are** 35p.
	only ['əʊnli]	nur, bloß	There aren't two books on the desk, there's **only** one. 
	(to) **take** 10c **off** [ˌteɪk_'ɒf]	10 Cent abziehen	£3? That's too much. Can you **take** 50p **off**?
	I'll take it. [aɪl 'teɪk_ɪt]	Ich werde es (ihn, sie) nehmen. / Ich nehme es (ihn, sie).	How much is the pencil case? – £2.50. – OK, **I'll take it**.
	change [tʃeɪndʒ]	Wechselgeld	

Unit 4: Party, party!

Wordbank

pp. 68/69 **Food and drink**

(to) **have ... for breakfast**	... zum Frühstück essen/trinken	I usually **have** toast and orange juice **for breakfast**.
chips *(pl)* [tʃɪps]	Pommes frites	
biscuit ['bɪskɪt]	Keks, Plätzchen	! Betonung auf der 1. Silbe: **biscuit** ['bɪskɪt]
crisps *(pl)* [krɪsps]	Kartoffelchips	! **crisps** = Kartoffelchips – **chips** = Pommes frites
fruit salad ['fruːt ˌsæləd]	Obstsalat	*French:* la salade de fruits

sausage ['sɒsɪdʒ]	(Brat-, Bock-)Würstchen, Wurst	**sausages** and **chips** 
sweets *(pl)* [swi:ts]	Süßigkeiten	
sweet [swi:t]	süß	I don't like bananas. They're too **sweet**.
behind [bɪ'haɪnd]	hinter	 **behind** the box
in front of [ɪn 'frʌnt_əv]	vor	**in front of** the box
next to	neben	**next to** the plate 
bottle ['bɒtl]	Flasche	a milk **bottle**   a **bottle of** milk *French:* la bouteille
glass [glɑ:s]	Glas	
jug [dʒʌg]	Krug	

a bottle of ..., a glass of ...

a bottle of milk

a glass of water

a jug of orange juice

a bowl of cornflakes

a plate of chips

a packet of crisps

a basket of apples

a piece of pizza

Would you like ...? [wəd, wʊd]	Möchtest du ...? / Möchten Sie ...?	**Would you like** a piece of pizza? – Yes, please.
I'd like ... (= I would like ...)	Ich hätte gern ... / Ich möchte gern ...	What would you like? – **I'd like** a hamburger, please.
some cheese/juice/money [səm, sʌm]	etwas Käse/Saft/Geld	! **some** = **1.** einige – **some** apples, chips, bottles, ... **2.** etwas – **some** cheese, milk, money, ...
hungry ['hʌŋgri]	hungrig	! Ich <u>habe</u> **Hunger**. = I<u>'m</u> **hungry**.
thirsty ['θɜ:sti]	durstig	! Ich <u>habe</u> **Durst**. = I<u>'m</u> **thirsty**.
p. 70/A 1 **invitation (to)** [ˌɪnvɪ'teɪʃn]	Einladung (zu)	*French:* l'invitation *(f)*
(to) **invite (to)** [ɪn'vaɪt]	einladen (zu)	Can I **invite** all my friends to my party? *French:* inviter
long [lɒŋ]	lang	Ananda's essay is very **long**. *French:* long, ue
short [ʃɔ:t]	kurz	Dan's essay is very **short**. short ◄► long
(to) **want to** do [wɒnt]	tun wollen	Do you really **want to** invite all your friends? ! (to) **want** = haben wollen: I **want** a new skateboard. (to) **want to do** = tun wollen: I **want to** buy it now.
both [bəʊθ]	beide	Do you want to listen to **both** CDs? We **both** like hamsters. I like **both** these T-shirts. Can we buy **both**?
real [rɪəl]	echt, wirklich	It's a party for **real** people, not for poltergeists.
p. 71/A 4 **present** ['preznt]	Geschenk	! **present** = **1.** Gegenwart; **2.** Geschenk
still [stɪl]	(immer) noch	After dinner Jo was **still** hungry.
soap [səʊp]	Seife	a piece of **soap** 
expensive [ɪk'spensɪv]	teuer	£60 for a T-shirt? That's too **expensive**.

	any …? ['eni]	(irgend)welche …?	! **any** bleibt oft unübersetzt: Are there **any** oranges? (= Gibt es Apfelsinen?)
	earring ['ɪərɪŋ]	Ohrring	
	not (…) any	kein, keine	There is**n't any** milk in the fridge. We have**n't** got **any** pets. What about you?
	(to) **be in a hurry** ['hʌri]	in Eile sein, es eilig haben	! **hurry**: **1. I'm in a hurry**. (= Ich habe es eilig.) **2. Hurry up**, please. (= Beeil dich, bitte.)
	(to) **follow** ['fɒləʊ]	folgen; verfolgen	My dog always **follows** me. The police **are following** the man to his house.
p. 71/A 5	**key word** ['ki: wɜ:d]	Stichwort, Schlüsselwort	
	another [ə'nʌðə]	ein(e) andere(r, s); noch ein(e)	I can't write with this pen. I need **another** pen. I'm still hungry. Let's eat **another** sandwich.
	reason ['ri:zn]	Grund, Begründung	*French:* la raison
p. 72/A 7	(to) **make a mess** [mes]	alles durcheinanderbringen, alles in Unordnung bringen	When the house is empty, Prunella often **makes a mess**.
	(to) **take** [teɪk]	(weg-, hin)bringen	Please **take** the plates into the kitchen, Sophie.
	to Jenny's	zu Jenny	Can we go **to Jenny's** now? (– to Jenny's house)
	later ['leɪtə]	später	
p. 73/A 9	**train** [treɪn]	Zug	! There was a funny man **on the train**. (= **im Zug**) *French:* le train
	station ['steɪʃn]	Bahnhof	! Betonung auf der 1. Silbe: **station** ['steɪʃn]
	somebody ['sʌmbədi]	jemand	Mr Green is talking to **somebody**.
	(to) **get off (the train/bus)** [ˌget‿'ɒf] **(-tt-)***	(aus dem Zug/Bus) aussteigen	This is where I live. We have to **get off** here.
	(to) **get on (the train/bus)** [ˌget‿'ɒn] **(-tt-)**	(in den Zug/Bus) einsteigen	! **in** den Bus **einsteigen** = (to) **get on** the bus; **aus** dem Bus **aussteigen** = (to) **get off** the bus
	parcel ['pɑ:sl]	Paket	
	(to) **look round** [ˌlʊk 'raʊnd]	sich umsehen	Mr Green **looks round**, then he starts to run.
	(to) **hide** [haɪd]	sich verstecken; *(etwas)* verstecken	Prunella often **hides** in the wardrobe. Can you **hide** this parcel for me, please?
p. 74/A 10	**Which** picture …? [wɪtʃ]	Welches Bild …?	**Which** cake would you like? The chocolate cake?

Wordbank

My body[1] (Mein Körper)

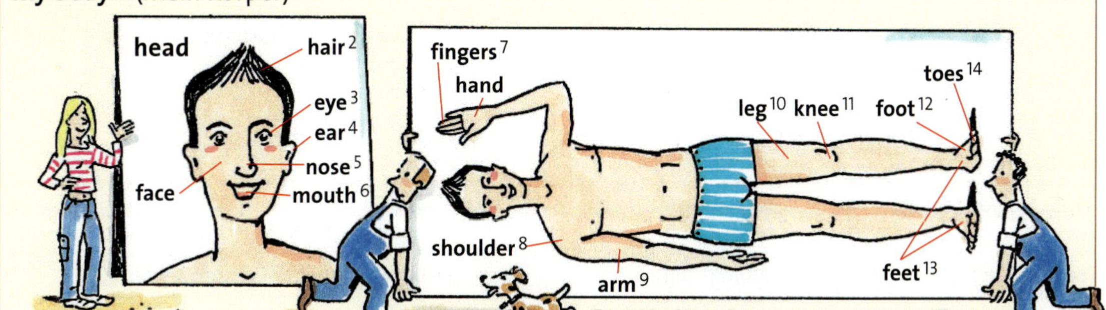

1['bɒdi] • 2[heə] • 3[aɪ] • 4[ɪə] • 5[nəʊz] • 6[maʊθ] • 7['fɪŋgəz] • 8['ʃəʊldə] • 9[ɑ:m] • 10[leg] • 11[ni:] • 12[fʊt] • 13[fi:t] • 14[təʊz]

*Die Angabe **(-tt-)** zeigt, dass der Endkonsonant bei der Bildung der *-ing*-Form verdoppelt wird: **get** – **getting**.

p. 76/P 6	**zoo** [zu:]	Zoo, Tierpark	**!** Aussprache: **zoo** [zu:] *French:* le zoo
	animal ['ænɪml]	Tier	*French:* l'animal *(m)*
p. 77/P 7	**muesli** ['mju:zli]	Müsli	
	egg [eg]	Ei	
p. 78/P 9	**minute** ['mɪnɪt]	Minute	 It's three **minutes** to six. **!** Betonung auf der 1. Silbe: **minute** ['mɪnɪt] *French:* la minute

Sophie's party – a play

p. 81	**play** [pleɪ]	Theaterstück	**!** **play** = **1.** *(verb)* spielen; **2.** *(noun)* Theaterstück
	scene [si:n]	Szene	**!** Das „c" wird nicht gesprochen: **scene** [si:n]. *French:* la scène
	... pm [ˌpi:‿'em]	... Uhr nachmittags/abends	**!** Man verwendet **am** oder **pm** nicht mit **o'clock**. Also nur: **at two pm** (nicht: ~~at two o'clock pm~~)
	... am [ˌeɪ‿'em]	... Uhr morgens/vormittags	
	Don't worry. ['wʌri]	Mach dir keine Sorgen.	
	(to) **worry (about)**	sich Sorgen machen (wegen, um)	When I come home late my mum always **worries about** me.
	doorbell ['dɔ:bel]	Türklingel	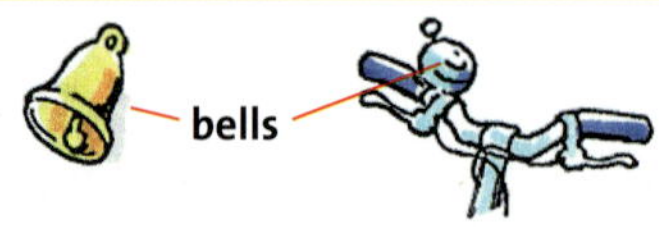
	bell [bel]	Klingel, Glocke	
	front door [ˌfrʌnt 'dɔ:]	Wohnungstür, Haustür	
	inside [ˌɪn'saɪd]	innen (drin), drinnen	Sophie isn't in the garden. She's **inside**. inside ◂▸ outside
	hole [həʊl]	Loch	a **hole** in my shoe 
	fantastic [fæn'tæstɪk]	fantastisch, toll	*French:* fantastique
	so sweet [səʊ]	so süß	
	(to) **be afraid (of)** [ə'freɪd]	Angst haben (vor)	My brother **is afraid of** big dogs. **I'm afraid of** mice.
	(to) **pass** [pɑ:s]	(herüber)reichen, weitergeben	Can you **pass** me the milk, please? You have to **pass** the parcel to the next student.
	(to) **pass round** [ˌpɑ:s 'raʊnd]	herumgeben	Now Sophie **is passing round** the party food.
	no more music	keine Musik mehr	
	no	kein, keine	I can't do my homework now. I've got **no** time.
p. 82	**note** [nəʊt]	Mitteilung, Notiz	Here's a **note** from Jack. Can you read it? I can't.
	(to) **take notes**	sich Notizen machen	
	prize [praɪz]	Preis, Gewinn	There's a **prize** for the best story.
	(to) **be over**	vorbei sein, zu Ende sein	
	What are you talking about?	Wovon redest du?	
	(to) **get** [get] **(-tt-)**	gelangen, (hin)kommen	How can we **get** to Cotham School?
	title ['taɪtl]	Titel, Überschrift	*French:* le titre

Unit 5: School: not just lessons

pp. 84/85	**rehearsal** [rɪ'hɜːsl]	Probe *(am Theater)*	
	(to) **rehearse** [rɪ'hɜːs]	proben *(am Theater)*	
	spring [sprɪŋ]	Frühling	
	autumn ['ɔːtəm]	Herbst	
	winter ['wɪntə]	Winter	
	show [ʃəʊ]	Show, Vorstellung	! **show** = **1.** *(verb)* zeigen; **2.** *(noun)* Show, Vorstellung
	may [meɪ]	dürfen	**May** I come in? (*höflich für:* Can I come in?)
	(to) **bring** [brɪŋ]	(mit-, her)bringen	 ! **Bring** me the newspaper. („herbringen")  Now **take** it to Dad. („hinbringen")
	(to) **use** [juːz]	benutzen, verwenden	May I **use** your phone, please?
	result [rɪ'zʌlt]	Ergebnis, Resultat	*French:* le résultat
	junior ['dʒuːniə]	Junioren-, Jugend-	
	choir ['kwaɪə]	Chor	! Schreibung: choir – Aussprache: ['kwaɪə]
	(to) **paint** [peɪnt]	malen, anmalen	Let's **paint** our faces for the party!
	pirate ['paɪrət]	Pirat, Piratin	! Betonung auf der 1. Silbe: **pirate** ['paɪrət]
	ship [ʃɪp]	Schiff	
	programme ['prəʊgræm]	Programm	! Betonung auf der 1. Silbe: **programme** ['prəʊgræm]
	(to) **practise** ['præktɪs]	üben; trainieren	
p. 86/A 1	**ticket** ['tɪkɪt]	Eintrittskarte	**Tickets** for the party are £2.50.
p. 86/A 2	(we/you/they) **were** [wə, wɜː]	*Vergangenheitsform von „be"*	I was at home last night. Where **were** you?
	Miss White [mɪs]	Frau White *(unverheiratet)*	
	(to) **sound** [saʊnd]	klingen, sich *(gut usw.)* anhören	A party in the park? That **sounds** very nice. ! **sound** = **1.** *(verb)* klingen; **2.** *(noun)* Laut; Klang
p. 87/A 4	**yesterday** ['jestədeɪ, 'jestədi]	gestern	**Yesterday** I was home late.
	terrible ['terəbl]	schrecklich, furchtbar	*French:* terrible
	mistake [mɪ'steɪk]	Fehler	There are three **mistakes** in your essay.
	I can't wait to see ...	ich kann es kaum erwarten, ... zu sehen	The band is great. **I can't wait** to see their next show.
	a minute **ago** [ə'gəʊ]	vor einer Minute	Where's Dan? – He was here **a minute ago**. ! **ago** steht hinter dem Nomen.
	voice [vɔɪs]	Stimme	*French:* la voix
	(to) **realize** ['rɪəlaɪz]	erkennen, merken	
	that [ðət, ðæt]	dass	Then I realized **that** Prunella was a poltergeist.
	part [pɑːt]	Teil	Cornwall is a pretty **part** of England. *Latin:* pars
p. 88/A 7	**king** [kɪŋ]	König	

Classroom English → S. 202 · Arbeitsanweisungen → S. 203 · Orts- und Personennamen → S. 204

p. 88/A 8	**diary** ['daɪəri]	Tagebuch; Terminkalender	
	had [hæd]	*Vergangenheitsform von „have" und von „have got"*	Yesterday I **had** breakfast at 6 o'clock. In 1998 we **had** a dog. Now we've got two cats.
	sang [sæŋ]	*Vergangenheitsform von „sing"*	
	way [weɪ]	Weg	We sang songs all the **way** to school yesterday.
	came [keɪm]	*Vergangenheitsform von „come"*	The teacher **came** into the classroom, and the students were quiet.
	did [dɪd]	*Vergangenheitsform von „do"*	Tell your partner what you **did** last Sunday.

Unregelmäßige Vergangenheitsformen

(to) find	**found** [faʊnd]	finden	(to) say	**said** [sed]	sagen
(to) go	**went** [went]	gehen	(to) see	**saw** [sɔː]	sehen
(to) make	**made** [meɪd]	machen, bauen, bilden	(to) think	**thought** [θɔːt]	glauben, meinen, denken
(to) put	**put** [pʊt]	legen, stellen, *(wohin)* tun			

	tired ['taɪəd]	müde	
	something ['sʌmθɪŋ]	etwas	I'm thirsty. I'd like **something** to drink.
	to [tə, tu]	um zu	Dan and Jo went to the park **to** play football.
	sure [ʃʊə, ʃɔː]	sicher	Ananda's dad is from Uganda? Are you **sure**?
	supermarket ['suːpəmɑːkɪt]	Supermarkt	*French:* le supermarché
	this morning/afternoon/ evening	heute Morgen/Nachmittag/ Abend	I can meet you at two o'clock **this afternoon**.
	(to) **hope** [həʊp]	hoffen	I **hope** you have a happy birthday.
p. 89/A 10	**article** ['ɑːtɪkl]	(Zeitungs-)Artikel	There was an **article** in the school magazine about the Spring Show. ! Betonung auf der 1. Silbe: **article** ['ɑːtɪkl]
	report (on) [rɪ'pɔːt]	Bericht, Reportage (über)	There's a **report on** the Spring Show on TV. *French:* le reportage
	stage [steɪdʒ]	Bühne	The band went on **stage** and started to play.
	(to) **design** [dɪ'zaɪn]	entwickeln, entwerfen	What is your dad's job? – He **designs** cars.
	twin town [ˌtwɪn 'taʊn]	Partnerstadt	
	town [taʊn]	Stadt	
	for example [ˌfər‿ɪg'zɑːmpl]	zum Beispiel	Toby likes ball games – football, **for example**.
	(to) **swap** [swɒp] **(-pp-)**	tauschen, austauschen	Friends sometimes **swap** clothes. We **swapped** information in a partner exercise.
	information (about/on) *(no pl)* [ˌɪnfə'meɪʃn]	Information(en) (über)	! • Hier sind die **Informationen** über die Show. = Here's the **information** about/on the show. *Nie:* ... the information~~s~~ • **eine** interessante Information = **some** interesting information
	Did you do **anything special?** [ˌeniθɪŋ 'speʃl]	Habt ihr irgendetwas Besonderes gemacht?	
	(to) **go on a trip**	einen Ausflug/eine Reise machen	Last summer we **went on a trip** to London.

Tipps zum Wörterlernen → S. 118–119 · Englische Laute → S. 147 · Alphabetische Wörterverzeichnisse → S. 179–191 / S. 192–201

p. 90/P 1	**flow chart** ['fləʊ tʃɑːt]	Flussdiagramm	
p. 90/P 2	**costume** ['kɒstjuːm]	Kostüm, Verkleidung	**!** Betonung auf der 1. Silbe: **costume** ['kɒstjuːm]
p. 91/P 4	your **best** friends [best]	deine besten Freunde/Freundinnen	
p. 92/P 8	**extra** ['ekstrə]	zusätzlich	Oh, here's Sophie. We need an **extra** plate.
	syllable ['sɪləbl]	Silbe	There are two **syllables** in *mistake*: *mis* and *take*.
p. 93/P 10	**elephant** ['elɪfənt]	Elefant	 *French:* l'éléphant *(m)*

A pirate story

Unregelmäßige Vergangenheitsformen

p. 96	(to) get	**got** [gɒt]	gelangen, (hin)kommen	(to) sit	**sat** [sæt]	sitzen; sich setzen
	(to) know	**knew** [njuː]	wissen; kennen	(to) take	**took** [tʊk]	nehmen; (weg-, hin)bringen
	(to) run	**ran** [ræn]	laufen, rennen	(to) tell	**told** [təʊld]	sagen; erzählen

dark [dɑːk]	dunkel	It's very **dark** in here. I can't find my pen.
windy ['wɪndi]	windig	
wind [wɪnd]	Wind	
young [jʌŋ]	jung	young ◂▸ old
many ['meni]	viele	Poor Peter. He hasn't got **many** friends.
how many ...?	wie viele ...?	**How many** kids are in the SHoCK Team? – Five.

„viel", „viele"

viel — **How much** orange juice have we got? – We haven't got **much** orange juice, but we've got **lots of** milk.
Wie viel Orangensaft ...? – ... nicht **viel** Orangensaft, ... **viel** Milch.

viele — **How many** CDs have you got? – I haven't got **many** CDs, but I've got **lots of** computer games.
Wie viele CDs ...? – ... nicht **viele** CDs, ... **viele** Computerspiele.

	(to) **kill** [kɪl]	töten	
	tonight [tə'naɪt]	heute Nacht, heute Abend	**!** heute Morgen = **this morning** heute Nachmittag = **this afternoon** heute Abend = **this evening** heute Nacht = **tonight**
p. 97	for three **days**	drei Tage (lang)	Sophie was in London **for five days** last year.
	at last [ət 'lɑːst]	endlich, schließlich	Jack waited for a long time. **At last** Ananda came.
	soon [suːn]	bald	It's my birthday **soon**. Let's have a party.
	when	als	

when

wann	**When**'s your birthday?	**Wann** hast du Geburtstag?
wenn	We can play cards **when** you come home.	Wir können Karten spielen, **wenn** du nach Hause kommst.
als	Jonah was scared **when** Mr Bonny saw him.	Jonah hatte Angst, **als** Mr Bonny ihn sah.

	beautiful ['bju:tɪfl]	schön	Ann Bonny was a **beautiful** woman.
	clear [klɪə]	klar, deutlich	*French:* clair, e
	sea [si:]	Meer, *(die)* See	
p. 98	(to) **be cold** [kəʊld]	frieren	It was very windy, and I **was cold**. (= Ich fror. / Mir war kalt.)
	I don't think so.	Das finde/glaube ich nicht.	This is a great book. – **I don't think so.** I think it's boring.
	I think so.	Ich glaube (ja).	Is he from Germany? – **I think so**, but I'm not sure.
	line [laɪn]	Zeile	Do you know the second word in **line** 12? *French:* la ligne
	danger ['deɪndʒə]	Gefahr	*French:* le danger

Unit 6: Great places for kids

p. 100	**kid** [kɪd]	Kind, Jugendliche(r)	
	near [nɪə]	in der Nähe von, nahe (bei)	! in der Nähe (von) = **near** (nicht: ~~in the near of~~): Our house is **near** the station.
	a long way (from) [weɪ]	weit entfernt (von)	a long way from ◄► near
	city centre [ˌsɪti 'sentə]	Stadtzentrum, Innenstadt	
	city ['sɪti]	Stadt, Großstadt	
	village ['vɪlɪdʒ]	Dorf	
	church [tʃɜ:tʃ]	Kirche	
	bridge [brɪdʒ]	Brücke	
	(to) **enjoy** [ɪn'dʒɔɪ]	genießen	
	heart [hɑ:t]	Herz	
	tower ['taʊə]	Turm	

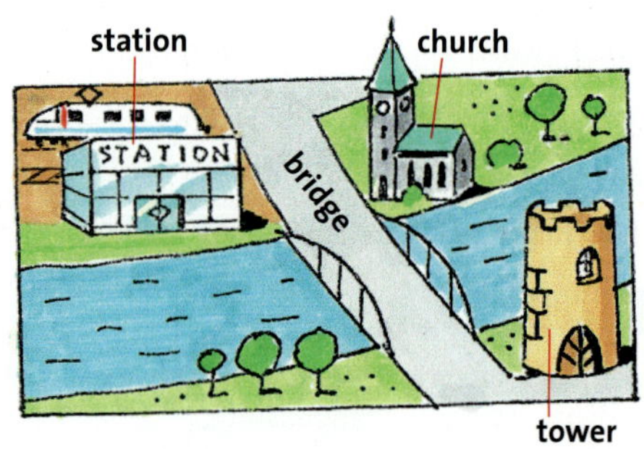

p. 101	(to) **explore** [ɪk'splɔ:]	erkunden, erforschen	It's very interesting to **explore** new places.
	(to) **touch** [tʌtʃ]	berühren, anfassen	Don't **touch** the cooker! It's hot.
	I'd like to go (= I would like to go)	ich würde gern gehen / ich möchte gehen	**I'd like to go** to the park this afternoon. What **would** you **like to do**?
	I wouldn't like to go	ich würde nicht gern gehen / ich möchte nicht gehen	**I wouldn't like to go** to the park. I'd like to watch a film on TV.
	museum [mju'zi:əm]	Museum	*French:* le musée
	fun [fʌn]	Spaß	

fun

Riding **is fun**. (*Nicht:* ... ~~makes fun~~.)	Reiten **macht Spaß**.
Prunella **has fun** with Sophie.	Prunella **hat viel Spaß / amüsiert sich** mit Sophie.
Have fun!	**Viel Spaß!**
Just **for fun**.	Nur **zum Spaß**.

! The play was **fun**. — Das Theaterstück **hat Spaß gemacht**.
The play was **funny**. — Das Theaterstück **war lustig/witzig**.

	price [praɪs]	(Kauf-)Preis	*French:* le prix

p. 102/A 1	(to) **begin** [bɪ'gɪn] **(-nn-),** *simple past:* **began** [bɪ'gæn]	beginnen, anfangen (mit)	(to) start
	each [iːtʃ]	jeder, jede, jedes (einzelne)	There are six guests at the party, so we need six little presents – one for **each** of them.
	must [mʌst]	müssen	❗ **müssen** = **1.** have to; **2.** must (*have to* wird häufiger verwendet als *must*.)
	corner ['kɔːnə]	Ecke	
	(to) **agree (on)** [ə'griː]	sich einigen (auf)	We have to **agree on** a day for our party.
	middle (of) ['mɪdl]	Mitte	
	library ['laɪbrəri]	Bibliothek, Bücherei	
p. 102/A 2	**far** [fɑː]	weit (entfernt)	Is it **far** to the station? – Yes, it's a long way. It's too **far** to walk.
	(to) **be right**	Recht haben	❗ Ananda **hat Recht**. = Ananda **is right**.
	against [ə'genst]	gegen	against ◂▸ for
	free	kostenlos	
	step [step]	Schritt	The first **step** is to choose an interesting place.
p. 103/A 3	(to) **whisper** ['wɪspə]	flüstern	'I think there's a poltergeist in this house!' Jo **whispered**.
	that's why	deshalb, darum	She's a poltergeist. **That's why** you can't see her.
	loud [laʊd]	laut	loud ◂▸ quiet
	towards Mr Green [tə'wɔːdz]	auf Mr Green zu, in Mr Greens Richtung	
	What **are** you **going to** do?	Was wirst du tun? / Was hast du vor zu tun?	What **are** you **going to** do? – **I'm going to** follow Mr Green.
p. 103/A 5	(to) **take photos**	Fotos machen, fotografieren	Learn to **take photos** at the camera club!
	better ['betə]	besser	Your essay is good, but my essay is **better**.
	(to) be/look **the same** [seɪm]	gleich sein/aussehen	All the cars in this museum **look the same**. the same ◂▸ different
	the same ...	der-/die-/dasselbe ...; dieselben	Sophie and her friends are at **the same** school.
	those [ðəʊz]	die (da), jene (dort)	

this, that – these, those

Wenn etwas **näher beim Sprecher** ist, verwendet man eher **this** und **these**.

Wenn etwas **weiter entfernt** ist, verwendet man eher **that** und **those**.

	(to) **finish** ['fɪnɪʃ]	beenden, zu Ende machen; enden	Let's **finish** the exercise and read the text again. Lessons **finish** at 3.30 pm. *Latin:* finire (to) finish ◂▸ (to) start
	(to) **smile** [smaɪl]	lächeln	
p. 104/A 6	(to) **stick on** [ˌstɪk_'ɒn], *simple past:* **stuck on** [stʌk]	aufkleben	First we **stuck** photos **on**. Then we put our poster on the wall.
	at the moment ['məʊmənt]	im Moment, gerade, zurzeit	right now ❗ Betonung auf der 1. Silbe: **moment** ['məʊmənt]

	presentation [ˌpreznˈteɪʃn]	Präsentation, Vorstellung	*French:* la présentation
	(to) **present (to)** [prɪˈzent]	*(jm. etwas)* präsentieren, vorstellen	**Present** your ideas **to** the class. *French:* présenter **!** Aussprache: (to) **present** [prɪˈzent] = präsentieren **the present** [ˈpreznt] = **1.** das Geschenk; **2.** die Gegenwart
	you **should** ... [ʃəd, ʃʊd]	du solltest ... / ihr solltet ...	You **should** ask me first before you go out.
	careful [ˈkeəfl]	vorsichtig	
	glue [gluː]	Klebstoff	
	(to) **suppose** [səˈpəʊz]	annehmen, vermuten	She's the boss, so I **suppose** she's right. *French:* supposer
p. 104/A 7	**nice and cool/clean/...**	schön kühl/sauber/...	Have a glass of lemonade. It's **nice and cool**.
p. 105/A 8	**one more**	noch ein(e), ein(e) weitere(r, s)	We need **two more** photos for the poster.
	to the front [frʌnt]	nach vorn	Go **to the front** and start your presentation.
	for lots of reasons	aus vielen Gründen	I ride my bike **for lots of reasons** – it's quick, it's fun, and it isn't expensive.

The Mr Green mystery

p. 110	**key** [kiː]	Schlüssel	I can't open the door. I can't find my **keys**.
	(to) **be out** [bi_ˈaʊt]	weg sein, nicht da sein	Dan **is out** – can you call back later?
	(to) **knock (on)** [nɒk]	(an)klopfen (an)	He **knocked on** the door and went in.
	(to) **be worried (about)** [ˈwʌrid]	beunruhigt sein, besorgt sein (wegen)	I'**m** very **worried about** the English test tomorrow.
p. 111	**hall** [hɔːl]	Flur, Diele	
	second [ˈsekənd]	Sekunde	60 **seconds** = 1 minute *French:* la seconde
	How do you know ...?	Woher weißt/kennst du ...?	**How do you know** my phone number?
	scared [skeəd]	verängstigt	
	(to) **be scared (of)**	Angst haben (vor)	My little brother is **scared of** poltergeists.
	(to) **turn on** the computer [ˌtɜːn_ˈɒn]	den Computer einschalten	
	(to) **turn off** the computer [ˌtɜːn_ˈɒf]	den Computer ausschalten	(to) turn on ◂▸ (to) turn off
	(to) **hurt** [hɜːt], *simple past:* **hurt**	wehtun; verletzen	Poor Ananda. She **hurt** her leg in a hockey match last week.
	(to) **cry in pain** [kraɪ], [peɪn]	vor Schmerzen schreien	Ananda **cried in pain** when she hurt her leg.
	(to) **lock** [lɒk]	abschließen, zuschließen	Please **lock** the door when you go outside.

Das Dictionary besteht aus zwei alphabetischen Wörterlisten:

Englisch – Deutsch (S. 179–191)
Deutsch – Englisch (S. 192–201).

Das **English – German Dictionary** enthält den gesamten Wortschatz dieses Bandes.
Wenn du wissen möchtest, was ein Wort bedeutet, wie man es ausspricht, wie es genau geschrieben wird oder wo es zum ersten Mal in *English G 21* vorkommt, kannst du hier nachschlagen.

Im **English – German Dictionary** werden folgende **Abkürzungen** und **Symbole** verwendet:

sb. = somebody	jm. = jemandem	pl = plural *(Mehrzahl)*
sth. = something	jn. = jemanden	no pl = no plural

° Mit diesem Kringel sind Wörter markiert, die nicht zum Lernwortschatz gehören.
► Der Pfeil verweist auf Kästchen im Vocabulary (S. 148–178), in denen du weitere Informationen zu diesem Wort findest.

Die **Fundstellenangaben** zeigen, wo ein Wort zum ersten Mal vorkommt.
Die Ziffern in Klammern bezeichnen Seitenzahlen:

Welc (8)	=	'Hello/Bonjour' and 'Welcome', Seite 8
Welc (8/148)	=	'Hello/Bonjour' and 'Welcome', Seite 148 (im Vocabulary, zu Seite 8)
1 (33)	=	Unit 1, Seite 33
1 (18/154)	=	Unit 1, Seite 154 (im Vocabulary, zu Seite 18)
TOP 2 (51)	=	Topic 2, Seite 51
TOP 2 (50/163)	=	Topic 2, Seite 163 (im Vocabulary, zu Seite 50)

Tipps zur Arbeit mit dem English – German Dictionary findest du im Skills File auf Seite 122.

A

a [ə] ein, eine Welc (8/148) • **°a few** ein paar, einige • **a lot** viel TOP 2 (51) **He likes her a lot.** Er mag sie sehr. 1 (33)

about [ə'baʊt] über Welc (8) • **ask about sth.** nach etwas fragen 5 (87) • **This is about Mr Green.** Es geht um Mr Green. 3 (65) • **What about ...?** **1.** Was ist mit ...? / Und ...? Welc (6); **2.** Wie wär's mit ...? TOP 3 (67) • **What are you talking about?** Wovon redest du? 4 (82)

act [ækt] aufführen, spielen 2 (38) **°Act out ...** Spiele/Spielt ... vor.

activity [æk'tɪvəti] Aktivität, Tätigkeit (3)

add (to) [æd] hinzufügen, ergänzen, addieren (zu) 3 (66)

afraid [ə'freɪd]**: be afraid (of)** Angst haben (vor) 4 (81)

after ['ɑːftə] **1.** nach *(zeitlich)* 1 (23) **after that** danach 2 (39) **2.** nachdem TOP 2 (51)

afternoon [,ɑːftə'nuːn] Nachmittag 2 (38) • **in the afternoon** nachmittags, am Nachmittag 2 (38/160) **on Friday afternoon** freitagnachmittags, am Freitagnachmittag 2 (38/160)

again [ə'gen] wieder; noch einmal 2 (48)

against [ə'genst] gegen 6 (102)

ago [ə'gəʊ]**: a minute ago** vor einer Minute 5 (87)

agree [ə'griː]**: agree (on)** sich einigen (auf) 6 (102) • **agree (with sb.)** (jm.) zustimmen 3 (65)

°ahoy [ə'hɔɪ]**: Ship ahoy!** Schiff ahoi!

alarm clock [ə'lɑːm klɒk] Wecker 2 (48)

°algebra ['ældʒɪbrə] Algebra

all [ɔːl] alle; alles 1 (24) • **all day** den ganzen Tag (lang) 2 (39) • **all the time** die ganze Zeit 2 (39) **This is all wrong.** Das ist ganz falsch. 2 (40)

alone [ə'ləʊn] allein 3 (55)

alphabet ['ælfəbet] Alphabet 1 (22)

°alphabetical [,ælfə'betɪkl] alphabetisch

always ['ɔːlweɪz] immer 3 (55)

am [,eɪ_'em]**: 7 am** 7 Uhr morgens/vormittags 4 (81/172)

American football [ə,merɪkən 'fʊtbɔːl] Football 3 (52/164)

an [ən] ein, eine 1 (18/154)

and [ənd, ænd] und Welc (8/148) **nice and cool/clean/...** schön kühl/sauber/... 6 (104)

animal ['ænɪml] Tier 4 (76)

°anonymous [ə'nɒnɪməs] anonym

another [ə'nʌðə] ein(e) andere(r, s); noch ein(e) 4 (71)

answer ['ɑːnsə] **1.** antworten; beantworten 3 (56); **2. answer (to)** Antwort (auf) 3 (56/166)

any ['eni]**: any ...?** (irgend)welche ...? 4 (71) • **not (...) any** kein(e) 4 (71)

anything ['eniθɪŋ]**: Did you do anything special?** Habt ihr irgendetwas Besonderes gemacht? 5 (89)

anyway ['eniweɪ] sowieso 3 (55)

apple ['æpl] Apfel Welc (8/148)

appointment [ə'pɔɪntmənt] Termin, Verabredung 3 (60)

April ['eɪprəl] April TOP 1 (35/158)

are [ɑː] bist; sind; seid Welc (8/148) **The pencils are 35p.** Die Bleistifte kosten 35 Pence. TOP 3 (67/169)

argue ['ɑːgjuː] sich streiten, sich zanken 2 (40)

arm [ɑːm] Arm 4 (74/171)

armchair ['ɑːmtʃeə] Sessel TOP 2 (50)

art [ɑːt] Kunst 1 (23/156)

article ['ɑːtɪkl] (Zeitungs-)Artikel 5 (89)

°as [əz, æz] während

°as many ... as you can [əz, æz] so viele ... wie du kannst

ask [ɑːsk] fragen 3 (55) • **ask about sth.** nach etwas fragen 5 (87) • **ask questions** Fragen stellen 3 (56/166)

°asleep [ə'sliːp]**: be asleep** schlafen

°assembly [ə'sembli] Schulversammlung

assistant [ə'sɪstənt] Verkäufer/in 3 (54)
at [ət, æt]: **at 7 Hamilton Street** in der Hamiltonstraße 7 Welc (12) • **at 8.45** um 8.45 1 (23) • **at home** daheim, zu Hause 2 (36) • **at last** endlich, schließlich 5 (97) • **at least** zumindest, wenigstens 3 (57) • **at night** nachts, in der Nacht 2 (38/160) **at school** in der Schule Welc (12/151) **at that table** an dem Tisch (dort) / an den Tisch (dort) 1 (24/157) • **at the end (of)** am Ende (von) 5 (86) **at the moment** im Moment, gerade, zurzeit 6 (104) • **at the Shaws' house** im Haus der Shaws / bei den Shaws zu Hause 2 (41) • **at the station** am Bahnhof 4 (73/171) **at the top (of)** oben, am oberen Ende, an der Spitze (von) 2 (41) • **at the weekend** am Wochenende 2 (38/160) • **at work** bei der Arbeit / am Arbeitsplatz Welc (16)
°**audience** ['ɔːdɪəns] Zuschauer/innen, Zuhörer/innen, Publikum
August ['ɔːgəst] August TOP 1 (35/158)
aunt [ɑːnt] Tante 2 (41)
autumn ['ɔːtəm] Herbst 5 (84/85/173)
°**avocado** [ˌævə'kɑːdəʊ] Avocado
away [ə'weɪ] weg, fort 3 (65)

B

baby ['beɪbi] Baby Welc (11)
back (to) [bæk] zurück (nach) Welc (16)
bad [bæd] schlecht, schlimm 1 (22)
°**bad luck** Pech
badminton ['bædmɪntən] Badminton, Federball 1 (22)
bag [bæg] Tasche, Beutel, Tüte Welc (12/151)
ball [bɔːl] Ball 1 (22/155)
banana [bə'nɑːnə] Banane Welc (8/148)
band [bænd] Band, (Musik-)Gruppe Welc (9/149)
°**Bang!** [bæŋ] Peng!
bank [bæŋk] Bank, Sparkasse 1 (24)
bank robber ['bæŋk ˌrɒbə] Bankräuber/in 1 (24)
°**barbecue** ['bɑːbɪkjuː] Grillparty
baseball ['beɪsbɔːl] Baseball 3 (52/164)
basket ['bɑːskɪt] Korb 2 (37) • **a basket of apples** ein Korb Äpfel 4 (69/170)
basketball ['bɑːskɪtbɔːl] Basketball 1 (22)

bath [bɑːθ] Badewanne TOP 2 (50)
bathroom ['bɑːθruːm] Badezimmer 2 (36/159)
be [biː] sein 1 (21)
beautiful ['bjuːtɪfl] schön 5 (97)
because [bɪ'kɒz] weil 2 (41)
bed [bed] Bett Welc (16) • **Bed and Breakfast (B&B)** [ˌbed‿ən 'brekfəst] Frühstückspension Welc (16) • **go to bed** ins Bett gehen 2 (38)
bedroom ['bedruːm] Schlafzimmer 2 (36/159)
before [bɪ'fɔː] **1.** vor *(zeitlich)* 1 (20); **2.** bevor TOP 2 (51/164)
began [bɪ'gæn] *Vergangenheitsform von „begin"* 6 (102/177)
begin (-nn-) [bɪ'gɪn] beginnen, anfangen (mit) 6 (102)
behind [bɪ'haɪnd] hinter 4 (69)
bell [bel] Klingel, Glocke 4 (81/172)
°**below** [bɪ'ləʊ] unten
°**bend** [bend] beugen
best [best]: **the best ...** der/die/das beste ...; die besten ... 5 (91)
better ['betə] besser 6 (103)
°**between** [bɪ'twiːn] zwischen
big [bɪg] groß Welc (9/149)
bike [baɪk] Fahrrad 3 (52/164) • **ride a bike** Rad fahren 3 (52/164)
biology [baɪ'ɒlədʒi] Biologie 1 (23/156)
bird [bɜːd] Vogel 2 (37/159)
birthday ['bɜːθdeɪ] Geburtstag TOP 1 (35) • **Happy birthday.** Herzlichen Glückwunsch zum Geburtstag. 4 (77) • **My birthday is in May.** Ich habe im Mai Geburtstag. TOP 1 (35/158) • **My birthday is on 13th June.** Ich habe am 13. Juni Geburtstag. TOP 1 (35/158) • **When's your birthday?** Wann hast du Geburtstag? TOP 1 (35/158)
► S.158 birthdays
biscuit ['bɪskɪt] Keks, Plätzchen 4 (69)
black [blæk] schwarz Welc (13/152)
°**blow sth. up** [ˌbləʊ‿'ʌp] etwas in die Luft sprengen
blue [bluː] blau Welc (13/152)
board [bɔːd] **1.** (Wand-)Tafel 1 (22/155) • **on the board** an der/die Tafel 1 (22/155)
°**2.** Brett
boat [bəʊt] Boot, Schiff Welc (9/149)
body ['bɒdi] Körper 4 (74/171)
book [bʊk] Buch Welc (12)
boot [buːt] Stiefel 3 (54/165)
boring ['bɔːrɪŋ] langweilig 1 (24)
boss [bɒs] Boss, Chef/in 6 (104)
both [bəʊθ] beide 4 (70)
bottle ['bɒtl] Flasche 4 (69) • **a bottle of milk** eine Flasche Milch 4 (69/170)

°**bottom** ['bɒtəm] Grund, Boden
°**at the bottom** unten, am unteren Ende
bowl [bəʊl] Schüssel 2 (39) • **a bowl of cornflakes** eine Schale Cornflakes 4 (69/170)
box [bɒks] Kasten, Kästchen, Kiste 1 (19)
boy [bɔɪ] Junge Welc (9/149)
°**bracket** ['brækɪt] Klammer *(in Texten)*
bread *(no pl)* [bred] Brot 4 (69/169)
break [breɪk] Pause 1 (23)
breakfast ['brekfəst] Frühstück Welc (15) • **have breakfast** frühstücken Welc (15)
°**breeze** [briːz] Brise
bridge [brɪdʒ] Brücke 6 (100)
bring [brɪŋ] (mit-, her)bringen 5 (84/85)
°**brochure** ['brəʊʃə] Broschüre
brother ['brʌðə] Bruder Welc (8/148)
brown [braʊn] braun Welc (13/152)
budgie ['bʌdʒi] Wellensittich 2 (37)
°**build** [bɪld] bauen
bus [bʌs] Bus 2 (38)
busy ['bɪzi] beschäftigt 3 (57)
but [bət, bʌt] aber Welc (10)
°**butter** ['bʌtə] Butter
buy [baɪ] kaufen 3 (54)
by [baɪ] von 2 (48)
Bye. [baɪ] Tschüs! 1 (33)

C

°**cabin** ['kæbɪn] Kajüte, Kabine
°**cabin boy** Schiffsjunge
café ['kæfeɪ] *(kleines)* Restaurant, Imbissstube, Café 4 (77)
cage [keɪdʒ] Käfig 2 (37)
cake [keɪk] Kuchen, Torte 4 (69/169)
calendar ['kælɪndə] Kalender TOP 1 (35)
call [kɔːl] rufen; anrufen; nennen 3 (65)
came [keɪm] *Vergangenheitsform von „come"* 5 (88)
camera ['kæmərə] Kamera, Fotoapparat 5 (84/85)
can [kən, kæn] **1.** können Welc (8/148)
I can't ... [kɑːnt] ich kann nicht ... Welc (8/148) • **Can I help you?** Kann ich Ihnen helfen? / Was kann ich für Sie tun? *(im Geschäft)* 3 (54)
2. dürfen 1 (22/129)
°**captain** ['kæptɪn] Kapitän/in
car [kɑː] Auto 3 (63)
°**caravan** ['kærəvæn] Wohnwagen
card [kɑːd] (Spiel-, Post-)Karte 3 (53)
careful ['keəfl] vorsichtig 6 (104)

°**Caribbean** [ˌkærəˈbiːən]: **in the Caribbean** in der Karibik
carrot [ˈkærət] Möhre, Karotte 2 (39)
cat [kæt] Katze Welc (12/151)
CD [ˌsiːˈdiː] CD 1 (29) • **CD player** CD-Spieler 4 (78)
cent (c) [sent] Cent TOP 3 (67)
centre [ˈsentə] Zentrum, Mitte 6 (100)
°**chain** [tʃeɪn] Kette
chair [tʃeə] Stuhl 1 (18/154)
champion [ˈtʃæmpiən] Meister/in, Champion 6 (106)
°**championship** [ˈtʃæmpiənʃɪp] Meisterschaft
change [tʃeɪndʒ] Wechselgeld TOP 3 (67)
°**chant** [tʃɑːnt] Sprechchor *(z.B. von Fußballfans)*
°**charity** [ˈtʃærəti] Wohltätigkeitsorganisation
°**chart** [tʃɑːt] Schaubild, Diagramm, Tabelle
°**chase** [tʃeɪs] jagen
check [tʃek] (über)prüfen, kontrollieren 1 (31)
checkpoint [ˈtʃekpɔɪnt] Kontrollpunkt *(hier: zur Selbstüberprüfung)* (3)
°**Cheers.** [tʃɪəz] Prost!
cheese [tʃiːz] Käse 4 (69/169)
chicken [ˈtʃɪkɪn] Huhn; (Brat-)Hähnchen 4 (69/169)
child [tʃaɪld], *pl* **children** [ˈtʃɪldrən] Kind 2 (41)
chips *(pl)* [tʃɪps] Pommes frites 4 (69)
chocolate [ˈtʃɒklət] Schokolade 4 (69/169)
choir [ˈkwaɪə] Chor 5 (84/85)
choose [tʃuːz] (sich) aussuchen, (aus)wählen 3 (54)
°**chorus** [ˈkɔːrəs] Refrain
°**Christmas** [ˈkrɪsməs] Weihnachten °**Father Christmas** der Weihnachtsmann • °**Merry Christmas.** Frohe Weihnachten.
church [tʃɜːtʃ] Kirche 6 (100)
°**chutney** [ˈtʃʌtni] Chutney *(Paste aus Früchten und Gewürzen)*
°**circle** [ˈsɜːkl] Kreis
city [ˈsɪti] Stadt, Großstadt 6 (100) **city centre** [ˌsɪti ˈsentə] Stadtzentrum, Innenstadt 6 (100)
°**clap (-pp-)** [klæp]: **Clap your hands.** Klatsch(t) in die Hände.
°**clarinet** [ˌklærəˈnet] Klarinette
class [klɑːs] (Schul-)Klasse 1 (24) **class teacher** Klassenlehrer/in 1 (24)
classmate [ˈklɑːsmeɪt] Klassenkamerad/in, Mitschüler/in 1 (32)
classroom [ˈklɑːsruːm] Klassenzimmer Welc (12/151)
clean [kliːn] **1.** sauber TOP 2 (51); **2.** sauber machen, putzen 2 (38) **I clean my teeth.** Ich putze mir die Zähne. 2 (38)
clear [klɪə] klar, deutlich 5 (97)
clever [ˈklevə] klug, schlau 1 (20)
climb [klaɪm] klettern; hinaufklettern (auf) 1 (22) • **Climb a tree.** Klettere auf einen Baum. 1 (22)
clock [klɒk] (Wand-, Stand-, Turm-) Uhr 3 (66/168)
close [kləʊz] schließen, zumachen Welc (10)
clothes *(pl)* [kləʊðz, kləʊz] Kleidung, Kleidungsstücke 3 (54)
°**cloud** [klaʊd] Wolke
clown [klaʊn] Clown/in 5 (92)
club [klʌb] Klub; Verein 4 (78)
°**cocktail stick** [ˈkɒkteɪl stɪk] Cocktailspieß(chen)
cold [kəʊld] kalt TOP 2 (51) • **be cold** frieren 5 (98)
collect [kəˈlekt] sammeln 3 (53)
colour [ˈkʌlə] Farbe Welc (8/148) **What colour is ...?** Welche Farbe hat ...? Welc (13)
°**combination** [ˌkɒmbɪˈneɪʃn] Kombination, Verbindung
come [kʌm] kommen 1 (20) • **come home** nach Hause kommen 2 (36/159) • **come in** hereinkommen 1 (32)
comfortable [ˈkʌmftəbl] bequem TOP 2 (51)
comic [ˈkɒmɪk] Comic-Heft 1 (18)
°**compare** [kəmˈpeə] vergleichen
°**complete** [kəmˈpliːt] vervollständigen, ergänzen
computer [kəmˈpjuːtə] Computer 1 (22/155)
°**consonant sound** [ˈkɒnsənənt saʊnd] konsonantischer Laut
°**context** [ˈkɒntekst]: **from the context** aus dem Zusammenhang, aus dem Kontext
cooker [ˈkʊkə] Herd TOP 2 (50)
cool [kuːl] **1.** kühl 6 (104); **2.** cool 4 (82)
°**copy** [ˈkɒpi] **1.** kopieren, übertragen, abschreiben; **2.** Kopie
corner [ˈkɔːnə] Ecke 6 (102)
cornflakes [ˈkɔːnfleɪks] Cornflakes 2 (42)
°**correct** [kəˈrekt] **1.** korrigieren, verbessern; **2.** korrekt, richtig
costume [ˈkɒstjuːm] Kostüm, Verkleidung 5 (90)
country [ˈkʌntri] Land 2 (48)
course: of course [əv ˈkɔːs] natürlich, selbstverständlich 2 (40)
cousin [ˈkʌzn] Cousin, Cousine 2 (41)
cover [ˈkʌvə] (CD-)Hülle 5 (89)
°**Crash.** [kræʃ] Krach!
crisps *(pl)* [krɪsps] Kartoffelchips 4 (69)
°**cross** [krɒs] Kreuz
°**crow** [krəʊ] Krähe
cry [kraɪ] schreien 6 (111) • **cry in pain** vor Schmerzen schreien 6 (111)
°**cucumber** [ˈkjuːkʌmbə] (Salat-)Gurke
cupboard [ˈkʌbəd] Schrank TOP 2 (50)
°**cut (-tt-)** [kʌt] schneiden

D

dad [dæd] Papa, Vati; Vater Welc (8/148)
dance [dɑːns] **1.** tanzen 3 (53/165); **2.** Tanz 5 (84/85) • **dancing** Tanzen 3 (52/164) • **dancing lessons** Tanzstunden, Tanzunterricht 3 (53)
danger [ˈdeɪndʒə] Gefahr 5 (98)
dark [dɑːk] dunkel 5 (96)
date [deɪt] Datum TOP 1 (35)
daughter [ˈdɔːtə] Tochter 2 (41)
day [deɪ] Tag Welc (12) • **one day** eines Tages 5 (90) • **days of the week** Wochentage Welc (14/152)
dead [ded] tot 2 (41)
dear [dɪə] **1.** Schatz, Liebling 4 (72); **2. Dear Jay ...** Lieber Jay, ... 3 (56)
December [dɪˈsembə] Dezember TOP 1 (35/158)
°**deck** [dek] Deck
design [dɪˈzaɪn] entwickeln, entwerfen 5 (89)
desk [desk] Schreibtisch 2 (36)
detective [dɪˈtektɪv] Detektiv/in 3 (65)
°**dialogue** [ˈdaɪəlɒg] Dialog
diary [ˈdaɪəri] Tagebuch; Terminkalender 5 (88)
dictionary [ˈdɪkʃənri] Wörterbuch, *(alphabetisches)* Wörterverzeichnis (3)
did [dɪd] *Vergangenheitsform von „do"* 5 (88) • **Did you go?** Bist du gegangen? / Gingst du? 5 (89) **we didn't go** [ˈdɪdnt] wir sind nicht gegangen / wir gingen nicht 5 (89)
different (from) [ˈdɪfrənt] verschieden, unterschiedlich; anders (als) 1 (25)
difficult [ˈdɪfɪkəlt] schwierig, schwer 2 (38/160)
dining room [ˈdaɪnɪŋ ruːm] Esszimmer TOP 2 (50)

dinner ['dɪnə] Abendessen, Abendbrot 3 (57) • **have dinner** Abendbrot essen 3 (57/167)
disco ['dɪskəʊ] Disko 4 (70)
dishes *(pl)* ['dɪʃɪz] Geschirr TOP 2 (51) **do the dishes** das Geschirr abwaschen TOP 2 (51)
dishwasher ['dɪʃwɒʃə] Geschirrspülmaschine TOP 2 (50)
divorced [dɪ'vɔːst] geschieden 2 (41)
do [duː] tun, machen 1 (22) • **Do what I do.** Tue, was ich tue. 1 (22) **Do you like ...?** Magst du ...? 1 (18/154) • **do sport** Sport treiben 3 (52/164) • **do the dishes** das Geschirr abwaschen TOP 2 (51)
doctor ['dɒktə] Arzt/Ärztin, Doktor 2 (45)
dog [dɒg] Hund Welc (12/151)
don't [dəʊnt]**: Don't listen to Dan.** Hör/Hört nicht auf Dan. 1 (20) • **I don't like ...** Ich mag ... nicht. / Ich mag kein(e) ... Welc (8/148)
door [dɔː] Tür 3 (65)
doorbell ['dɔːbel] Türklingel 4 (81)
°**doorstopper** ['dɔːstɒpə] Türstopper; *hier:* mehrschichtiges Sandwich
dossier ['dɒsieɪ] Mappe, Dossier *(des Sprachenportfolios)* (3)
double ['dʌbl] zweimal, doppelt, Doppel- Welc (15)
down [daʊn] hinunter, herunter, nach unten 3 (65)
downstairs [ˌdaʊn'steəz] unten; nach unten TOP 2 (50)
drama ['drɑːmə] Schauspiel, darstellende Kunst 1 (23/154)
°**draw** [drɔː] zeichnen
dream [driːm] Traum TOP 2 (51) **dream house** Traumhaus TOP 2 (51)
dress [dres] Kleid 3 (54/165)
°**dress rehearsal** ['dres rɪˌhɜːsl] Generalprobe, Kostümprobe
dressed [drest]**: get dressed** sich anziehen 2 (39)
drink [drɪŋk] **1.** trinken 2 (39); **2.** Getränk 4 (69)
drop (-pp-) [drɒp] **1.** fallen lassen Welc (10); **2.** fallen 6 (111)
°**drum** [drʌm] Trommel
DVD [ˌdiː viː' diː] DVD 4 (71)

E

each [iːtʃ] jeder, jede, jedes (einzelne) 6 (102)
ear [ɪə] Ohr 4 (74/171)
early ['ɜːli] früh 2 (40)
earring ['ɪərɪŋ] Ohrring 4 (71)
easy ['iːzi] leicht, einfach 2 (38)
eat [iːt] essen 1 (18/154)
e-friend ['iːfrend] Brieffreund/in *(im Internet)* 5 (89)
°**e.g.** [ˌiː'dʒiː] z.B. (zum Beispiel)
egg [eg] Ei 4 (77)
elephant ['elɪfənt] Elefant 5 (93)
e-mail ['iːmeɪl] E-Mail 2 (42)
empty ['empti] leer Welc (10)
end [end] Ende 1 (32) • **at the end (of)** am Ende (von) 5 (86)
English ['ɪŋglɪʃ] Englisch; englisch Welc (8/148)
enjoy [ɪn'dʒɔɪ] genießen 6 (100)
enough [ɪ'nʌf] genug 1 (22)
essay (about, on) ['eseɪ] Aufsatz (über) 2 (38)
euro (€) ['jʊərəʊ] Euro TOP 3 (67)
evening ['iːvnɪŋ] Abend 2 (38/160) **in the evening** abends, am Abend 2 (38/160) • **on Friday evening** freitagabends, am Freitagabend 2 (38/160)
°**ever so small** ['evə] unheimlich klein
every ['evri] jeder, jede, jedes 2 (38)
everything ['evriθɪŋ] alles 1 (32)
everywhere ['evriweə] überall 2 (39)
example [ɪg'zɑːmpl] Beispiel 5 (89) **for example** zum Beispiel 5 (89)
Excuse me, ... [ɪk'skjuːz miː] Entschuldigung, ... / Entschuldigen Sie, ... Welc (16)
► S.153 „Entschuldigung"
exercise ['eksəsaɪz] Übung, Aufgabe Welc (12/152) • **exercise book** ['eksəsaɪz bʊk] Schulheft, Übungsheft Welc (12)
expensive [ɪk'spensɪv] teuer 4 (71)
explore [ɪk'splɔː] erkunden, erforschen 6 (101)
°**explosive** [ɪk'spləʊsɪv] Sprengstoff
extra ['ekstrə] zusätzlich 5 (92)
eye [aɪ] Auge 4 (74/171)

F

face [feɪs] Gesicht 1 (22/155)
°**fair** [feə] Jahrmarkt
family ['fæməli] Familie Welc (12/151) **family tree** (Familien-)Stammbaum 2 (41)
°**fancy-dress party** [ˌfænsi'dres] Kostümfest
fantastic [fæn'tæstɪk] fantastisch, toll 4 (81)
far [fɑː] weit (entfernt) 6 (102) °**so far** bis jetzt, bis hierher
father ['fɑːðə] Vater Welc (12/151) °**Father Christmas** der Weihnachtsmann
favourite ['feɪvərɪt] Lieblings- Welc (8/148) • **my favourite colour** meine Lieblingsfarbe Welc (8/148)
February ['februəri] Februar TOP 1 (35/158)
feed [fiːd] füttern 2 (39)
feet [fiːt] *Plural von „foot"* 4 (74/171)
felt tip ['felt tɪp] Filzstift Welc (12/151)
°**few** [fjuː]**: a few** ein paar, einige
file [faɪl]**: grammar file** *Grammatik-anhang* (3/126) • **skills file** *Anhang mit Lern- und Arbeitstechniken* (3/118)
°**fill in** [ˌfɪl‿'ɪn] einsetzen
film [fɪlm] Film 2 (48) • **film star** Filmstar 2 (48)
find [faɪnd] finden Welc (10) • **find out (about)** herausfinden (über) 3 (65)
finger ['fɪŋgə] Finger 4 (74/171)
finish ['fɪnɪʃ] beenden, zu Ende machen; enden 6 (103)
first [fɜːst] **1.** erste(r, s) Welc (14) **the first day** der erste Tag Welc (14) **be first** der/die Erste sein 6 (105) **2.** zuerst, als Erstes 1 (20)
fish, *pl* **fish** [fɪʃ] Fisch 2 (37/159)
fit (-tt-) [fɪt] passen 2 (48)
flat [flæt] Wohnung Welc (14)
floor [flɔː] Fußboden TOP 2 (51)
flow chart ['fləʊ tʃɑːt] Flussdiagramm 5 (90)
follow ['fɒləʊ] folgen; verfolgen 4 (71)
food [fuːd] **1.** Essen; Lebensmittel 1 (24); **2.** Futter 2 (39)
foot [fʊt], *pl* **feet** [fiːt] Fuß 4 (74/171)
football ['fʊtbɔːl] Fußball Welc (9/149) • **football boots** Fußballschuhe, -stiefel 3 (54/165)
for [fə, fɔː] **1.** für Welc (12) • **for breakfast/lunch/dinner** zum Frühstück/Mittagessen/Abendbrot 4 (69) • **for example** zum Beispiel 5 (89) • **for lots of reasons** aus vielen Gründen 6 (105) • **for three days** drei Tage (lang) 5 (97) • **just for fun** nur zum Spaß 6 (101/176) **What's for homework?** Was haben wir als Hausaufgabe auf? 1 (28/157) °**2.** denn
form [fɔːm] **1.** (Schul-)Klasse 1 (22) **form teacher** Klassenlehrer/in 1 (22) °**2.** Form
found [faʊnd] *Vergangenheitsform von „find"* 5 (88/174)
free [friː] **1.** frei 3 (52) • **free time** Freizeit, freie Zeit 3 (52) **2.** kostenlos 6 (102)
French [frentʃ] Französisch 1 (23/156)

Friday ['fraɪdeɪ, 'fraɪdi] Freitag Welc (14/152)
fridge [frɪdʒ] Kühlschrank TOP 2 (50)
friend [frend] Freund/in Welc (12/151)
from [frəm, frɒm] **1.** aus Welc (8/148); **2.** von 2 (46) • **I'm from ...** Ich komme/bin aus ... Welc (8/148) **Where are you from?** Wo kommst du her? Welc (8/148)
front [frʌnt]: **in front of** vor *(räumlich)* 4 (69) • **to the front** nach vorn 6 (105) • **front door** [ˌfrʌnt 'dɔː] Wohnungstür, Haustür 4 (81)
fruit [fruːt] Obst, Früchte; Frucht 4 (69) • **fruit salad** Obstsalat 4 (69)
full [fʊl] voll Welc (10)
fun [fʌn] Spaß 6 (101) • **have fun** Spaß haben, sich amüsieren 6 (101/176) • **Have fun!** Viel Spaß! 6 (101/176) • **just for fun** nur zum Spaß 6 (101/176) • **Riding is fun.** Reiten macht Spaß. 6 (101/176)
► S.174 fun
funny ['fʌni] witzig, komisch 4 (71)

G

°**galleon** ['gæliən] Galeone
game [geɪm] Spiel (3)
garden ['gɑːdn] Garten 2 (36)
geography [dʒi'ɒgrəfi] Geografie, Erdkunde 1 (23/156)
German ['dʒɜːmən] Deutsch; deutsch; Deutsche(r) 1 (23/156)
Germany ['dʒɜːməni] Deutschland Welc (17)
get (-tt-) [get] **1.** gelangen, (hin-) kommen 4 (82) • **get home** nach Hause kommen 6 (106) **2. get dressed** sich anziehen 2 (39) **3. get off (the train/bus)** (aus dem Zug/Bus) aussteigen 4 (73) • **get on (the train/bus)** (in den Zug/ Bus) einsteigen 4 (73/171) **4. get ready (for)** sich fertig machen (für), sich vorbereiten (auf) 4 (72) • **get things ready** Dinge fertig machen, vorbereiten 2 (48) **5. get up** aufstehen 2 (38)
getting by in English [ˌgetɪŋ 'baɪ] *etwa:* auf Englisch zurechtkommen (3)
°**ghost train** ['gəʊst treɪn] Geisterbahn
girl [gɜːl] Mädchen Welc (9/149)
give [gɪv] geben 2 (39) • **give sth. back** etwas zurückgeben 5 (93)
glass [glɑːs] Glas 4 (69) • **a glass of water** ein Glas Wasser 4 (69/170)
glasses *(pl)* ['glɑːsɪz] (eine) Brille 2 (48/163)
°**glorious** ['glɔːriəs] herrlich; ruhmreich
glue [gluː] Klebstoff 6 (104) • **glue stick** ['gluː stɪk] Klebestift Welc (12/151)
go (to) [gəʊ] gehen (zu, nach) Welc (14) • **What are you going to do?** Was wirst du tun? / Was hast du vor zu tun? 6 (103) • **go home** nach Hause gehen 2 (36/159) • **go on** weitermachen 1 (33) • **Go on.** Mach weiter. / Erzähl weiter. 1 (33) **go on a trip** einen Ausflug/eine Reise machen 5 (89) • **go out** weg-, raus-, ausgehen 4 (79) • **go riding** reiten gehen 3 (53) • **go shopping** einkaufen gehen 3 (57) **go swimming** schwimmen gehen 3 (52/164) • **go to bed** ins Bett gehen 2 (38) • **Let's go.** Auf geht's! *(wörtlich:* Lass uns gehen.) Welc (12) • °**go with** passen zu
°**gold** [gəʊld] Gold
good [gʊd] gut Welc (14/152) **Good afternoon.** Guten Tag. *(nachmittags)* 3 (54) • **Good luck (with ...)!** Viel Glück (bei/mit ...)! Welc (16) • **Good morning.** Guten Morgen. Welc (14/152)
Goodbye. [ˌgʊd'baɪ] Auf Wiedersehen. Welc (14/152) • **say goodbye** sich verabschieden Welc (17)
got [gɒt]: **I've got ...** Ich habe ... Welc (8/148) • **I haven't got a chair.** Ich habe keinen Stuhl. 1 (24)
got [gɒt] *Vergangenheitsform von „get"* 5 (96/175)
grammar ['græmə] Grammatik (3) **grammar file** *Grammatikanhang* (3/126)
grandchild ['græntʃaɪld], *pl* **grandchildren** ['-tʃɪldrən] Enkel/in 2 (41)
grandfather ['grænfɑːðə] Großvater 2 (41/161)
grandma ['grænmɑː] Oma 2 (41)
grandmother ['grænmʌðə] Großmutter 2 (41/161)
grandpa ['grænpɑː] Opa 2 (41)
grandparents ['grænpeərənts] Großeltern 2 (41)
°**grass** [grɑːs] Gras
great [greɪt] großartig, toll Welc (9)
green [griːn] grün Welc (13/152)
°**ground** [graʊnd] (Erd-)Boden, Erde
group [gruːp] Gruppe 3 (66)
°**guess** [ges] raten, erraten
guest [gest] Gast 2 (47)
guinea pig ['gɪni pɪg] Meerschweinchen 2 (37/159)
guitar [gɪ'tɑː] Gitarre 3 (53) • **play the guitar** Gitarre spielen 3 (53/165)

H

had [hæd] *Vergangenheitsform von „have" und von „have got"* 5 (88)
hair *(no pl)* [heə] Haar, Haare 4 (74/171)
half [hɑːf]: **half past 11** halb zwölf (11.30 / 23.30) Welc (17/153)
°**halfway** ['hɑːfweɪ] halb, auf halbem Weg
hall [hɔːl] **1.** Flur, Diele 6 (111); °**2.** Halle, Saal
°**ham** [hæm] Schinken
hamburger ['hæmbɜːgə] Hamburger 2 (45)
hamster ['hæmstə] Hamster 2 (37/159)
hand [hænd] Hand 2 (38)
happen (to) ['hæpən] geschehen, passieren (mit) TOP 2 (50)
happy ['hæpi] glücklich, froh Welc (9/149) • **Happy birthday.** Herzlichen Glückwunsch zum Geburtstag. 4 (77)
°**harbour** ['hɑːbə] Hafen
hat [hæt] Hut 3 (54/165)
hate [heɪt] hassen, gar nicht mögen 1 (24)
have [hæv]: **have a shower** (sich) duschen 2 (48) • **have breakfast** frühstücken Welc (15) • **have dinner** Abendbrot essen 3 (57/167) **have ... for breakfast** ... zum Frühstück essen/trinken 4 (69) **have fun** Spaß haben, sich amüsieren 6 (101/176) • **Have fun!** Viel Spaß! 6 (101/176) • **have to do** tun müssen 3 (57)
have got: I've got ... [aɪv 'gɒt] Ich habe ... Welc (8/148) • **I haven't got a chair.** ['hævnt gɒt] Ich habe keinen Stuhl. 1 (24)
°**hay** [heɪ] Heu
he [hiː] er Welc (8)
head [hed] Kopf 3 (55)
hear [hɪə] hören 2 (48)
heart [hɑːt] Herz 6 (100)
Hello. [hə'ləʊ] Hallo. / Guten Tag. Welc (8/148)
help [help] **1.** helfen Welc (11) • **Can I help you?** Kann ich Ihnen helfen? / Was kann ich für Sie tun? *(im Geschäft)* 3 (54) **2.** Hilfe 2 (40)
her [hə, hɜː] **1.** ihr, ihre 1 (21); **2.** sie; ihr 1 (33)
here [hɪə] **1.** hier Welc (11); **2.** hierher 2 (39/161) • **Here you are.** Bitte sehr. / Hier bitte. 2 (40)
► S.161 „bitte"
Hi! [haɪ] Hallo! Welc (8/148) • **Say hi to Dilip for me.** Grüß Dilip von mir. 3 (56)

hide [haɪd] sich verstecken; *(etwas)* verstecken 4 (73)
°**highlight** ['haɪlaɪt] Höhepunkt
him [hɪm] ihn; ihm 1 (24)
his [hɪz] sein, seine Welc (8)
history ['hɪstri] Geschichte 1 (23/156)
hobby ['hɒbi] Hobby 3 (52/164)
hockey ['hɒki] Hockey 1 (22)
hockey shoes Hockeyschuhe 3 (54/165)
°**hold** [həʊld]: **hold hands** sich an den Händen halten • **hold up** hochhalten
hole [həʊl] Loch 4 (81)
holidays ['hɒlədeɪz] Ferien Welc (12)
home [həʊm] Heim, Zuhause 2 (36)
at home daheim, zu Hause 2 (36)
come home nach Hause kommen 2 (36/159) • **get home** nach Hause kommen 6 (106) • **go home** nach Hause gehen 2 (36/159)
homework *(no pl)* ['həʊmwɜːk] Hausaufgabe(n) 1 (28/157) • **do homework** die Hausaufgabe(n) machen 2 (48) • **What's for homework?** Was haben wir als Hausaufgabe auf? 1 (28/157)
°**Hooray!** [hu'reɪ] Hurra!
hope [həʊp] hoffen 5 (88)
horse [hɔːs] Pferd 2 (37/159)
°**hospital** ['hɒspɪtl] Krankenhaus
hot [hɒt] heiß TOP 2 (51) • **hot chocolate** heiße Schokolade 4 (69/169)
hour ['aʊə] Stunde TOP 2 (51)
house [haʊs] Haus Welc (9/149)
at the Shaws' house im Haus der Shaws / bei den Shaws zu Hause 2 (41)
how [haʊ] wie Welc (8/148) • **How do you know ...?** Woher weißt/kennst du ...? 6 (111) • **how many?** wie viele? 5 (96/175) • **how much?** wie viel? 5 (96/175) • **How much is/are ...?** Was kostet/kosten ...? / Wie viel kostet/kosten ...? TOP 3 (67)
How old are you? Wie alt bist du? Welc (8/148) • **How was ...?** Wie war ...? 1 (33)
hundred ['hʌndrəd] hundert Welc (15)
hungry ['hʌŋgri] hungrig 4 (69)
be hungry Hunger haben, hungrig sein 4 (69)
°**hurrah** [hə'rɑː] hurra
hurry ['hʌri]: **1. hurry up** sich beeilen 1 (32); **2. be in a hurry** in Eile sein, es eilig haben 4 (71)
hurt [hɜːt] **1.** wehtun; verletzen 6 (111); **2.** *Vergangenheitsform von „hurt"* 6 (111)
hutch [hʌtʃ] (Kaninchen-)Stall 2 (37)

I

I [aɪ] ich Welc (8/148) • **I'm** [aɪm] ich bin Welc (8/148) • **I'm from ...** Ich komme aus ... / Ich bin aus ... Welc (8/148) • **I'm ... years old.** Ich bin ... Jahre alt. Welc (8/148) • **I'm sorry.** Entschuldigung. / Tut mir leid. 1 (21)
ice: ice cream [ˌaɪs 'kriːm] (Speise-) Eis 4 (69/169) • °**ice rink** ['aɪs rɪŋk] Schlittschuhbahn
idea [aɪ'dɪə] Idee, Einfall 1 (24)
°**if** [ɪf] falls, wenn • °**if you're happy** wenn du glücklich bist
°**imagine sth.** [ɪ'mædʒɪn] sich etwas vorstellen
°**important** [ɪm'pɔːtnt] wichtig
in [ɪn] in Welc (8/148) • **in ... Street** in der ...straße Welc (8/148) • **in English** auf Englisch Welc (8/148)
in front of vor *(räumlich)* 4 (69)
in here hier drinnen Welc (11) • **in the afternoon** nachmittags, am Nachmittag 2 (38/160) • **in the evening** abends, am Abend 2 (38/160) • **in the morning** am Morgen, morgens 1 (19) • **in the photo** auf dem Foto Welc (9/150)
in the picture auf dem Bild Welc (11/151) • **in there** dort drinnen 5 (87)
°**Indian** ['ɪndiən] indisch
°**industrial museum** [ɪnˌdʌstriəl mju'ziːəm] Industriemuseum
infinitive [ɪn'fɪnətɪv] Infinitiv *(Grundform des Verbs)* 5 (88)
information (about/on) *(no pl)* [ˌɪnfə'meɪʃn] Information(en) (über) 5 (89)
°**ingredient** [ɪn'griːdiənt] Zutat *(beim Kochen)*
inside [ˌɪn'saɪd] innen (drin), drinnen 4 (81)
interesting ['ɪntrəstɪŋ] interessant 2 (48)
internet ['ɪntənet] Internet 5 (89)
into ['ɪntə, 'ɪntʊ] in ... (hinein) 3 (65)
°**invent** [ɪn'vent] erfinden
invitation (to) [ˌɪnvɪ'teɪʃn] Einladung (zu) 4 (70)
invite (to) [ɪn'vaɪt] einladen (zu) 4 (70/170)
is [ɪz] ist Welc (8/148)
it [ɪt] er/sie/es Welc (9) • **It's £1.** Er/Sie/Es kostet 1 Pfund. TOP 3 (67)
its [ɪts] sein/seine; ihr/ihre 2 (41/134)

J

January ['dʒænjuəri] Januar TOP 1 (35/158)
jeans *(pl)* [dʒiːnz] Jeans 3 (54/165)
°**jingle** ['dʒɪŋgl] klingeln, bimmeln
job [dʒɒb] Aufgabe, Job 3 (63)
joke [dʒəʊk] Witz 1 (22)
judo ['dʒuːdəʊ] Judo 2 (40) • **do judo** Judo machen 2 (40)
jug [dʒʌg] Krug 4 (69) • **a jug of orange juice** ein Krug Orangensaft 4 (69/170)
juice [dʒuːs] Saft 4 (69/169)
July [dʒu'laɪ] Juli TOP 1 (35/158)
°**jumble** ['dʒʌmbl] gebrauchte Sachen, Trödel
jumble sale ['dʒʌmbl seɪl] Wohltätigkeitsbasar TOP 3 (67)
°**jump** [dʒʌmp] springen
June [dʒuːn] Juni TOP 1 (35/158)
junior ['dʒuːniə] Junioren-, Jugend- 5 (84/85)
just [dʒʌst] (einfach) nur, bloß 2 (41)

K

key [kiː] Schlüssel 6 (110) • **key word** Stichwort, Schlüsselwort 4 (71)
kid [kɪd] Kind, Jugendliche(r) 6 (100)
kill [kɪl] töten 5 (96)
king [kɪŋ] König 5 (88)
kitchen ['kɪtʃɪn] Küche 2 (36/159)
kite [kaɪt] Drachen Welc (9)
knee [niː] Knie 4 (74/171)
knew [njuː] *Vergangenheitsform von „know"* 5 (96/175)
°**knife** [naɪf], *pl* **knives** [naɪvz] Messer
knock (on) [nɒk] (an)klopfen (an) 6 (110)
know [nəʊ] **1.** wissen 3 (54/165); **2.** kennen 3 (60) • **How do you know ...?** Woher weißt du ...? / Woher kennst du ...? 6 (111)
..., you know. ..., wissen Sie. / ..., weißt du. 3 (54) • **You know what, Sophie?** Weißt du was, Sophie? 6 (104)

L

°**label** ['leɪbl] beschriften, etikettieren
°**ladder** ['lædə] *(die)* Leiter
lamp [læmp] Lampe 2 (36/159)
language ['læŋgwɪdʒ] Sprache (3)
lasagne [lə'zænjə] Lasagne 1 (24)

last [lɑːst] letzte(r, s) Welc (12)
the last day der letzte Tag Welc (12)
at last endlich, schließlich 5 (97)
late [leɪt] spät; zu spät Welc (12)
be late zu spät sein/kommen Welc (12) • **Sorry, I'm late.** Entschuldigung, dass ich zu spät bin/komme. Welc (12)
later ['leɪtə] später 4 (72)
laugh [lɑːf] lachen Welc (10)
lay the table [leɪ] den Tisch decken 3 (57)
°**lazy** ['leɪzi] faul
learn [lɜːn] lernen 3 (57)
least: at least [ət 'liːst] zumindest, wenigstens 3 (57)
°**leave** [liːv] verlassen
left [left] linke(r, s) 3 (65/168) • **look left** nach links schauen 3 (65)
on the left links, auf der linken Seite 3 (65/168)
► S.168 left – right
leg [leg] Bein 4 (74/171)
lemonade [ˌlemə'neɪd] Limonade 4 (69/169)
lesson ['lesn] (Unterrichts-)Stunde 1 (20) • **lessons** *(pl)* Unterricht 1 (20)
Let's ... [lets] Lass uns ... / Lasst uns ... Welc (12) • **Let's go.** Auf geht's! (*wörtlich:* Lass uns gehen.) Welc (12)
Let's look at the list. Sehen wir uns die Liste an. / Lasst uns die Liste ansehen. Welc (12)
letter ['letə] **1.** Buchstabe 2 (40); °**2. letter (to)** Brief (an)
°**lettuce** ['letɪs] (grüner) Salat
library ['laɪbrəri] Bibliothek, Bücherei 6 (102)
life [laɪf], *pl* **lives** [laɪvz] Leben 2 (38)
like [laɪk] wie 1 (24) • °**like this** so
like [laɪk] mögen, gernhaben Welc (8/148) • **I like ...** Ich mag ... Welc (8/148) • **I don't like ...** Ich mag ... nicht. / Ich mag kein(e) ... Welc (8/148) • **Do you like ...?** Magst du ...? 1 (18/154) • **Dilip likes ...** Dilip mag ... 1 (33) • **I like swimming/dancing/...** Ich schwimme/tanze/... gern. 3 (53) • **I'd like ... (= I would like ...)** Ich hätte gern ... / Ich möchte gern ... 4 (69) • **I'd like to go (= I would like to go)** Ich würde gern gehen / Ich möchte gehen 6 (101)
I wouldn't like to go Ich würde nicht gern gehen / Ich möchte nicht gehen 6 (101) • **Would you like ...?** Möchtest du ...? / Möchten Sie ...? 4 (69)
line [laɪn] Zeile 5 (98)
link [lɪŋk] verbinden, verknüpfen 3 (63) • °**link up (with)** sich *(über das Internet)* in Verbindung setzen (mit)
list [lɪst] Liste Welc (12)
listen (to) ['lɪsn] zuhören; sich *etwas* anhören Welc (9/149)
little ['lɪtl] klein 1 (33)
live [lɪv] leben, wohnen Welc (8/148)
lives [laɪvz] *Plural von „life"* 2 (38)
living room ['lɪvɪŋ ruːm] Wohnzimmer 2 (36/159)
°**local** ['ləʊkl] lokal, örtlich, Lokal-
°**locked** [lɒkt] abgeschlossen, verschlossen
long [lɒŋ] lang 4 (70) • **a long way (from)** weit entfernt (von) 6 (100)
look [lʊk] schauen, gucken Welc (10) • **look at** ansehen, anschauen Welc (12/151) • **Look at the board.** Sieh/Seht an die Tafel. 1 (24/157) • **look different/great/old** anders/toll/alt aussehen TOP 2 (50)
look left and right nach links und rechts schauen 3 (65) • **look round** sich umsehen 4 (73) • °**look for** suchen
► S.161 (to) look – (to) see – (to) watch
°**look-out** ['lʊkaʊt] Ausguck
lot: a lot [ə 'lɒt] viel TOP 2 (50)
Thanks a lot! Vielen Dank! 3 (56)
He likes her a lot. Er mag sie sehr. 1 (33) • **lots more** [lɒts] viel mehr 6 (101) • **lots of ...** eine Menge ..., viele ..., viel ... 1 (18)
loud [laʊd] laut 6 (103)
love [lʌv] lieben, sehr mögen 3 (56/166)
Love ... [lʌv] Liebe Grüße, ... *(Briefschluss)* 3 (56)
luck [lʌk]: **Good luck (with ...)!** Viel Glück (bei/mit ...)! Welc (16) • °**bad luck** Pech
lunch [lʌntʃ] Mittagessen 1 (23)
lunch break Mittagspause 1 (23)

M

mad [mæd] verrückt 1 (20)
made [meɪd] *Vergangenheitsform von „make"* 5 (88/174)
magazine [ˌmægə'ziːn] Zeitschrift, Magazin 4 (79)
make [meɪk] machen; bauen TOP 1 (35) • **make a mess** alles durcheinanderbringen, alles in Unordnung bringen 4 (72)
man [mæn], *pl* **men** [men] Mann 2 (41)
many ['meni] viele 5 (96) • **how many?** wie viele? 5 (96/175)
► S.175 „viel", „viele"
March [mɑːtʃ] März TOP 1 (35/158)
°**mark** [mɑːk] markieren, kennzeichnen
marmalade ['mɑːməleɪd] Orangenmarmelade 1 (18)
married (to) ['mærɪd] verheiratet (mit) 2 (41)
match [mætʃ] Spiel, Wettkampf 3 (56)
°**match** [mætʃ] zuordnen • °**Match the letters and numbers.** Ordne die Buchstaben den Zahlen zu.
maths [mæθs] Mathematik 1 (23/156)
may [meɪ] dürfen 5 (84/85)
May [meɪ] Mai TOP 1 (35/158)
maybe ['meɪbi] vielleicht 3 (65)
me [miː] mir; mich Welc (10) • **Me too.** Ich auch. Welc (12) • **That's me.** Das bin ich. Welc (10) • **Why me?** Warum ich? Welc (14)
mean [miːn] meinen, sagen wollen 3 (65)
meaning ['miːnɪŋ] Bedeutung 3 (61)
meat [miːt] Fleisch 2 (39)
meet [miːt] **1.** treffen; kennenlernen 1 (22); **2.** sich treffen 3 (60)
men [men] *Plural von „man"* 3 (65)
°**Merry Christmas.** [ˌmeri 'krɪsməs] Frohe Weihnachten.
mess [mes]: **make a mess** alles durcheinanderbringen, alles in Unordnung bringen 4 (72)
°**message** ['mesɪdʒ] Nachricht, Botschaft
°**miaow** [mi'aʊ] miauen
mice [maɪs] *Plural von „mouse"* 2 (37/159)
middle (of) ['mɪdl] Mitte 6 (102)
milk [mɪlk] Milch 1 (19)
milkshake ['mɪlkʃeɪk] Milchshake 4 (69)
°**mime** [maɪm] vorspielen, pantomimisch darstellen
mind map ['maɪnd mæp] Mindmap („Gedankenkarte", „Wissensnetz") 2 (38)
mints *(pl)* [mɪnts] Pfefferminzbonbons 1 (33)
minute ['mɪnɪt] Minute 4 (78)
Miss White [mɪs] Frau White *(unverheiratet)* 5 (86)
°**missing** ['mɪsɪŋ]: **be missing** fehlen
the missing information/words die fehlenden Informationen/Wörter
mistake [mɪ'steɪk] Fehler 5 (87)
°**mix (with)** [mɪks] sich vermischen (mit) • °**mix up** durcheinanderbringen
mobile (phone) ['məʊbaɪl] Mobiltelefon, Handy 1 (19)
model ['mɒdl] Modell*(-flugzeug, -schiff usw.)* 3 (53)

moment ['məʊmənt] Augenblick, Moment 6 (104) • **at the moment** im Moment, gerade, zurzeit 6 (104)
Monday ['mʌndeɪ, 'mʌndi] Montag Welc (14/152) • **Monday morning** Montagmorgen Welc (14/152)
money ['mʌni] Geld TOP 3 (67)
°**monster** ['mɒnstə] Monster
month [mʌnθ] Monat TOP 1 (35/158)
more [mɔː] mehr 1 (33) • **lots more** viel mehr 6 (101) • **no more music** keine Musik mehr 4 (81) **one more** noch ein(e), ein(e) weitere(r, s) 6 (105)
morning ['mɔːnɪŋ] Morgen, Vormittag Welc (14/152) • **in the morning** morgens, am Morgen 1 (19) • **Monday morning** Montagmorgen Welc (14/152) • **on Friday morning** freitagmorgens, am Freitagmorgen 2 (38/160)
most [məʊst]: **most people** die meisten Leute 3 (57)
mother ['mʌðə] Mutter Welc (12/151)
°**mountain** ['maʊntən] Berg
mouse [maʊs], *pl* **mice** [maɪs] Maus 2 (37/159)
mouth [maʊθ] Mund 4 (74/171)
°**mozzarella** [ˌmɒtsə'relə] Mozzarella
MP3 player [ˌempiː'θriː ˌpleɪə] MP3-Spieler Welc (12)
Mr ... ['mɪstə] Herr ... Welc (12/151)
Mrs ... ['mɪsɪz] Frau ... Welc (12/151)
°**Ms ...** [mɪz, məz] Frau ...
much [mʌtʃ] viel TOP 3 (67) • **how much?** wie viel? 5 (96/175) • **How much is/are ...?** Was kostet/kosten ...? / Wie viel kostet/kosten ...? TOP 3 (67)
► S.175 „viel", „viele"
muesli ['mjuːzli] Müsli 4 (77)
mum [mʌm] Mama, Mutti; Mutter Welc (8/148)
museum [mju'ziːəm] Museum 6 (101)
music ['mjuːzɪk] Musik 1 (23/156)
musical ['mjuːzɪkl] **1.** Musical 5 (86); °**2.** musikalisch
must [mʌst] müssen 6 (102)
my [maɪ] mein/e Welc (8/148) • **My name is ...** Ich heiße ... / Mein Name ist ... Welc (8/148) • **It's my turn.** Ich bin dran / an der Reihe. 1 (20)
°**mystery** ['mɪstri] Rätsel, Geheimnis

N

name [neɪm] Name Welc (8/148) **My name is ...** Ich heiße ... / Mein Name ist ... Welc (8/148) • **What's your name?** Wie heißt du? Welc (8/148)
near [nɪə] in der Nähe von, nahe (bei) 6 (100)
°**necessary** ['nesəsəri] nötig, notwendig
°**necklace** ['nekləs] Halskette
need [niːd] brauchen, benötigen Welc (12)
neighbour ['neɪbə] Nachbar/in 3 (55)
nervous ['nɜːvəs] nervös, aufgeregt 1 (20)
°**network** ['netwɜːk] (Wörter-)Netz
never ['nevə] nie, niemals 3 (56)
new [njuː] neu Welc (8)
news *(no pl)* [njuːz] Nachrichten 3 (63)
newspaper ['njuːspeɪpə] Zeitung Welc (15)
next [nekst]: **be next** der/die Nächste sein 6 (105) • **the next morning/day** am nächsten Morgen/Tag 3 (56) • **the next photo** das nächste Foto 6 (104) **What have we got next?** Was haben wir als Nächstes? 1 (24)
next to [nekst] neben 4 (69)
nice [naɪs] schön, nett Welc (11) **nice and cool/clean/...** schön kühl/sauber/... 6 (104)
°**nickname** ['nɪkneɪm] Spitzname
night [naɪt] Nacht, später Abend 2 (38/160) • **at night** nachts, in der Nacht 2 (38/160) • **on Friday night** freitagnachts, Freitagnacht 2 (38/160)
no [nəʊ] **1.** nein Welc (8/148); **2.** kein, keine 4 (81/172) • **no more music** keine Musik mehr 4 (81)
noise [nɔɪz] Geräusch; Lärm 3 (65)
nose [nəʊz] Nase 4 (74/171)
not [nɒt] nicht Welc (9/149) • **not (...) any** kein, keine 4 (71)
note [nəʊt] Mitteilung, Notiz 4 (82) **take notes** sich Notizen machen 4 (82/172)
°**notice** ['nəʊtɪs] Notiz, Mitteilung
November [nəʊ'vembə] November TOP 1 (35/158)
now [naʊ] nun, jetzt Welc (13)
number ['nʌmbə] Zahl, Ziffer, Nummer Welc (9/149)

O

o [əʊ] null Welc (15)
o'clock [ə'klɒk]: **eleven o'clock** elf Uhr Welc (17/153)
October [ɒk'təʊbə] Oktober TOP 1 (35/158)
°**odd** [ɒd]: **What word is the odd one out?** Welches Wort passt nicht dazu? / Welches Wort gehört nicht dazu?
of [əv, ɒv] von 2 (38) • **of the summer holidays** der Sommerferien Welc (12)
of course [əv 'kɔːs] natürlich, selbstverständlich 2 (40)
off [ɒf]: **take 10c off** 10 Cent abziehen TOP 3 (67)
often ['ɒfn] oft, häufig 3 (56)
Oh well ... [əʊ 'wel] Na ja ... / Na gut ... Welc (13)
OK [əʊ'keɪ] okay, gut, in Ordnung Welc (12)
old [əʊld] alt Welc (8/148) • **How old are you?** Wie alt bist du? Welc (8/148) • **I'm ... years old.** Ich bin ... Jahre alt. Welc (8/148)
on [ɒn] auf 1 (23/156) • **on 13th June** am 13. Juni TOP 1 (35/158) • **on Friday** am Freitag 1 (23) • **on Friday afternoon** freitagnachmittags, am Freitagnachmittag 2 (38/160) • **on Friday evening** freitagabends, am Freitagabend 2 (38/160) • **on Friday morning** freitagmorgens, am Freitagmorgen 2 (38/160) • **on Friday night** freitagnachts, Freitagnacht 2 (38/160) **on the board** an die Tafel 1 (22/155) **on the left** links, auf der linken Seite 3 (65/168) • **on the phone** am Telefon 4 (78) • **on the radio** im Radio 3 (62) • **on the right** rechts, auf der rechten Seite 3 (65/168) • **on the train** im Zug 4 (73/171) • **on TV** im Fernsehen 2 (39/161) • **What page are we on?** Auf welcher Seite sind wir? 1 (28/157)
°**once** [wʌns] einmal
one ['wʌn] eins, ein, eine Welc (14) **one day** eines Tages 5 (90) • **one more** noch ein/e, ein/e weitere(r, s) 6 (105)
only ['əʊnli] **1.** nur, bloß TOP 3 (67); **2. the only guest** der einzige Gast 3 (65)
°**onto** ['ɒntə, 'ɒntu] auf (... hinauf)
open ['əʊpən] **1.** öffnen, aufmachen Welc (10); **2.** sich öffnen 6 (111); **3.** geöffnet 6 (101)
or [ɔː] oder 1 (28)
orange ['ɒrɪndʒ] **1.** orange(farben) Welc (13/152); **2.** Orange, Apfelsine 4 (69/169) • **orange juice** ['ɒrɪndʒ dʒuːs] Orangensaft 4 (69/169)
°**order** ['ɔːdə] Reihenfolge • °**word order** Wortstellung
other ['ʌðə] andere(r, s) 2 (48) **the others** die anderen 3 (66)

Ouch! [aʊtʃ] Autsch! 4 (82)
our ['aʊə] unser, unsere 1 (21)
out [aʊt]**: be out** weg sein, nicht da sein 6 (110)
out of ... ['aʊt‿əv] aus ... (heraus/hinaus) 3 (65/168)
outside [ˌaʊt'saɪd] draußen 3 (65)
outside the room vor dem Zimmer; außerhalb des Zimmers 3 (65)
over ['əʊvə] **1.** über, oberhalb von Welc (14) • **over there** da drüben, dort drüben TOP 2 (51)
2. be over vorbei sein, zu Ende sein 4 (82)
°**own** [əʊn]**: your own song** dein eigenes Lied
°**owner** ['əʊnə] Besitzer/in
°**Oxfam** ['ɒksfæm] *bekannteste Wohltätigkeitsorganisation Großbritanniens mit einer Kette von Gebrauchtwarengeschäften*

P

packet ['pækɪt] Päckchen, Packung, Schachtel 1 (33) • **a packet of mints** ein Päckchen/eine Packung Pfefferminzbonbons 1 (33)
page [peɪdʒ] (Buch-, Heft-)Seite Welc (8) • **What page are we on?** Auf welcher Seite sind wir? 1 (28/157)
pain [peɪn] Schmerz(en) 6 (111)
cry in pain vor Schmerzen schreien 6 (111)
paint [peɪnt] malen, anmalen 5 (84/85)
paper ['peɪpə] Papier 3 (66)
parcel ['pɑːsl] Paket 4 (73)
parents ['peərənts] Eltern 2 (41/162)
park [pɑːk] Park Welc (10)
parrot ['pærət] Papagei Welc (16)
part [pɑːt] Teil 5 (87)
partner ['pɑːtnə] Partner/in Welc (8)
party ['pɑːti] Party 4 (68)
pass [pɑːs] **1.** (herüber)reichen, weitergeben 4 (81) • **pass round** herumgeben 4 (81)
°**2.** vorbei-, vorüberziehen *(Wolken)*
°**past** [pɑːst] Vergangenheit
past [pɑːst]**: half past 11** halb zwölf (11.30 / 23.30) Welc (17/153)
quarter past 11 Viertel nach 11 (11.15 / 23.15) Welc (17/153)
°**patch** [pætʃ] Augenklappe
PE [ˌpiː‿'iː]**, Physical Education** [ˌfɪzɪkəl‿edʒu'keɪʃn] Sportunterricht, Turnen 1 (23/156)
pen [pen] Kugelschreiber, Füller Welc (12/151)
pence (p) *(pl)* [pens] Pence *(Plural von „penny")* TOP 3 (67)

pencil ['pensl] Bleistift Welc (12/151)
pencil case ['pensl keɪs] Federmäppchen Welc (12/151) • **pencil sharpener** ['pensl ʃɑːpnə] Bleistiftanspitzer Welc (12)
penny ['peni] *kleinste britische Münze* TOP 3 (67/169)
people ['piːpl] Menschen, Leute 2 (36)
°**pepper** ['pepə] Pfeffer
person ['pɜːsn] Person 3 (61)
pet [pet] Haustier Welc (12/151)
pet shop Tierhandlung 2 (44)
phone [fəʊn] **1.** Telefon 1 (19) • **on the phone** am Telefon 4 (78)
phone number Telefonnummer Welc (15)
2. anrufen 3 (65)
photo ['fəʊtəʊ] Foto Welc (9) • **in the photo** auf dem Foto Welc (9/150) • **take photos** Fotos machen, fotografieren 6 (103)
°**phrase** [freɪz] Ausdruck, (Rede-)Wendung
piano [pi'ænəʊ] Klavier, Piano 3 (55)
play the piano Klavier spielen 3 (55/166)
picture ['pɪktʃə] Bild Welc (11) • **in the picture** auf dem Bild Welc (11/151)
piece [piːs]**: a piece of** ein Stück 3 (66) • **a piece of paper** ein Stück Papier 3 (66)
pink [pɪŋk] pink(farben), rosa Welc (13/152)
pirate ['paɪrət] Pirat, Piratin 5 (84/85)
°**pistol** ['pɪstl] Pistole
pizza ['piːtsə] Pizza 1 (24)
place [pleɪs] Ort, Platz Welc (9)
°**placemat** ['pleɪsmæt] Set, Platzdeckchen
plan [plæn] **1.** Plan 2 (38); °**2. plan to do (-nn-)** planen zu tun
°**plank** [plæŋk] Brett, Planke
°**plastic explosive** [ˌplæstɪk ɪk'spləʊsɪv] Plastiksprengstoff
plate [pleɪt] Teller Welc (13) • **a plate of chips** ein Teller Pommes frites 4 (69/170)
play [pleɪ] **1.** spielen Welc (9/149)
play football Fußball spielen Welc (9/149) • **play the guitar** Gitarre spielen 3 (53/165) • **play the piano** Klavier spielen 3 (55/166)
2. Theaterstück 4 (81)
player ['pleɪə] Spieler/in 6 (106)
please [pliːz] bitte *(in Fragen und Aufforderungen)* Welc (12/151)
► S.161 „bitte"
pm [ˌpiː‿'em]**: 7 pm** 7 Uhr nachmittags/abends 4 (81)
poem ['pəʊɪm] Gedicht Welc (14)

°**poetry** ['pəʊətri] *hier:* Gedichte
police *(pl)* [pə'liːs] Polizei 3 (65)
poltergeist ['pəʊltəgaɪst] Poltergeist Welc (10)
poor [pɔː, pʊə] arm 1 (32) • **poor Sophie** (die) arme Sophie 1 (32)
poster ['pəʊstə] Poster 1 (24)
potato [pə'teɪtəʊ], *pl* **potatoes** Kartoffel 4 (69/169)
pound (£) [paʊnd] Pfund *(britische Währung)* TOP 3 (67)
practice ['præktɪs] *hier:* Übungsteil (3)
practise ['præktɪs] üben; trainieren 5 (84/85)
°**prepare** [prɪ'peə] vorbereiten
present ['preznt] **1.** Gegenwart 4 (71/170); **2.** Geschenk 4 (71)
present sth. (to sb.) [prɪ'zent] (jm.) etwas präsentieren, vorstellen 6 (104/178)
presentation [ˌprezn'teɪʃn] Präsentation, Vorstellung 6 (104)
pretty ['prɪti] hübsch Welc (6)
price [praɪs] (Kauf-)Preis 6 (101)
prize [praɪz] Preis, Gewinn 4 (82)
programme ['prəʊgræm] Programm 5 (84/85)
project (about, on) ['prɒdʒekt] Projekt (über, zu) 3 (55)
pronunciation [prəˌnʌnsi'eɪʃn] Aussprache (3)
pull [pʊl] ziehen Welc (10)
purple ['pɜːpl] violett; lila Welc (13/152)
push [pʊʃ] drücken, schieben, stoßen Welc (10)
put (-tt-) [pʊt] **1.** legen, stellen, *(etwas wohin)* tun 2 (39); **2.** *Vergangenheitsform von „put"* 5 (88/174)
°**puzzle** ['pʌzl] Rätsel

Q

quarter ['kwɔːtə]**: quarter past 11** Viertel nach 11 (11.15 / 23.15) Welc (17/153) • **quarter to 12** Viertel vor 12 (11.45 / 23.45) Welc (17/153)
question ['kwestʃn] Frage 3 (56)
ask questions Fragen stellen 3 (56/166)
quick [kwɪk] schnell 3 (56)
quiet ['kwaɪət] leise, still, ruhig 1 (22)
°**quite like it** [kwaɪt] ganz so wie diese(r, s), genau wie diese(r, s)
quiz [kwɪz], *pl* **quizzes** ['kwɪzɪz] Quiz, Ratespiel 2 (45)

R

rabbit ['ræbɪt] Kaninchen 2 (37/159)

°**racket** ['rækɪt] (Tennis-, Federball-, Squash-)Schläger

radio ['reɪdiəʊ] Radio 3 (62) • **on the radio** im Radio 3 (62)

°**rain** [reɪn] Regen

°**ram (-mm-)** [ræm] rammen

ran [ræn] *Vergangenheitsform von „run“* 5 (96/175)

rap [ræp] Rap *(rhythmischer Sprechgesang)* 1 (22)

RE [ˌɑːr_ˈiː], **Religious Education** [rɪˌlɪdʒəs_edʒuˈkeɪʃn] Religion, Religionsunterricht 1 (23/156)

read [riːd] lesen 2 (38) • °**read on** weiterlesen • °**read out** vorlesen °**Read out loud.** Lies laut vor.

ready ['redi] bereit, fertig 2 (48) **get ready (for)** sich fertig machen (für), sich vorbereiten (auf) 4 (72) **get things ready** Dinge fertig machen, vorbereiten 2 (48)

real [rɪəl] echt, wirklich 4 (70)

realize ['rɪəlaɪz] erkennen, merken 5 (87)

really ['rɪəli] wirklich 1 (24)

reason ['riːzn] Grund, Begründung 4 (71) • **for lots of reasons** aus vielen Gründen 6 (105)

°**recipe** ['resəpi] (Koch-)Rezept

red [red] rot Welc (13/152)

rehearsal [rɪ'hɜːsl] Probe *(am Theater)* 5 (84/85)

rehearse [rɪ'hɜːs] proben *(am Theater)* 5 (84/85/173)

remember sth. [rɪ'membə] **1.** sich an etwas erinnern 2 (45); **2.** sich etwas merken 1 (22) • **Can you remember that?** Kannst du dir das merken? 1 (22)

report [rɪ'pɔːt]**: 1. report (on)** Bericht, Reportage (über) 5 (89) °**2. report (to sb.)** (jm.) berichten

result [rɪ'zʌlt] Ergebnis, Resultat 5 (84/85)

revision [rɪ'vɪʒn] Wiederholung *(des Lernstoffs)* (3)

°**rhyming words** ['raɪmɪŋ wɜːdz] Reimwörter

°**rhythm** ['rɪðəm] Rhythmus

ride [raɪd] reiten 3 (53/165) • **go riding** ['raɪdɪŋ] reiten gehen 3 (53) **ride a bike** Rad fahren 3 (52/164)

right [raɪt] **1.** richtig Welc (11) • **be right** Recht haben 6 (102) • **That's right.** Das ist richtig. / Das stimmt. Welc (11) • **You need a school bag, right?** Du brauchst eine Schultasche, stimmt's? / nicht wahr? Welc (12) **2.** rechte(r, s) 3 (65/168) • **look right** nach rechts schauen 3 (65) • **on the right** rechts, auf der rechten Seite 3 (65/168)

► S.168 left – right

3. right now jetzt sofort; jetzt gerade 3 (57)

°**river** ['rɪvə] Fluss

road [rəʊd] Straße Welc (10) • **Park Road** [ˌpɑːk 'rəʊd] Parkstraße Welc (10)

°**roll up** [ˌrəʊl_'ʌp] aufrollen

room [ruːm, rʊm] Raum, Zimmer Welc (9/149)

rubber ['rʌbə] Radiergummi Welc (12/151)

ruler ['ruːlə] Lineal Welc (12/151)

run (-nn-) [rʌn] laufen, rennen 3 (65)

S

said [sed] *Vergangenheitsform von „say“* 5 (88/174)

°**sail** [seɪl] **1.** segeln; **2.** Segel

°**sailor** ['seɪlə] Seemann, Matrose

salad ['sæləd] Salat *(als Gericht oder Beilage)* 4 (69)

°**salami** [sə'lɑːmi] Salami

°**salt** [sɔːlt] Salz

same [seɪm]**: the same ...** der-/die-/dasselbe ...; dieselben ... 6 (103/177) **be/look the same** gleich sein/aussehen 6 (103)

sandwich ['sænwɪtʃ, 'sænwɪdʒ] Sandwich, *(zusammengeklapptes)* belegtes Brot 2 (45)

sang [sæŋ] *Vergangenheitsform von „sing“* 5 (88)

sat [sæt] *Vergangenheitsform von „sit“* 5 (96/175)

Saturday ['sætədeɪ, 'sætədi] Samstag, Sonnabend Welc (14/152)

sausage ['sɒsɪdʒ] (Brat-, Bock-) Würstchen, Wurst 4 (69)

°**save** [seɪv] retten

saw [sɔː] *Vergangenheitsform von „see“* 5 (88/174)

say [seɪ] sagen Welc (12) • **say goodbye** sich verabschieden Welc (17) • **Say hi to Dilip for me.** Grüß Dilip von mir. 3 (56)

°**scare away** [ˌskeər_ə'weɪ] verscheuchen, verjagen

scared [skeəd] verängstigt 6 (111) **be scared (of)** Angst haben (vor) 6 (111/178)

scary ['skeəri] unheimlich; gruselig 3 (65)

scene [siːn] Szene 4 (81)

school [skuːl] Schule Welc (12/151) **at school** in der Schule Welc (12/151) **school bag** Schultasche Welc (12/151) **school subject** Schulfach 1 (23/156)

► S.156 School subjects

science ['saɪəns] Naturwissenschaft 1 (23/156)

sea [siː] Meer, *(die)* See 5 (97)

second ['sekənd] Sekunde 6 (111)

second ['sekənd] zweite(r, s) TOP 1 (35)

°**secret** ['siːkrət] Geheimnis

°**section** ['sekʃn] Abschnitt

see [siː] sehen Welc (9) • **See?** Siehst du? 4 (81) • **See you.** Bis bald. / Tschüs. 1 (33)

► S.161 (to) look – (to) see – (to) watch

sell [sel] verkaufen 3 (54/165)

°**send** [send] senden, schicken

sentence ['sentəns] Satz 1 (28/157)

September [sep'tembə] September TOP 1 (35/158)

°**shadow** ['ʃædəʊ] Schatten

°**shake** [ʃeɪk] schütteln

share sth. (with sb.) [ʃeə] sich etwas teilen (mit jm.) 2 (36)

she [ʃiː] sie Welc (8)

shelf [ʃelf], *pl* **shelves** [ʃelvz] Regal(brett) 2 (36/159)

ship [ʃɪp] Schiff 5 (84/85)

shirt [ʃɜːt] Hemd 3 (54/165)

shoe [ʃuː] Schuh 3 (54/165)

shop [ʃɒp] Laden, Geschäft Welc (14) **shop assistant** ['ʃɒp_əˌsɪstənt] Verkäufer/in 3 (54) • **shopping** (das) Einkaufen Welc (12) • **go shopping** einkaufen gehen 3 (57) **shopping list** Einkaufsliste Welc (12)

short [ʃɔːt] kurz 4 (70/170)

shorts *(pl)* [ʃɔːts] Shorts, kurze Hose 3 (54/165)

should [ʃəd, ʃʊd]**: you should ...** du solltest ... / ihr solltet ... 6 (104)

shoulder ['ʃəʊldə] Schulter 4 (74/171)

shout [ʃaʊt] schreien, rufen 3 (57) **shout at sb.** jn. anschreien 3 (57/167)

show [ʃəʊ] **1.** zeigen 3 (66); **2.** Show, Vorstellung 5 (84/85)

shower ['ʃaʊə] Dusche 2 (48) • **have a shower** (sich) duschen 2 (48)

°**Shush!** [ʃʊʃ] Pst!

°**signal** ['sɪgnəl] Signal, Zeichen

°**silver** ['sɪlvə] Silber

sing [sɪŋ] singen Welc (8/148)

single ['sɪŋgl] ledig, alleinstehend 2 (41)

sink [sɪŋk] Spüle, Spülbecken TOP 2 (50)

°**sir** [sɜː] Sir

sister ['sɪstə] Schwester Welc (8/148)

sit (-tt-) [sɪt] sitzen; sich setzen 1 (20) • **Sit with me.** Setz dich zu mir. / Setzt euch zu mir. 1 (20)

size [saɪz] Größe 3 (54)

skate [skeɪt] Inliner/Skateboard fahren 3 (55) • **skates** [skeɪts] Inliner 3 (55/166)
skateboard ['skeɪtbɔːd] Skateboard Welc (9/149)
sketch [sketʃ] Sketch 5 (86)
skills file ['skɪlz faɪl] *Anhang mit Lern- und Arbeitstechniken* (3/118)
°**sky** [skaɪ] Himmel
sleep [sliːp] schlafen 2 (38)
°**sleepover** ['sliːpəʊvə] Schlafparty
°**sleigh** [sleɪ] (Pferde-)Schlitten
°**slowly** ['sləʊli] langsam
°**small** [smɔːl] klein
smile [smaɪl] lächeln 6 (103)
snake [sneɪk] Schlange 3 (58)
so [səʊ] **1.** also; deshalb, daher 2 (41); **2. so sweet** so süß 4 (81) • °**so far** bis jetzt, bis hierher **3. I think so.** Ich glaube (ja). 5 (98/176) • **I don't think so.** Das finde/glaube ich nicht. 5 (98)
soap [səʊp] Seife 4 (71)
sock [sɒk] Socke, Strumpf 3 (54/165)
sofa ['səʊfə] Sofa TOP 2 (50)
some [səm, sʌm] einige, ein paar 3 (56) • **some cheese/juice/money** etwas Käse/Saft/Geld 4 (69)
somebody ['sʌmbədi] jemand 4 (73)
something ['sʌmθɪŋ] etwas 5 (88)
sometimes ['sʌmtaɪmz] manchmal 2 (39)
son [sʌn] Sohn 2 (41)
song [sɒŋ] Lied, Song Welc (8/148)
soon [suːn] bald 5 (97)
sorry ['sɒri]: **(I'm) sorry.** Entschuldigung. / Tut mir leid. 1 (21) **Sorry, I'm late.** Entschuldigung, dass ich zu spät bin/komme. Welc (12) • **Sorry?** Wie bitte? 1 (21/155) ▸ S.153 „Entschuldigung" / S.155 sorry
sound [saʊnd] **1.** klingen, sich *(gut usw.)* anhören 5 (86); **2.** Laut; Klang 1 (30)
°**Spanish** ['spænɪʃ] spanisch
°**speak** [spiːk] sprechen
special ['speʃl]: **Did you do anything special?** Habt ihr irgendetwas Besonderes gemacht? 5 (89)
°**speech bubble** ['spiːtʃ bʌbl] Sprechblase
spell [spel] buchstabieren 1 (23)
°**spelling** ['spelɪŋ] Schreibung, Schreibweise
sport [spɔːt] Sport; Sportart 3 (52) **do sport** Sport treiben 3 (52/164) ▸ S.164 Sports
spring [sprɪŋ] Frühling 5 (84/85)
spy [spaɪ] Spion/in 2 (48)
stage [steɪdʒ] Bühne 5 (89)
stairs *(pl)* [steəz] Treppe; Treppenstufen TOP 2 (50/163)
stamp [stæmp] Briefmarke 3 (53)
°**stand** [stænd] stehen
star [stɑː] (Film-, Pop-)Star 2 (48)
start [stɑːt] starten, anfangen, beginnen (mit) 3 (66)
°**statement** ['steɪtmənt] Aussage, Aussagesatz
station ['steɪʃn] Bahnhof 4 (73) **at the station** am Bahnhof 4 (73/171)
°**statue** ['stætʃuː] Statue
°**stay (with)** [steɪ] wohnen (bei)
step [step] Schritt 6 (102) • °**take a step** einen Schritt tun
stick on [ˌstɪk_'ɒn] aufkleben 6 (104)
still [stɪl] (immer) noch 4 (71)
stop (-pp-) [stɒp] **1.** aufhören Welc (14) • **Stop that!** Hör auf damit! / Lass das! Welc (14) **2.** anhalten 1 (31)
story ['stɔːri] Geschichte, Erzählung 2 (48)
strange [streɪndʒ] seltsam, sonderbar TOP 2 (51)
street [striːt] Straße Welc (12) • **at 7 Hamilton Street** in der Hamiltonstraße 7 Welc (12)
°**stretch** [stretʃ] strecken, dehnen
stuck [stʌk] *Vergangenheitsform von „stick"* 6 (104)
student ['stjuːdənt] Schüler/in; Student/in 1 (20)
studio ['stjuːdiəʊ] Studio 5 (84/85)
study skills *(pl)* ['stʌdi skɪlz] Lern- und Arbeitstechniken (3)
stuff [stʌf] Zeug, Kram 3 (54)
subject ['sʌbdʒɪkt] **1.** Subjekt 4 (72); **2.** Schulfach 1 (23/156) ▸ S.156 School subjects
suddenly ['sʌdnli] plötzlich, auf einmal 3 (65)
summer ['sʌmə] Sommer Welc (12)
Sunday ['sʌndeɪ, 'sʌndi] Sonntag Welc (14/152)
sunglasses *(pl)* ['sʌnglɑːsɪz] (eine) Sonnenbrille 2 (48)
supermarket ['suːpəmɑːkɪt] Supermarkt 5 (88)
suppose [sə'pəʊz] annehmen, vermuten 6 (104)
sure [ʃʊə, ʃɔː] sicher 5 (88)
°**survey (on)** ['sɜːveɪ] Umfrage (über, zu)
°**suspension bridge** [sə'spenʃn brɪdʒ] Hängebrücke
swap (-pp-) [swɒp] tauschen 5 (89)
sweatshirt ['swetʃɜːt] Sweatshirt 3 (54/165)
sweet [swiːt] süß 4 (69/170) **sweets** *(pl)* Süßigkeiten 4 (69)
swim (-mm-) [swɪm] schwimmen 3 (52/164) • **go swimming** schwimmen gehen 3 (52/164)
°**sword** [sɔːd] Schwert
°**swordfish** ['sɔːdfɪʃ] Schwertfisch
syllable ['sɪləbl] Silbe 5 (92)
°**synchronize watches** ['sɪŋkrənaɪz] Uhren gleichstellen

T

table ['teɪbl] Tisch 1 (18/154) • **table tennis** ['teɪbl tenɪs] Tischtennis 3 (52/164)
take [teɪk] **1.** nehmen Welc (11); **2.** (weg-, hin)bringen 4 (72) • **take 10c off** 10 Cent abziehen TOP 3 (67) **take notes** sich Notizen machen 4 (82/172) • **take out** herausnehmen 1 (23) • **take photos** Fotos machen, fotografieren 6 (103) °**take a step** einen Schritt tun **I'll take it.** [aɪl 'teɪk_ɪt] *(beim Einkaufen)* Ich werde es (ihn, sie) nehmen. / Ich nehme es (ihn, sie). TOP 3 (67)
talk [tɔːk]: **talk (about)** reden (über), sich unterhalten (über) Welc (8) **talk (to)** reden (mit), sich unterhalten (mit) Welc (8)
°**tavern** ['tævən] Schenke, Kneipe
tea [tiː] Tee; *(auch:) leichte Nachmittags- oder Abendmahlzeit* 1 (32)
teach [tiːtʃ] unterrichten, lehren 3 (57) • **teacher** ['tiːtʃə] Lehrer/in 1 (21)
team [tiːm] Team, Mannschaft 3 (53)
teeth [tiːθ] *Plural von „tooth"* 2 (38)
telephone ['telɪfəʊn] Telefon Welc (15) • **telephone number** Telefonnummer Welc (15)
television (TV) ['telɪvɪʒn] Fernsehen 2 (39/161)
tell (about) [tel] erzählen (von), berichten (über) 1 (22/156) • **Tell me your names.** Sagt mir eure Namen. 1 (22)
tennis ['tenɪs] Tennis 1 (22)
terrible ['terəbl] schrecklich, furchtbar 5 (87)
text [tekst] Text (3)
Thank you. ['θæŋk juː] Danke (schön). Welc (12/151) • **Thanks.** [θæŋks] Danke. 2 (40) • **Thanks a lot!** Vielen Dank! 3 (56)
that [ðət, ðæt] **1.** das (dort) Welc (11); **2.** jene(r, s) 1 (24) • **That's me.** Das bin ich. Welc (10) • **That's right.** Das ist richtig. / Das stimmt. Welc (11) • **that's why** deshalb, darum 6 (103) **3.** dass 5 (87) ▸ S.177 this, that – these, those

the [ðə, ði] der, die, das; die Welc (9/149)
their [ðeə] ihr, ihre *(Plural)* Welc (12)
them [ðəm, ðem] sie; ihnen TOP 2 (51)
then [ðen] dann, danach Welc (10)
there [ðeə] **1.** da, dort Welc (11); **2.** dahin, dorthin 2 (39/161) • **in there** dort drinnen 5 (87) • **over there** da drüben, dort drüben TOP 2 (51) **there are** es sind (vorhanden); es gibt 1 (18) • **there's** es ist (vorhanden); es gibt 1 (18) • **there isn't a ...** es ist kein/e ...; es gibt kein/e ... 1 (18/154)
► S.154 There's ... / There are ...
these [ði:z] diese, die (hier) 3 (54)
► S.177 this, that – these, those
they [ðeɪ] sie *(Plural)* Welc (8)
°thin [θɪn] dünn
thing [θɪŋ] Ding, Sache Welc (10)
think [θɪŋk] glauben, meinen, denken Welc (11) • **I think so.** Ich glaube (ja). 5 (98/176) • **I don't think so.** Das finde/glaube ich nicht. 5 (98) • **°think of** sich ausdenken
third [θɜ:d] dritte(r, s) TOP 1 (35)
thirsty ['θɜ:sti] durstig 4 (69) • **be thirsty** Durst haben, durstig sein 4 (69)
this [ðɪs] **1.** dies (hier) Welc (8); **2.** diese(r, s) 1 (34) • **this morning/afternoon/evening** heute Morgen/Nachmittag/Abend 5 (88) • **°This is the way ...** So ... / Auf diese Weise ...
► S.177 this, that – these, those
those [ðəʊz] die (da), jene (dort) 6 (103)
► S.177 this, that – these, those
thought [θɔ:t] *Vergangenheitsform von „think"* 5 (88/174)
thousand ['θaʊznd] tausend TOP 1 (35)
throw [θrəʊ] werfen 1 (22)
°Thud! [θʌd] Rums!
Thursday ['θɜ:zdeɪ, 'θɜ:zdi] Donnerstag Welc (14/152)
°tick [tɪk] Häkchen
ticket ['tɪkɪt] Eintrittskarte 5 (86) **°ticket inspector** ['tɪkɪt‿ɪn,spektə] Fahrkartenkontrolleur/in
tidy ['taɪdi] aufräumen 2 (39)
°tie [taɪ] zusammenbinden
till [tɪl] bis *(zeitlich)* 2 (40)
time [taɪm] Zeit; Uhrzeit Welc (17/153) • **What's the time?** Wie spät ist es? Welc (17/153) • **°The Times** *britische Tageszeitung*
timetable ['taɪmteɪbl] Stundenplan 1 (23)
tired ['taɪəd] müde 5 (88)
title ['taɪtl] Titel, Überschrift 4 (82)
to [tə, tu] **1.** zu, nach Welc (14) • **to Jenny's** zu Jenny 4 (72) • **to the front** nach vorn 6 (105) **2. an e-mail to** eine E-Mail an 3 (56) **write to** schreiben an 3 (56) **3. quarter to 12** Viertel vor 12 (11.45 / 23.45) Welc (17/153) **4. try to do** versuchen, zu tun 2 (39) **5.** um zu 5 (88)
toast [təʊst] Toast(brot) 2 (39)
today [tə'deɪ] heute Welc (12)
toe [təʊ] Zeh 4 (74/171)
together [tə'geðə] zusammen 1 (21)
toilet ['tɔɪlət] Toilette 1 (28/157)
told [təʊld] *Vergangenheitsform von „tell"* 5 (96/175)
°tomato [tə'mɑ:təʊ], *pl* **tomatoes** Tomate
tomorrow [tə'mɒrəʊ] morgen Welc (14)
tonight [tə'naɪt] heute Nacht, heute Abend 5 (96)
too [tu:]: **1. from Bristol too** auch aus Bristol Welc (8) • **Me too.** Ich auch. Welc (12) **2. too much/big/expensive** zu viel/groß/teuer TOP 3 (67)
took [tʊk] *Vergangenheitsform von „take"* 5 (96/175)
tooth [tu:θ], *pl* **teeth** [ti:θ] Zahn 2 (38)
top [tɒp] **1.** Spitze, oberes Ende 2 (41) • **at the top (of)** oben, am oberen Ende, an der Spitze (von) 2 (41) **2.** Top, Oberteil 3 (54/165)
topic ['tɒpɪk] Thema, Themenbereich (3)
°tornado [tɔ:'neɪdəʊ] Tornado, Wirbelsturm
tortoise ['tɔ:təs] Schildkröte 2 (37)
touch [tʌtʃ] berühren, anfassen 6 (101)
tour (of the house) [tʊə] Rundgang, Tour (durch das Haus) TOP 2 (50)
towards Mr Green [tə'wɔ:dz] auf Mr Green zu, in Mr Greens Richtung 6 (103)
tower ['taʊə] Turm 6 (100)
town [taʊn] Stadt 5 (89)
°toy [tɔɪ] Spielzeug
train [treɪn] Zug 4 (73) • **on the train** im Zug 4 (73/171)
°train [treɪn] trainieren • **°trainer** ['treɪnə] Trainer/in
tree [tri:] Baum Welc (9/149)
trick [trɪk] (Zauber-)Kunststück, Trick Welc (15) • **do tricks** (Zauber-) Kunststücke machen Welc (15)
trip [trɪp] Reise; Ausflug Welc (16) **go on a trip** einen Ausflug/eine Reise machen 5 (89)
°true [tru:] wahr
try [traɪ] **1.** versuchen 2 (39); **2.** probieren, kosten 4 (76) • **try and do / try to do** versuchen, zu tun 2 (39) **try on** anprobieren *(Kleidung)* 3 (54)
T-shirt ['ti:ʃɜ:t] T-Shirt 2 (46)
Tuesday ['tju:zdeɪ, 'tju:zdi] Dienstag Welc (14/152)
turn [tɜ:n]: **°turn around** sich umdrehen • **turn off the computer** den Computer ausschalten 6 (111/178) **turn on the computer** den Computer einschalten 6 (111)
turn [tɜ:n]: **(It's) my turn.** Ich bin dran / an der Reihe. 1 (20)
TV [ti:'vi:] Fernsehen 2 (39/161) **on TV** im Fernsehen 2 (39/161) **watch TV** fernsehen 2 (39/161)
twin [twɪn]: **twin brother** Zwillingsbruder Welc (8) • **twins** *(pl)* Zwillinge Welc (8/149) • **twin town** Partnerstadt 5 (89)

U

uncle ['ʌŋkl] Onkel 2 (41)
under ['ʌndə] unter 3 (61)
understand [,ʌndə'stænd] verstehen, begreifen 3 (57)
uniform ['ju:nɪfɔ:m] Uniform Welc (14)
unit ['ju:nɪt] Kapitel, Lektion (3)
up [ʌp] hinauf, herauf, nach oben 3 (65/167)
°update [,ʌp'deɪt] aktualisieren, auf den neuesten Stand bringen
upstairs [,ʌp'steəz] oben; nach oben TOP 2 (50)
us [əs, ʌs] uns 2 (48)
use [ju:z] benutzen, verwenden 5 (84/85) • **°used** [ju:zd] gebraucht
°usual ['ju:ʒuəl] üblich, gewöhnlich
usually ['ju:ʒuəli] meistens, gewöhnlich, normalerweise 3 (56)

V

very ['veri] sehr Welc (11)
village ['vɪlɪdʒ] Dorf 6 (100)
°visit ['vɪzɪt] besuchen; besichtigen
visitor ['vɪzɪtə] Besucher/in, Gast 3 (65)
vocabulary [və'kæbjələri] Vokabelverzeichnis, Wörterverzeichnis (3)
voice [vɔɪs] Stimme 5 (87)

volleyball ['vɒlibɔːl] Volleyball 3 (52/164)
°**vowel sound** ['vaʊəl saʊnd] Vokallaut

W

wait (for) ['weɪt fɔː] warten (auf) 3 (66) • **I can't wait to see ...** ich kann es kaum erwarten, ... zu sehen 5 (87)
walk [wɔːk] (zu Fuß) gehen 3 (56)
°**wall** [wɔːl] Wand, Mauer
°**Wallop!** ['wɒləp] Schepper!
want [wɒnt] (haben) wollen 3 (54)
want to do tun wollen 4 (70)
°**wanted** ['wɒntɪd] *(polizeilich)* gesucht
wardrobe ['wɔːdrəʊb] Kleiderschrank 2 (36/159)
warm [wɔːm] warm TOP 2 (51)
was [wəz, wɒz]: **(I/he/she/it) was** *Vergangenheitsform von „be"* 1 (33)
How was ...? Wie war ...? 1 (33)
wash [wɒʃ] waschen 2 (38) • **I wash my hands.** Ich wasche mir die Hände. 2 (38)
watch [wɒtʃ] beobachten, sich *etwas* ansehen; zusehen 2 (39)
watch TV fernsehen 2 (39/161)
► S.161 (to) look – (to) see – (to) watch
watch [wɒtʃ] Armbanduhr 3 (66)
water ['wɔːtə] Wasser Welc (9/149)
way [weɪ] Weg 5 (88) • **a long way (from)** weit entfernt (von) 6 (100)
°**way** [weɪ]: **This is the way ...** So ... / Auf diese Weise ...
we [wiː] wir Welc (8/148)
wear [weə] tragen, anhaben *(Kleidung)* 2 (48)
Wednesday ['wenzdeɪ, 'wenzdi] Mittwoch Welc (14/152)
week [wiːk] Woche Welc (14)
days of the week Wochentage Welc (14/152)
weekend [ˌwiːk'end] Wochenende 2 (36) • **at the weekend** am Wochenende 2 (38/160)
welcome ['welkəm]: **1. welcome sb. (to)** jn. begrüßen, willkommen heißen (in) Welc (16) • **They welcome you to ...** Sie heißen dich in ... willkommen Welc (16)
2. Welcome (to Bristol). Willkommen (in Bristol). Welc (8);
3. You're welcome. Gern geschehen. / Nichts zu danken. Welc (17)
► S.154 welcome
well [wel]: **Well, ...** Nun, ... / Also, ... Welc (14) • **Oh well ...** Na ja ... / Na gut ... Welc (13)

went [went] *Vergangenheitsform von „go"* 5 (88/174)
were [wə, wɜː]: **(we/you/they) were** *Vergangenheitsform von „be"* 5 (86)
what [wɒt] **1.** was Welc (8/148); **2.** welche(r, s) Welc (13) • **What about ...?** **1.** Was ist mit ...? / Und ...? Welc (6); **2.** Wie wär's mit ...? TOP 3 (67) • **What are you talking about?** Wovon redest du? 4 (82)
What colour is ...? Welche Farbe hat ...? Welc (13) • **What have we got next?** Was haben wir als Nächstes? 1 (24) • **What page are we on?** Auf welcher Seite sind wir? 1 (28/157) • **What's for homework?** Was haben wir als Hausaufgabe auf? 1 (28/157) • **What's the time?** Wie spät ist es? Welc (17/153)
What's your name? Wie heißt du? Welc (8/148)
wheelchair ['wiːltʃeə] Rollstuhl Welc (16)
when [wen] **1.** wann TOP 1 (35)
When's your birthday? Wann hast du Geburtstag? TOP 1 (35/158)
2. wenn Welc (10); **3.** als 5 (97)
where [weə] **1.** wo Welc (8/148); **2.** wohin 2 (39/161) • **Where are you from?** Wo kommst du her? Welc (8/148)
which [wɪtʃ]: **Which picture ...?** Welches Bild ...? 4 (74)
whisper ['wɪspə] flüstern 6 (103)
white [waɪt] weiß Welc (13/152)
who [huː] wer Welc (11) • **Who are you?** Wer bist du? Welc (11)
why [waɪ] warum Welc (14) • **Why me?** Warum ich? Welc (14) • **that's why** deshalb, darum 6 (103)
win (-nn-) [wɪn] gewinnen 3 (55)
wind [wɪnd] Wind 5 (96/175)
window ['wɪndəʊ] Fenster 1 (28/157)
windy ['wɪndi] windig 5 (96)
winter ['wɪntə] Winter 5 (84/85/173)
with [wɪð] **1.** mit Welc (8); **2.** bei 1 (23) • **Sit with me.** Setz dich zu mir. / Setzt euch zu mir. 1 (20)
without [wɪ'ðaʊt] ohne 2 (41)
woman ['wʊmən], *pl* **women** ['wɪmɪn] Frau 2 (41)
°**wonder** ['wʌndə] sich fragen
°**wonderful** ['wʌndəfəl] wunderbar
word [wɜːd] Wort 1 (19) • °**word order** Wortstellung
work [wɜːk] **1.** arbeiten 1 (28/157)
work on sth. an etwas arbeiten 5 (92)
2. Arbeit Welc (16) • **at work** bei der Arbeit / am Arbeitsplatz Welc (16)

worksheet ['wɜːkʃiːt] Arbeitsblatt 1 (28/157)
world [wɜːld] Welt 1 (33)
worried ['wʌrid]: **be worried (about)** beunruhigt sein, besorgt sein (wegen) 6 (110)
worry (about) ['wʌri] sich Sorgen machen (wegen, um) 4 (81)
Don't worry. Mach dir keine Sorgen. 4 (81)
would [wəd, wʊd]: **I'd like ... (= I would like ...)** Ich hätte gern ... / Ich möchte gern ... 4 (69) • **Would you like ...?** Möchtest du ...? / Möchten Sie ...? 4 (69) • **I'd like to go (= I would like to go)** ich würde gern gehen / ich möchte gehen 6 (101)
I wouldn't like to go ich würde nicht gern gehen / ich möchte nicht gehen 6 (101)
write [raɪt] schreiben 1 (22)
write down aufschreiben 1 (23)
write to schreiben an 3 (56)
wrong [rɒŋ] falsch, verkehrt 1 (20)

Y

year [jɪə] **1.** Jahr Welc (8/148); **2.** Jahrgangsstufe 5 (84/85)
yellow ['jeləʊ] gelb Welc (13/152)
yes [jes] ja Welc (8/148)
yesterday ['jestədeɪ, 'jestədi] gestern 5 (87) • **yesterday morning/afternoon/evening** gestern Morgen/Nachmittag/Abend 5 (87)
yoga ['jəʊgə] Yoga 3 (57)
you [juː] **1.** du; Sie Welc (8/148)
You're welcome. Gern geschehen. / Nichts zu danken. Welc (17)
2. ihr Welc (10) • **you two** ihr zwei Welc (12)
3. dir; dich; euch Welc (10)
► S.150 you – I/me
young [jʌŋ] jung 5 (96)
your [jɔː] **1.** dein/e Welc (8/148)
What's your name? Wie heißt du? Welc (8/148)
2. Ihr Welc (17); **3.** euer/eure 1 (21)
°**yourself** [jə'self, jɔː'self]: **about yourself** über dich selbst
°**youth** [juːθ] Jugend, Jugend-

Z

zero ['zɪərəʊ] null Welc (15)
zoo [zuː] Zoo, Tierpark 4 (76)

Das **German – English Dictionary** enthält den **Lernwortschatz** dieses Bandes. Es kann dir eine erste Hilfe sein, wenn du vergessen hast, wie etwas auf Englisch heißt.
Wenn du wissen möchtest, wo das englische Wort zum ersten Mal in *English G 21* vorkommt, dann kannst du im **English – German Dictionary** (S. 179–191) nachschlagen.

► Der Pfeil verweist auf Kästchen im Vocabulary (S. 148–178), in denen du weitere Informationen findest.

A

Abend evening ['i:vnɪŋ]; *(später Abend)* night [naɪt] • **am Abend, abends** in the evening
Abendbrot, -essen dinner ['dɪnə] **Abendbrot essen** have dinner **zum Abendbrot** for dinner
aber but [bət, bʌt]
abwaschen: das Geschirr abwaschen do the dishes ['dɪʃɪz]
abziehen: 10 Cent abziehen take 10c off [ˌteɪk_'ɒf]
addieren (zu) add (to) [æd]
Aktivität activity [æk'tɪvəti]
alle *(die ganze Gruppe)* all [ɔ:l]
allein alone [ə'ləʊn]
alleinstehend single ['sɪŋgl]
alles everything ['evriθɪŋ]; all [ɔ:l]
Alphabet alphabet ['ælfəbet]
als *(zeitlich)* when [wen]
also *(daher, deshalb)* so [səʊ] **Also, ...** Well, ... [wel]
alt old [əʊld]
am 1. am Bahnhof at the station **am oberen Ende / an der Spitze (von)** at the top (of) • **am Telefon** on the phone **2.** *(zeitlich)* **am 13. Juni** on 13th June **am Morgen/Nachmittag/Abend** in the morning/afternoon/evening **am Ende (von)** at the end (of) **am Freitag** on Friday • **am Freitagmorgen** on Friday morning **am nächsten Morgen/Tag** the next morning/day • **am Wochenende** at the weekend
amüsieren: sich amüsieren have fun [hæv 'fʌn]
an: an dem/den Tisch (dort) at that table • **an der Spitze** at the top (of) • **an der/die Tafel** on the board • **schreiben an** write to
andere(r, s) other ['ʌðə] • **die anderen** the others • **ein(e) andere(r, s) ...** another ... [ə'nʌðə]
anders (als) different (from) ['dɪfrənt]
anfangen (mit) start [stɑ:t]
anfassen touch [tʌtʃ]
Angst haben (vor) be afraid (of) [ə'freɪd]; be scared (of) [skeəd]
anhaben *(Kleidung)* wear [weə]
anhalten stop [stɒp]
anhören 1. sich etwas anhören listen to sth. ['lɪsn]; **2. sich gut anhören** sound good [saʊnd]
anklopfen (an) knock (on) [nɒk]
anmalen paint [peɪnt]
annehmen *(vermuten)* suppose [sə'pəʊz]
anprobieren *(Kleidung)* try on [ˌtraɪ_'ɒn]
anrufen call [kɔ:l]; phone [fəʊn]
anschauen look at [lʊk]
anschreien: jn. anschreien shout at sb. [ʃaʊt]
ansehen: sich etwas ansehen look at sth. [lʊk]; watch sth. [wɒtʃ]
Antwort (auf) answer (to) ['ɑ:nsə]
antworten answer ['ɑ:nsə]
anziehen: sich anziehen get dressed [get 'drest]
Apfel apple ['æpl]
Apfelsine orange ['ɒrɪndʒ]
April April ['eɪprəl]
Arbeit work [wɜ:k] • **bei der Arbeit/ am Arbeitsplatz** at work
arbeiten (an) work (on) [wɜ:k]
Arbeitsblatt worksheet ['wɜ:kʃi:t]
Arbeits- und Lerntechniken study skills ['stʌdi skɪlz]
arm poor [pɔ:, pʊə]
Arm arm [ɑ:m]
Armbanduhr watch [wɒtʃ]
Artikel article ['ɑ:tɪkl]
Arzt/Ärztin doctor ['dɒktə]
auch: auch aus Bristol from Bristol too [tu:] • **Ich auch.** Me too.
auf on [ɒn] • **auf dem Bild/Foto** in the picture/photo • **auf einmal** suddenly ['sʌdnli] • **auf Englisch** in English • **Auf geht's!** Let's go. **auf jn. zu** towards sb. [tə'wɔ:dz] **Auf welcher Seite sind wir?** What page are we on? • **Auf Wiedersehen.** Goodbye. [ˌgʊd'baɪ]
aufführen *(Szene, Dialog)* act [ækt]
Aufgabe *(im Schulbuch)* exercise ['eksəsaɪz]; *(Job)* job [dʒɒb]
aufgeregt *(nervös)* nervous ['nɜ:vəs]
aufhören stop [stɒp]
aufkleben stick on [ˌstɪk_'ɒn]
aufmachen open ['əʊpən]
aufräumen tidy ['taɪdi]
Aufsatz essay ['eseɪ]
aufschreiben write down [ˌraɪt 'daʊn]
aufstehen get up [ˌget_'ʌp]
Auge eye [aɪ]
Augenblick moment ['məʊmənt]
August August ['ɔ:gəst]
aus: Ich komme/bin aus ... I'm from ... [frəm, frɒm] • **aus ... (heraus/hinaus)** out of ... ['aʊt_əv] • **aus dem Zug/Bus aussteigen** get off the train/bus • **aus vielen Gründen** for lots of reasons
Ausflug trip [trɪp] • **einen Ausflug machen** go on a trip
ausgehen *(weg-, rausgehen)* go out [ˌgəʊ_'aʊt]
ausschalten: den Computer ausschalten turn off the computer [ˌtɜ:n_'ɒf]
aussehen: anders/toll/alt aussehen look different/great/old [lʊk] **gleich aussehen** look the same
außerhalb seines Zimmers outside his room [ˌaʊt'saɪd]
Aussprache pronunciation [prəˌnʌnsi'eɪʃn]
aussteigen (aus dem Zug/Bus) get off (the train/bus) [ˌget_'ɒf]
aussuchen: (sich) etwas aussuchen choose sth. [tʃu:z]
auswählen choose [tʃu:z]
Auto car [kɑ:]
Autsch! Ouch! [aʊtʃ]

B

Baby baby ['beɪbi]
Badewanne bath [bɑ:θ]
Badezimmer bathroom ['bɑ:θru:m]
Badminton badminton ['bædmɪntən]
Bahnhof station ['steɪʃn] • **am Bahnhof** at the station
bald soon [su:n] • **Bis bald.** See you. ['si: ju:]
Ball ball [bɔ:l]
Banane banana [bə'nɑ:nə]
Band *(Musikgruppe)* band [bænd]
Bank *(Sparkasse)* bank [bæŋk]
Bankräuber/in bank robber ['rɒbə]
Baseball baseball ['beɪsbɔ:l]
Basketball basketball ['bɑ:skɪtbɔ:l]
Baum tree [tri:]
beantworten answer ['ɑ:nsə]
Bedeutung meaning ['mi:nɪŋ]
beeilen: sich beeilen hurry up [ˌhʌri_'ʌp]

beenden finish ['fɪnɪʃ]
beginnen (mit) start [stɑ:t]; begin [bɪ'gɪn]
begreifen understand [ˌʌndə'stænd]
Begründung reason ['ri:zn]
bei: bei den Shaws zu Hause at the Shaws' house • **bei der Arbeit** at work • **Englisch bei Mr Kingsley** English with Mr Kingsley
beide both [bəʊθ]
Bein leg [leg]
Beispiel example [ɪg'zɑ:mpl] • **zum Beispiel** for example
benötigen need [ni:d]
benutzen use [ju:z]
beobachten watch [wɒtʃ]
bequem comfortable ['kʌmftəbl]
bereit ready ['redi]
Bericht (über) report (on) [rɪ'pɔ:t]
berichten (über) tell (about) [tel]
berühren touch [tʌtʃ]
beschäftigt busy ['bɪzi]
besorgt sein (wegen) be worried (about) ['wʌrid]
besser better ['betə]
beste: der/die/das beste ...; die besten ... the best ... [best]
Besucher/in visitor ['vɪzɪtə]
Bett bed [bed]
beunruhigt sein (wegen) be worried (about) ['wʌrid]
Beutel bag [bæg]
bevor before [bɪ'fɔ:]
Bibliothek library ['laɪbrəri]
Bild picture ['pɪktʃə] • **auf dem Bild** in the picture
Biologie biology [baɪ'ɒlədʒi]
bis *(zeitlich)* till [tɪl] • **Bis bald.** See you. ['si: ju:]
bitte 1. *(in Fragen und Aufforderungen)* please [pli:z]; **2. Bitte sehr. / Hier bitte.** Here you are.; **3. Bitte, gern geschehen.** You're welcome. ['welkəm]; **4. Wie bitte?** Sorry? ['sɒri] ▶ S.161 „bitte“
blau blue [blu:]
Bleistift pencil ['pensl]
Bleistiftanspitzer pencil sharpener ['pensl ʃɑ:pnə]
bloß just [dʒʌst]; only ['əʊnli]
Boot boat [bəʊt]
Boss boss [bɒs]
brauchen need [ni:d]
braun brown [braʊn]
Brieffreund/in *(im Internet)* e-friend ['i:frend]
Briefmarke stamp [stæmp]
Brille: (eine) Brille glasses *(pl)* ['glɑ:sɪz]
bringen: (mit-, her)bringen bring [brɪŋ] • **(weg-, hin)bringen** take [teɪk]
Brot bread *(no pl)* [bred]
Brücke bridge [brɪdʒ]
Bruder brother ['brʌðə]
Buch book [bʊk]
Bücherei library ['laɪbrəri]
Buchstabe letter ['letə]
buchstabieren spell [spel]
Bühne stage [steɪdʒ]
Bus bus [bʌs]

C

Café café ['kæfeɪ]
CD CD [ˌsi:'di:] • **CD-Spieler** CD player [ˌsi:'di: ˌpleɪə]
Cent cent (c) [sent]
Champion champion ['tʃæmpiən]
Chef/in boss [bɒs]
Chor choir ['kwaɪə]
Cola cola ['kəʊlə]
Clown/in clown [klaʊn]
Comic-Heft comic ['kɒmɪk]
Computer computer [kəm'pju:tə]
cool cool [ku:l]
Cornflakes cornflakes ['kɔ:nfleɪks]
Cousin, Cousine cousin ['kʌzn]

D

da, dahin *(dort, dorthin)* there [ðeə] • **da drüben** over there [ˌəʊvə 'ðeə]
daheim at home [ət 'həʊm]
daher so [səʊ]
danach *(zeitlich)* after that [ˌɑ:ftə 'ðæt]
Danke. Thank you. ['θæŋk ju:]; Thanks. **Vielen Dank!** Thanks a lot!
dann then [ðen]
darstellende Kunst drama ['drɑ:mə]
darum that's why ['ðæts ˌwaɪ]
das *(Artikel)* the [ðə, ði]
das (dort) *(Singular)* that [ðət, ðæt]; *(Plural)* those [ðəʊz] • **Das bin ich.** That's me.
dass that [ðət, ðæt]
dasselbe the same [seɪm]
Datum date [deɪt]
decken: den Tisch decken lay the table [ˌleɪ ðə 'teɪbl]
dein(e) your [jɔ:]
denken think [θɪŋk]
der *(Artikel)* the [ðə, ði]
derselbe the same [seɪm]
deshalb so [səʊ]; that's why ['ðæts ˌwaɪ]
Detektiv/in detective [dɪ'tektɪv]
deutlich clear [klɪə]
Deutsch; deutsch; Deutsche(r) German ['dʒɜ:mən]
Deutschland Germany ['dʒɜ:məni]
Dezember December [dɪ'sembə]
dich you [ju:]
die *(Artikel)* the [ðə, ði]
die (dort) *(Singular)* that [ðət, ðæt]; *(Plural)* those [ðəʊz] • **die (hier)** *(Singular)* this [ðɪs]; *(Plural)* these [ði:z] ▶ S.177 this, that – these, those
Diele hall [hɔ:l]
Dienstag Tuesday ['tju:zdeɪ, 'tju:zdi] *(siehe auch unter „Freitag“)*
dies (hier); diese(r, s) *(Singular)* this [ðɪs]; *(Plural)* these [ði:z]
dieselbe(n) the same [seɪm]
Ding thing [θɪŋ]
dir you [ju:]
Disko disco ['dɪskəʊ]
Donnerstag Thursday ['θɜ:zdeɪ, 'θɜ:zdi] *(siehe auch unter „Freitag“)*
doppelt, Doppel- double ['dʌbl]
Dorf village ['vɪlɪdʒ]
dort, dorthin there [ðeə] • **dort drinnen** in there [ˌɪn 'ðeə] • **dort drüben** over there [ˌəʊvə 'ðeə]
Dossier dossier ['dɒsieɪ]
Drachen kite [kaɪt]
dran: Ich bin dran. It's my turn. [tɜ:n]
draußen outside [ˌaʊt'saɪd]
drinnen inside [ˌɪn'saɪd] • **dort drinnen** in there [ˌɪn 'ðeə] • **hier drinnen** in here [ˌɪn 'hɪə]
dritte(r, s) third [θɜ:d]
drüben: da/dort drüben over there [ˌəʊvə 'ðeə]
drücken push [pʊʃ]
du you [ju:]
dunkel dark [dɑ:k]
durcheinander: alles durcheinanderbringen make a mess [ˌmeɪk‿ə 'mes]
dürfen can [kən, kæn]; may [meɪ]
Durst haben, durstig sein be thirsty ['θɜ:sti]
Dusche shower ['ʃaʊə]
duschen; sich duschen have a shower ['ʃaʊə]
DVD DVD [ˌdi: vi:' di:]

E

echt real [rɪəl]
Ecke corner ['kɔ:nə]
Ei egg [eg]
Eile: in Eile sein be in a hurry ['hʌri]
eilig: es eilig haben be in a hurry ['hʌri]
ein(e) a, an [ə, ən]; one ['wʌn] • **ein(e) andere(r, s) ...** another ... [ə'nʌðə] • **eine Menge ...** lots of ... ['lɒts‿əv] • **ein paar** some [səm, sʌm] • **eines Tages** one day
einfach *(nicht schwierig)* easy ['i:zi] • **einfach nur** just [dʒʌst]
Einfall *(Idee)* idea [aɪ'dɪə]
einige some [səm, sʌm]

einigen: sich einigen (auf) agree (on) [ə'griː]
einkaufen: einkaufen gehen go shopping [ˌgəʊ 'ʃɒpɪŋ] • **(das) Einkaufen** shopping • **Einkaufsliste** shopping list
einladen (zu) invite (to) [ɪn'vaɪt]
Einladung (zu) invitation (to) [ˌɪnvɪ'teɪʃn]
einmal: auf einmal suddenly ['sʌdnli]
eins, ein, eine one ['wʌn]
einschalten: den Computer einschalten turn on the computer [ˌtɜːn_'ɒn]
einsteigen (in den Zug/Bus) get on (the train/bus) [ˌget_'ɒn]
Eintrittskarte ticket ['tɪkɪt]
einzig: der einzige Gast the only guest ['əʊnli]
Eis *(Speiseeis)* ice cream [ˌaɪs 'kriːm]
Elefant elephant ['elɪfənt]
Eltern parents ['peərənts]
E-Mail (an) e-mail (to) ['iːmeɪl]
Ende 1. end [end] • **am Ende (von)** at the end (of) • **zu Ende machen** finish ['fɪnɪʃ] • **zu Ende sein** be over ['əʊvə]
2. oberes Ende *(Spitze)* top [tɒp] **am oberen Ende** at the top
enden finish ['fɪnɪʃ]
endlich at last [ət 'lɑːst]
Englisch; englisch English ['ɪŋglɪʃ]
Enkel/in grandchild ['græntʃaɪld], *pl* grandchildren ['græntʃɪldrən]
Entschuldigung 1. *(Tut mir leid)* I'm sorry. ['sɒri] • **Entschuldigung, dass ich zu spät komme.** Sorry, I'm late.
2. Entschuldigung, ... / Entschuldigen Sie, ... *(Darf ich mal stören?)* Excuse me, ... [ɪk'skjuːz miː]
▸ S.153 „Entschuldigung"
entwerfen design [dɪ'zaɪn]
entwickeln *(entwerfen)* design [dɪ'zaɪn]
er 1. *(männliche Person)* he [hiː]; **2.** *(Ding, Tier)* it [ɪt]
Erdkunde geography [dʒi'ɒgrəfi]
erforschen explore [ɪk'splɔː]
ergänzen add (to) [æd]
Ergebnis result [rɪ'zʌlt]
erinnern: sich erinnern (an) remember [rɪ'membə]
erkennen *(merken)* realize ['rɪəlaɪz]
erkunden explore [ɪk'splɔː]
erste(r, s) first [fɜːst] • **als Erstes** first • **der erste Tag** the first day **der/die Erste sein** be first
erwarten: ich kann es kaum erwarten, ... zu sehen I can't wait to see ... [weɪt]
erzählen (von) tell (about) [tel]
Erzählung story ['stɔːri]

es it [ɪt] • **es gibt** *(es ist vorhanden)* there's; *(es sind vorhanden)* there are ▸ S.154 There's ... / There are ...
Essen food [fuːd]
essen eat [iːt] • **Abendbrot essen** have dinner • **Toast zum Frühstück essen** have toast for breakfast
Esszimmer dining room ['daɪnɪŋ ruːm]
etwas 1. something ['sʌmθɪŋ]; **2.** *(ein bisschen)* **etwas Käse/Saft** some cheese/juice [səm, sʌm]
euch you [juː]
euer, eure your [jɔː]
Euro euro ['jʊərəʊ]

F

fahren: Inliner/Skateboard fahren skate [skeɪt] • **Rad fahren** ride a bike [ˌraɪd ə 'baɪk]
Fahrrad bike [baɪk]
fallen; fallen lassen drop [drɒp]
falsch wrong [rɒŋ]
Familie family ['fæməli]
fantastisch fantastic [fæn'tæstɪk]
Farbe colour ['kʌlə] • **Welche Farbe hat ...?** What colour is ...?
Februar February ['februəri]
Federball badminton ['bædmɪntən]
Federmäppchen pencil case ['pensl keɪs]
Fehler mistake [mɪ'steɪk]
Fenster window ['wɪndəʊ]
Ferien holidays ['hɒlədeɪz]
Fernsehen television ['telɪvɪʒn]; TV [tiː'viː] • **im Fernsehen** on TV
fernsehen watch TV [ˌwɒtʃ tiː'viː]
fertig *(bereit)* ready ['redi] • **sich fertig machen (für)** *(sich vorbereiten)* get ready (for) • **Dinge fertig machen (für)** *(vorbereiten)* get things ready (for)
Film film [fɪlm]
Filmstar film star ['fɪlm stɑː]
Filzstift felt tip ['felt tɪp]
finden *(entdecken)* find [faɪnd]
Finger finger ['fɪŋgə]
Fisch fish, *pl* fish [fɪʃ]
Flasche bottle ['bɒtl] • **eine Flasche Milch** a bottle of milk
Fleisch meat [miːt]
Flur hall [hɔːl]
Flussdiagramm flow chart ['fləʊ tʃɑːt]
flüstern whisper ['wɪspə]
folgen follow ['fɒləʊ]
Football American football [əˌmerɪkən 'fʊtbɔːl]
fort away [ə'weɪ]
Foto photo ['fəʊtəʊ] • **auf dem Foto** in the photo • **Fotos machen** take photos

Fotoapparat camera ['kæmərə]
fotografieren take photos [teɪk 'fəʊtəʊz]
Frage question ['kwestʃn] • **Fragen stellen** ask questions
fragen ask [ɑːsk] • **nach etwas fragen** ask about sth.
Französisch French [frentʃ]
Frau woman ['wʊmən], *pl* women ['wɪmɪn] • **Frau Brown** Mrs Brown ['mɪsɪz] • **Frau White** *(unverheiratet)* Miss White [mɪs]
frei [friː] free • **freie Zeit** free time
Freitag Friday ['fraɪdeɪ, 'fraɪdi] **freitagabends, am Freitagabend** on Friday evening • **freitagnachts, Freitagnacht** on Friday night
Freizeit free time [ˌfriː 'taɪm]
Freund/in friend [frend]
frieren be cold [kəʊld]
froh happy ['hæpi]
Frucht, Früchte fruit [fruːt]
früh early ['ɜːli]
Frühling spring [sprɪŋ]
Frühstück breakfast ['brekfəst] **zum Frühstück** for breakfast
frühstücken have breakfast
Frühstückspension Bed and Breakfast (B&B) [ˌbed_ən 'brekfəst]
Füller pen [pen]
für for [fə, fɔː]
furchtbar terrible ['terəbl]
Fuß foot [fʊt], *pl* feet [fiːt]
Fußball football ['fʊtbɔːl]
Fußballschuhe, -stiefel football boots ['fʊtbɔːl buːts]
Fußboden floor [flɔː]
Futter food [fuːd]
füttern feed [fiːd]

G

ganz: den ganzen Tag (lang) all day **die ganze Zeit** all the time • **Das ist ganz falsch.** This is all wrong.
Garten garden ['gɑːdn]
Gast guest [gest]; *(Besucher/in)* visitor ['vɪzɪtə]
geben give [gɪv] • **es gibt** *(es ist vorhanden)* there's; *(es sind vorhanden)* there are
▸ S.154 There's ... / There are ...
Geburtstag birthday ['bɜːθdeɪ] **Herzlichen Glückwunsch zum Geburtstag.** Happy birthday. **Ich habe im Mai / am 13. Juni Geburtstag.** My birthday is in May / on 13th June. • **Wann hast du Geburtstag?** When's your birthday?
Gedicht poem ['pəʊɪm]
Gefahr danger ['deɪndʒə]

gegen against [ə'genst]
Gegenwart present ['preznt]
gehen **1. gehen (nach, zu)** go (to) [gəʊ] • **(zu Fuß) gehen** walk [wɔ:k] **Auf geht's!** Let's go. • **einkaufen gehen** go shopping • **ins Bett gehen** go to bed • **nach Hause gehen** go home • **reiten/ schwimmen gehen** go riding/ swimming
2. Es geht um Mr Green. This is about Mr Green.
gelangen *(hinkommen)* get [get]
gelb yellow ['jeləʊ]
Geld money ['mʌni]
genießen enjoy [ɪn'dʒɔɪ]
genug enough [ɪ'nʌf]
geöffnet open ['əʊpən]
Geografie geography [dʒi'ɒgrəfi]
gerade: jetzt gerade right now [raɪt 'naʊ]; at the moment ['məʊmənt]
Geräusch noise [nɔɪz]
gern: Ich hätte gern ... / Ich möchte gern ... I'd like ... (= I would like ...) [laɪk] • **Ich schwimme/tanze/... gern.** I like swimming/dancing/... **Ich würde gern gehen** I'd like to go **Ich würde nicht gern gehen** I wouldn't like to go • **Gern geschehen.** You're welcome. ['welkəm]
gernhaben like [laɪk]
Geschäft shop [ʃɒp]
geschehen (mit) happen (to) ['hæpən]
Geschenk present ['preznt]
Geschichte **1.** story ['stɔ:ri]; **2.** *(vergangene Zeiten)* history ['hɪstri]
geschieden divorced [dɪ'vɔ:st]
Geschirr dishes *(pl)* ['dɪʃɪz] • **das Geschirr abwaschen** do the dishes
Geschirrspülmaschine dishwasher ['dɪʃwɒʃə]
Gesicht face [feɪs]
gestern yesterday ['jestədeɪ, 'jestədi] **gestern Morgen/Nachmittag/ Abend** yesterday morning/afternoon/evening
Getränk drink [drɪŋk]
Gewinn prize [praɪz]
gewinnen win [wɪn]
gewöhnlich usually ['ju:ʒuəli]
Gitarre guitar [gɪ'tɑ:] • **Gitarre spielen** play the guitar
Glas glass [glɑ:s] • **ein Glas Wasser** a glass of water
glauben think [θɪŋk] • **Das glaube ich nicht. / Ich glaube nicht.** I don't think so. • **Ich glaube (ja).** I think so.
gleich sein/aussehen be/look the same [seɪm]
Glocke bell [bel]
Glück: Viel Glück (bei/mit ...)! Good luck (with ...)! [gʊd 'lʌk]
glücklich happy ['hæpi]
Grammatik grammar ['græmə]
groß big [bɪg]
großartig great [greɪt]
Größe *(Schuhgröße usw.)* size [saɪz]
Großeltern grandparents ['grænpeərənts]
Großmutter grandmother ['grænmʌðə]
Großstadt city ['sɪti]
Großvater grandfather ['grænfɑ:ðə]
grün green [gri:n]
Grund reason ['ri:zn] • **aus vielen Gründen** for lots of reasons
Gruppe group [gru:p]; *(Musikgruppe)* band [bænd]
gruselig scary ['skeəri]
Gruß: Liebe Grüße, ... *(Briefschluss)* Love ... [lʌv]
Grüß Dilip von mir. Say hi to Dilip for me.
gucken look [lʊk]
gut good [gʊd]; *(okay)* OK [əʊ'keɪ] **Guten Morgen.** Good morning. **Guten Tag.** Hello.; *(nachmittags)* Good afternoon.

H

Haar, Haare hair *(no pl)* [heə]
haben have got ['hæv gɒt] • **Ich habe keinen Stuhl.** I haven't got a chair. • **Ich habe am 13. Juni/im Mai Geburtstag.** My birthday is on 13th June/in May. • **Wann hast du Geburtstag?** When's your birthday? • **haben wollen** want [wɒnt] **Was haben wir als Hausaufgabe auf?** What's for homework?
Hähnchen chicken ['tʃɪkɪn]
halb zwölf half past 11 [hɑ:f]
Hallo! Hi! [haɪ]; Hello. [hə'ləʊ]
Hamburger hamburger ['hæmbɜ:gə]
Hamster hamster ['hæmstə]
Hand hand [hænd]
Handy mobile (phone) ['məʊbaɪl]
hassen hate [heɪt]
häufig often ['ɒfn]
Haus house [haʊs] • **im Haus der Shaws / bei den Shaws zu Hause** at the Shaws' house • **nach Hause gehen** go home [həʊm] • **nach Hause kommen** come home; get home • **zu Hause** at home
Hausaufgabe(n) homework *(no pl)* ['həʊmwɜ:k] • **die Hausaufgabe(n) machen** do homework • **Was haben wir als Hausaufgabe auf?** What's for homework?
Haustier pet [pet]
Haustür front door [ˌfrʌnt 'dɔ:]
Heim home [həʊm]
heiß hot [hɒt]
heißen **1. Ich heiße ...** My name is ... **Wie heißt du?** What's your name? **2. Sie heißen dich in ... willkommen** They welcome you to ... ['welkəm]
helfen help [help]
Hemd shirt [ʃɜ:t]
herauf up [ʌp]
heraus: aus ... heraus out of ... ['aʊt‿əv]
herausfinden find out [ˌfaɪnd‿'aʊt]
herausnehmen take out [ˌteɪk‿'aʊt]
herbringen bring [brɪŋ]
Herbst autumn ['ɔ:təm]
Herd cooker ['kʊkə]
hereinkommen come in [ˌkʌm‿'ɪn]
Herr Brown Mr Brown ['mɪstə]
herumgeben pass round [ˌpɑ:s 'raʊnd]
herunter down [daʊn]
Herzlichen Glückwunsch zum Geburtstag. Happy birthday. [ˌhæpi 'bɜ:θdeɪ]
heute today [tə'deɪ] • **heute Morgen/Nachmittag/Abend** this morning/afternoon/evening **heute Nacht** tonight [tə'naɪt]
hier here [hɪə] • **Hier bitte.** *(Bitte sehr.)* Here you are. • **hier drinnen** in here [ˌɪn 'hɪə]
hierher here [hɪə]
Hilfe help [help]
hinauf up [ʌp]
hinaufklettern (auf) climb [klaɪm] **Klettere auf einen Baum.** Climb a tree.
hinaus: aus ... hinaus out of ... ['aʊt‿əv]
hinein: in ... hinein into ... ['ɪntə, 'ɪntʊ]
hinkommen *(gelangen)* get [get]
hinter behind [bɪ'haɪnd]
hinunter down [daʊn]
hinzufügen (zu) add (to) [æd]
Hobby hobby ['hɒbi], *pl* hobbies
Hockey hockey ['hɒki]
Hockeyschuhe hockey shoes ['hɒki ʃu:z]
hoffen hope [həʊp]
hören hear [hɪə]
hübsch pretty ['prɪti]
Huhn chicken ['tʃɪkɪn]
Hülle cover ['kʌvə]
Hund dog [dɒg]
hundert hundred ['hʌndrəd]
Hunger haben, hungrig sein be hungry ['hʌŋgri]
Hut hat [hæt]

I

ich I [aɪ] • **Ich auch.** Me too. [ˌmiː ˈtuː] • **Das bin ich.** That's me. **Warum ich?** Why me?
Idee idea [aɪˈdɪə]
ihm him; *(bei Dingen, Tieren)* it
ihn him; *(bei Dingen, Tieren)* it
ihnen them [ðəm, ðem]
Ihnen *(höfliche Anrede)* you [juː]
ihr *(Plural von „du")* you [juː]
ihr: Hilf ihr. Help her. [hə, hɜː]
ihr(e) *(besitzanzeigend)* *(zu „she")* her [hə, hɜː]; *(zu „they")* their [ðeə] **Ihr(e)** your [jɔː]
im: im Fernsehen on TV • **im Haus der Shaws** at the Shaws' house **im Mai** in May • **im Radio** on the radio • **im Zug** on the train
immer always [ˈɔːlweɪz] • **immer noch** still [stɪl]
in in • **in ... (hinein)** into ... [ˈɪntə, ˈɪntʊ] • **in der ...straße** in ... Street **in der Hamiltonstraße 7** at 7 Hamilton Street • **in der Nacht** at night • **in der Nähe von** near **in der Schule** at school • **in Eile sein** be in a hurry • **in den Zug/ Bus einsteigen** get on the train/ bus • **ins Bett gehen** go to bed
Infinitiv infinitive [ɪnˈfɪnətɪv]
Information(en) (über) information (about/on) *(no pl)* [ˌɪnfəˈmeɪʃn]
Inliner skates [skeɪts] • **Inliner fahren** skate
innen (drin) inside [ˌɪnˈsaɪd]
Innenstadt city centre [ˌsɪti ˈsentə]
interessant interesting [ˈɪntrəstɪŋ]
Internet internet [ˈɪntənet]
irgendetwas: Habt ihr irgendetwas Besonderes gemacht? Did you do anything special? [ˌeniθɪŋ ˈspeʃl]
irgendwelche any [ˈeni]

J

ja yes [jes]
Jahr year [jɪə]
Jahrgangsstufe year [jɪə]
Januar January [ˈdʒænjuəri]
Jeans jeans *(pl)* [dʒiːnz]
jede(r, s) ... *(Begleiter)* **1.** every ... [ˈevri] **2.** *(jeder einzelne)* each ... [iːtʃ]
jemand somebody [ˈsʌmbədi]
jene(r, s) *(Singular)* that [ðət, ðæt]; *(Plural)* those [ðəʊz]
jetzt now [naʊ] • **jetzt gerade, jetzt sofort** right now
Job job [dʒɒb]
Judo judo [ˈdʒuːdəʊ] • **Judo machen** do judo
Jugend- junior [ˈdʒuːniə]
Jugendliche(r) kid [kɪd]
Juli July [dʒuˈlaɪ]
jung young [jʌŋ]
Junge boy [bɔɪ]
Juni June [dʒuːn]
Junioren- junior [ˈdʒuːniə]

K

Käfig cage [keɪdʒ]
Kalender calendar [ˈkælɪndə]
kalt cold [kəʊld]
Kamera camera [ˈkæmərə]
Kaninchen rabbit [ˈræbɪt]
Karotte carrot [ˈkærət]
Karte *(Post-, Spielkarte)* card [kɑːd]
Kartoffel potato [pəˈteɪtəʊ], *pl* potatoes
Kartoffelchips crisps *(pl)* [krɪsps]
Käse cheese [tʃiːz]
Kästchen, Kasten box [bɒks]
Katze cat [kæt]
kaufen buy [baɪ]
kein(e) no; not a; not (...) any • **Ich habe keinen Stuhl.** I haven't got a chair. • **Ich mag kein(e) ...** I don't like ... • **keine Musik mehr** no more music
Keks biscuit [ˈbɪskɪt]
kennen know [nəʊ]
kennenlernen meet [miːt]
Kind child [tʃaɪld], *pl* children [ˈtʃɪldrən]; kid [kɪd]
Kirche church [tʃɜːtʃ]
Kiste box [bɒks]
Klang sound [saʊnd]
klar clear [klɪə]
Klasse class [klɑːs]; form [fɔːm]
Klassenkamerad/in classmate [ˈklɑːsmeɪt]
Klassenlehrer/in class teacher; form teacher
Klassenzimmer classroom [ˈklɑːsruːm]
Klavier piano [piˈænəʊ] • **Klavier spielen** play the piano
Klebestift glue stick [ˈgluː stɪk]
Klebstoff glue [gluː]
Kleid dress [dres]
Kleiderschrank wardrobe [ˈwɔːdrəʊb]
Kleidung, Kleidungsstücke clothes *(pl)* [kləʊðz, kləʊz]
klein little [ˈlɪtl]
Kleinstadt town [taʊn]
klettern climb [klaɪm] • **Klettere auf einen Baum.** Climb a tree.
Klingel bell [bel]
klingen sound [saʊnd]
klopfen (an) knock (on) [nɒk]
Klub club [klʌb]
klug clever [ˈklevə]
Knie knee [niː]
komisch *(witzig)* funny [ˈfʌni]
kommen come [kʌm]; *(hinkommen)* get [get] • **Ich komme aus ...** I'm from ... • **Wo kommst du her?** Where are you from? • **nach Hause kommen** come home; get home • **zu spät kommen** be late
König king [kɪŋ]
können can [kən, kæn] • **ich kann nicht ...** I can't ... [kɑːnt]
kontrollieren *(prüfen)* check [tʃek]
Kopf head [hed]
Korb basket [ˈbɑːskɪt] • **ein Korb Äpfel** a basket of apples
Körper body [ˈbɒdi]
kosten *(Essen probieren)* try [traɪ]
kosten: Er/Sie/Es kostet 1 Pfund. It's £1. • **Sie kosten 35 Pence.** They are 35p. • **Wie viel kostet/kosten ...?** How much is/are ...?
kostenlos free [friː]
Kostüm *(Verkleidung)* costume [ˈkɒstjuːm]
Kram stuff [stʌf]
Krug jug [dʒʌg] • **ein Krug Orangensaft** a jug of orange juice
Küche kitchen [ˈkɪtʃɪn]
Kuchen cake [keɪk]
Kugelschreiber pen [pen]
kühl cool [kuːl]
Kühlschrank fridge [frɪdʒ]
Kunst art [ɑːt]
kurz short [ʃɔːt] • **kurze Hose** shorts *(pl)* [ʃɔːts]

L

lächeln smile [smaɪl]
lachen laugh [lɑːf]
Laden *(Geschäft)* shop [ʃɒp]
Lampe lamp [læmp]
Land country [ˈkʌntri]
lang long [lɒŋ] • **drei Tage lang** for three days
langweilig boring [ˈbɔːrɪŋ]
Lärm noise [nɔɪz]
Lasagne lasagne [ləˈzænjə]
lassen: Lass das! Stop that! • **Lass uns ... / Lasst uns ...** Let's ... [lets]
laufen run [rʌn]
laut loud [laʊd]
Laut sound [saʊnd]
leben live [lɪv]
Leben life [laɪf], *pl* lives [laɪvz]
Lebensmittel food [fuːd]
ledig single [ˈsɪŋgl]
leer empty [ˈempti]
legen *(hin-, ablegen)* put [pʊt]
lehren teach [tiːtʃ]
Lehrer/in teacher [ˈtiːtʃə]

leicht *(nicht schwierig)* easy ['i:zi]
leid: Tut mir leid. I'm sorry. ['sɒri]
leise quiet ['kwaɪət]
Lektion *(im Schulbuch)* unit ['ju:nɪt]
lernen learn [lɜ:n]
Lern- und Arbeitstechniken study skills ['stʌdi skɪlz]
lesen read [ri:d]
letzte(r, s) last [lɑ:st]
Leute people ['pi:pl]
Liebe Grüße, ... *(Briefschluss)* Love ... [lʌv]
Lieber Jay, ... Dear Jay ... [dɪə]
Liebling dear [dɪə]
Lieblings-: meine Lieblingsfarbe my favourite colour ['feɪvərɪt]
Lied song [sɒŋ]
lila purple ['pɜ:pl]
Limonade lemonade [ˌlemə'neɪd]
Lineal ruler ['ru:lə]
linke(r, s) left [left] • **nach links schauen** look left • **links, auf der linken Seite** on the left
Liste list [lɪst]
Loch hole [həʊl]

M

machen do [du:]; make [meɪk] • **die Hausaufgabe(n) machen** do homework • **einen Ausflug/eine Reise machen** go on a trip • **Fotos machen** take photos • **Judo machen** do judo • **sich Notizen machen** take notes • **sich Sorgen machen (wegen, um)** worry (about) ['wʌri] • **(Zauber-)Kunststücke machen** do tricks • **Reiten macht Spaß.** Riding is fun.
Mädchen girl [gɜ:l]
Magazin *(Zeitschrift)* magazine [ˌmægə'zi:n]
Magst du ...? Do you like ...? *(siehe auch unter „mögen")*
Mai May [meɪ]
malen paint [peɪnt]
Mama mum [mʌm]
manchmal sometimes ['sʌmtaɪmz]
Mann man [mæn], *pl* men [men]
Mannschaft team [ti:m]
Mappe *(des Sprachenportfolios)* dossier ['dɒsieɪ]
Marmelade *(Orangenmarmelade)* marmalade ['mɑ:məleɪd]
März March [mɑ:tʃ]
Mathematik maths [mæθs]
Maus mouse [maʊs], *pl* mice [maɪs]
Meer sea [si:]
Meerschweinchen guinea pig ['gɪni pɪg]

mehr more [mɔ:] • **viel mehr** lots more • **keine Musik mehr** no more music
mein(e) my [maɪ]
meinen *(glauben, denken)* think [θɪŋk]; *(sagen wollen) mean* [mi:n]
meist: die meisten Leute most people [məʊst]
meistens usually ['ju:ʒuəli]
Meister/in *(Champion)* champion ['tʃæmpiən]
Menschen people ['pi:pl]
merken 1. *(erkennen)* realize ['rɪəlaɪz]; **2. sich etwas merken** remember sth. [rɪ'membə]
mich me [mi:]
Milch milk [mɪlk] • **Milchshake** milkshake ['mɪlkʃeɪk]
Mindmap mind map ['maɪnd mæp]
Minute minute ['mɪnɪt]
mir me [mi:]
mit with [wɪð]
mitbringen bring [brɪŋ]
Mitschüler/in classmate ['klɑ:smeɪt]
Mittagessen lunch [lʌntʃ] • **zum Mittagessen** for lunch
Mittagspause lunch break ['lʌntʃ breɪk]
Mitte centre ['sentə]; middle ['mɪdl]
Mitteilung *(Notiz)* note [nəʊt]
Mittwoch Wednesday ['wenzdeɪ, 'wenzdi] *(siehe auch unter „Freitag")*
Mobiltelefon mobile phone [ˌməʊbaɪl 'fəʊn]; mobile ['məʊbaɪl]
möchte: Ich möchte gern ... (haben) I'd like ... (= I would like ...) [laɪk]
Ich möchte gehen I'd like to go
Ich möchte nicht gehen I wouldn't like to go • **Möchtest du / Möchten Sie ...?** Would you like ...?
Modell *(-auto, -schiff)* model ['mɒdl]
mögen like [laɪk]; *(sehr mögen)* love [lʌv] • **Ich mag ...** I like ... • **Ich mag ... nicht./ Ich mag kein(e) ...** I don't like ... • **Magst du ...?** Do you like ...?
Möhre carrot ['kærət]
Moment moment ['məʊmənt] • **im Moment** at the moment
Monat month [mʌnθ]
Montag Monday ['mʌndeɪ, 'mʌndi] *(siehe auch unter „Freitag")*
morgen tomorrow [tə'mɒrəʊ]
Morgen morning ['mɔ:nɪŋ] • **am Morgen, morgens** in the morning
MP3-Spieler MP3 player [ˌempi:'θri: ˌpleɪə]
müde tired ['taɪəd]
Mund mouth [maʊθ]
Museum museum [mju'zi:əm]
Musical musical ['mju:zɪkl]
Musik music ['mju:zɪk]

Müsli muesli ['mju:zli]
müssen have to; must [mʌst]
Mutter mother ['mʌðə]
Mutti mum [mʌm]

N

Na ja ... / Na gut ... Oh well ... [əʊ 'wel]
nach 1. *(örtlich)* to [tə, tu] • **nach Hause gehen** go home • **nach Hause kommen** come home; get home • **nach oben** up; *(im Haus)* upstairs [ˌʌp'steəz] • **nach unten** down; *(im Haus)* downstairs [ˌdaʊn'steəz] • **nach vorn** to the front [frʌnt]
2. *(zeitlich)* after • **Viertel nach 11** quarter past 11 [pɑ:st]
3. nach etwas fragen ask about sth. [ə'baʊt]
Nachbar/in neighbour ['neɪbə]
nachdem after ['ɑ:ftə]
Nachmittag afternoon [ˌɑ:ftə'nu:n]
am Nachmittag, nachmittags in the afternoon
Nachrichten news *(no pl)* [nju:z]
nächste(r, s): am nächsten Tag the next day [nekst] • **der Nächste sein** be next • **Was haben wir als Nächstes?** What have we got next?
Nacht night [naɪt] • **heute Nacht** tonight [tə'naɪt] • **in der Nacht, nachts** at night
nahe (bei) near [nɪə]
Nähe: in der Nähe von near [nɪə]
Name name [neɪm]
Nase nose [nəʊz]
natürlich of course [əv 'kɔ:s]
Naturwissenschaft science ['saɪəns]
neben next to [nekst]
nehmen take [teɪk] • **Ich nehme es.** *(beim Einkaufen)* I'll take it.
nein no [nəʊ]
nennen call [kɔ:l]
nervös nervous ['nɜ:vəs]
nett nice [naɪs]
neu new [nju:]
nicht not [nɒt] • **Das glaube ich nicht. / Ich glaube nicht.** I don't think so. • **Du brauchst ein ..., nicht wahr?** You need a ..., right?
Nichts zu danken. You're welcome. ['welkəm]
nie, niemals never ['nevə]
noch: noch ein(e) ... another ... [ə'nʌðə]; one more ... [mɔ:] • **noch einmal** again [ə'gen] • **(immer) noch** still [stɪl]
normalerweise usually ['ju:ʒuəli]
Notiz note [nəʊt] • **sich Notizen machen** take notes

November November [nəʊ'vembə]
null o [əʊ]; zero ['zɪərəʊ]
Nummer number ['nʌmbə]
nun now [naʊ] • **Nun, ...** Well, ... [wel]
nur only ['əʊnli]; just [dʒʌst] • **nur zum Spaß** just for fun

O

oben *(an der Spitze)* at the top (of) [tɒp]; *(im Haus)* upstairs [ˌʌp'steəz] **nach oben** up; *(im Haus)* upstairs
oberhalb von over ['əʊvə]
Oberteil top [tɒp]
Obst fruit [fru:t]
Obstsalat fruit salad ['fru:t ˌsæləd]
oder or [ɔ:]
öffnen open ['əʊpən]
oft often ['ɒfn]
ohne without [wɪ'ðaʊt]
Ohr ear [ɪə]
Ohrring earring ['ɪərɪŋ]
okay OK [əʊ'keɪ]
Oktober October [ɒk'təʊbə]
Oma grandma ['grænmɑ:]
Onkel uncle ['ʌŋkl]
Opa grandpa ['grænpɑ:]
Orange orange ['ɒrɪndʒ]
orange(farben) orange ['ɒrɪndʒ]
Orangenmarmelade marmalade ['mɑ:məleɪd]
Orangensaft orange juice ['ɒrɪndʒ dʒu:s]
Ort place [pleɪs]

P

paar: ein paar some [səm, sʌm]
Päckchen, Packung packet ['pækɪt] **ein Päckchen / eine Packung Pfefferminzbonbons** a packet of mints
Paket parcel ['pɑ:sl]
Papa dad [dæd]
Papagei parrot ['pærət]
Papier paper ['peɪpə]
Park park [pɑ:k]
Partner/in partner ['pɑ:tnə]
Partnerstadt twin town [ˌtwɪn 'taʊn]
Party party ['pɑ:ti]
passen fit [fɪt]
passieren (mit) happen (to) ['hæpən]
Pause break [breɪk]
Pence pence (p) [pens]
Person person ['pɜ:sn]
Pfefferminzbonbons mints [mɪnts]
Pferd horse [hɔ:s]
Pfund *(britische Währung)* pound (£) [paʊnd] • **Es kostet 1 Pfund.** It's £1.
Piano piano [pi'ænəʊ]
pink(farben) pink [pɪŋk]
Pirat/in pirate ['paɪrət]
Pizza pizza ['pi:tsə]
Plan plan [plæn]
Platz *(Ort, Stelle)* place [pleɪs]
Plätzchen biscuit ['bɪskɪt]
plötzlich suddenly ['sʌdnli]
Polizei police *(pl)* [pə'li:s]
Poltergeist poltergeist ['pəʊltəgaɪst]
Pommes frites chips *(pl)* [tʃɪps]
Poster poster ['pəʊstə]
Präsentation presentation [ˌprezn'teɪʃn]
präsentieren: (jm.) etwas präsentieren present sth. (to sb.) [prɪ'zent]
Preis *(Kaufpreis)* price [praɪs]; *(Gewinn)* prize [praɪz]
Probe *(am Theater)* rehearsal [rɪ'hɜ:sl]
proben *(am Theater)* rehearse [rɪ'hɜ:s]
probieren try [traɪ]
Programm programme ['prəʊgræm]
Projekt (über, zu) project (on, about) ['prɒdʒekt]
prüfen *(überprüfen)* check [tʃek]
putzen clean [kli:n] • **Ich putze mir die Zähne.** I clean my teeth.

Q

Quiz quiz [kwɪz], *pl* quizzes ['kwɪzɪz]

R

Rad fahren ride a bike [ˌraɪd‿ə 'baɪk]
Radiergummi rubber ['rʌbə]
Radio radio ['reɪdiəʊ] • **im Radio** on the radio
Rap rap [ræp]
Ratespiel quiz [kwɪz], *pl* quizzes ['kwɪzɪz]
Raum room [ru:m]
Recht haben be right [raɪt]
rechte(r, s) right [raɪt] • **nach rechts schauen** look right • **rechts, auf der rechten Seite** on the right
reden (mit, über) talk (to, about) [tɔ:k] • **Wovon redest du?** What are you talking about?
Regal(brett) shelf [ʃelf], *pl* shelves [ʃelvz]
reichen *(weitergeben)* pass [pɑ:s]
Reihe: Du bist an der Reihe. It's your turn. [tɜ:n]
Reise trip [trɪp] • **eine Reise machen** go on a trip
reiten ride [raɪd] • **reiten gehen** go riding
Religion *(Religionsunterricht)* RE [ˌɑ:r‿'i:], Religious Education [rɪˌlɪdʒəs‿edʒu'keɪʃn]
rennen run [rʌn]
Reportage (über) report (on) [rɪ'pɔ:t]
Resultat result [rɪ'zʌlt]
richtig right [raɪt]
Rollstuhl wheelchair ['wi:ltʃeə]
rosa pink [pɪŋk]
rot red [red]
rufen call [kɔ:l]; shout [ʃaʊt] • **die Polizei rufen** call the police
ruhig quiet ['kwaɪət]
Rundgang (durch das Haus) tour (of the house) [tʊə]

S

Sache thing [θɪŋ]
Saft juice [dʒu:s]
sagen say [seɪ] • **Sagt mir eure Namen.** Tell me your names. [tel]
Salat *(Gericht, Beilage)* salad ['sæləd]
sammeln collect [kə'lekt]
Samstag Saturday ['sætədeɪ, 'sætədi] *(siehe auch unter „Freitag")*
Sandwich sandwich ['sænwɪtʃ]
Satz sentence ['sentəns]
sauber clean [kli:n] • **sauber machen** clean
Schachtel packet ['pækɪt]
Schale bowl [bəʊl] • **eine Schale Cornflakes** a bowl of cornflakes
Schatz dear [dɪə]
schauen look [lʊk]
Schauspiel drama ['drɑ:mə]
schieben push [pʊʃ]
Schiff boat [bəʊt]; ship [ʃɪp]
Schildkröte tortoise ['tɔ:təs]
schlafen sleep [sli:p]
Schlafzimmer bedroom ['bedru:m]
Schlange snake [sneɪk]
schlau clever ['klevə]
schlecht bad [bæd]
schließen *(zumachen)* close [kləʊz]
schließlich at last [ət 'lɑ:st]
schlimm bad [bæd]
Schlüssel key [ki:]
Schlüsselwort key word ['ki: wɜ:d]
Schmerz(en) pain [peɪn] • **schreien vor Schmerzen** cry in pain [kraɪ]
schnell quick [kwɪk]
Schokolade chocolate ['tʃɒklət]
schön beautiful ['bju:tɪfl]; *(nett)* nice [naɪs] • **schön kühl/sauber/...** nice and cool/clean/...
Schrank cupboard ['kʌbəd]; *(Kleiderschrank)* wardrobe ['wɔ:drəʊb]
schrecklich terrible ['terəbl]
schreiben (an) write (to) [raɪt]
Schreibtisch desk [desk]
schreien shout [ʃaʊt]; cry [kraɪ] **schreien vor Schmerzen** cry in pain
Schritt step [step]

Schuh shoe [ʃu:]
Schule school [sku:l] • **in der Schule** at school
Schüler/in student ['stju:dənt]
Schulfach (school) subject ['sʌbdʒɪkt]
Schulheft exercise book ['eksəsaɪz bʊk]
Schulklasse class [klɑ:s]; form [fɔ:m]
Schultasche school bag ['sku:l bæg]
Schulter shoulder ['ʃəʊldə]
Schüssel bowl [bəʊl]
schwarz black [blæk]
schwer *(schwierig)* difficult ['dɪfɪkəlt]
Schwester sister ['sɪstə]
schwierig difficult ['dɪfɪkəlt]
schwimmen swim [swɪm]
schwimmen gehen go swimming
See *(die See, das Meer)* sea [si:]
sehen see [si:] • **Siehst du?** See?
sehr very ['veri] • **Er mag sie sehr.** He likes her a lot. [ə 'lɒt]
Seife soap [səʊp]
sein *(Verb)* be [bi:]
sein(e) *(besitzanzeigend)* *(zu „he")* his; *(zu „it")* its
Seite *(Buch-, Heftseite)* page [peɪdʒ] **Auf welcher Seite sind wir?** What page are we on?
Sekunde second ['sekənd]
selbstverständlich of course [əv 'kɔ:s]
seltsam strange [streɪndʒ]
September September [sep'tembə]
Sessel armchair ['ɑ:mtʃeə]
setzen: sich setzen sit [sɪt] • **Setz dich / Setzt euch zu mir.** Sit with me.
Shorts shorts *(pl)* [ʃɔ:ts]
Show show [ʃəʊ]
sicher sein *(keine Zweifel haben)* be sure [ʃʊə, ʃɔ:]
sie 1. *(weibliche Person)* she [ʃi:] **Frag sie.** Ask her. [hə, hɜ:]
2. *(Ding, Tier)* it [ɪt]
3. *(Plural)* they [ðeɪ] • **Frag sie.** Ask them. [ðəm, ðem]
4. **Sie** *(höfliche Anrede)* you [ju:]
Silbe syllable ['sɪləbl]
singen sing [sɪŋ]
sitzen sit [sɪt]
Skateboard skateboard ['skeɪtbɔ:d]
Skateboard fahren skate [skeɪt]
Sketch sketch [sketʃ]
so süß so sweet [səʊ]
Socke sock [sɒk]
Sofa sofa ['səʊfə]
Sohn son [sʌn]
sollte(n, st, t) should [ʃəd, ʃʊd]
Sommer summer ['sʌmə]
sonderbar strange [streɪndʒ]
Song song [sɒŋ]
Sonnabend Saturday ['sætədeɪ, 'sætədi] *(siehe auch unter „Freitag")*
Sonnenbrille: (eine) Sonnenbrille sunglasses *(pl)* ['sʌnglɑ:sɪz]
Sonntag Sunday ['sʌndeɪ, 'sʌndi] *(siehe auch unter „Freitag")*
Sorgen: sich Sorgen machen (wegen, um) worry (about) ['wʌri] • **Mach dir keine Sorgen.** Don't worry.
sowieso anyway ['eniweɪ]
Spaß fun [fʌn] • **Spaß haben** have fun • **nur zum Spaß** just for fun **Reiten macht Spaß.** Riding is fun. **Viel Spaß!** Have fun! ► S.174 fun
spät late [leɪt] • **Wie spät ist es?** What's the time? • **zu spät sein/kommen** be late
später later ['leɪtə]
Spiel game [geɪm]; *(Wettkampf)* match [mætʃ]
spielen play [pleɪ]; *(Szene, Dialog)* act [ækt] • **Fußball spielen** play football • **Gitarre/Klavier spielen** play the guitar/the piano
Spieler/in player ['pleɪə]
Spion/in spy [spaɪ]
Spitze *(oberes Ende)* top [tɒp] • **an der Spitze (von)** at the top (of)
Sport; Sportart sport [spɔ:t] • **Sport treiben** do sport ► S.164 Sports
Sportunterricht PE [ˌpi:_'i:], Physical Education [ˌfɪzɪkəl_edʒu'keɪʃn]
Sprache language ['læŋgwɪdʒ]
Spülbecken, Spüle sink [sɪŋk]
Stadt *(Großstadt)* city ['sɪti]; *(Kleinstadt)* town [taʊn]
Stadtzentrum city centre [ˌsɪti 'sentə]
Stall *(für Kaninchen)* hutch [hʌtʃ]
Stammbaum family tree ['fæməli tri:]
Star *(Film-, Popstar)* star [stɑ:]
starten start [stɑ:t]
stellen *(hin-, abstellen)* put [pʊt] **Fragen stellen** ask questions
Stichwort *(Schlüsselwort)* key word ['ki: wɜ:d]
Stiefel boot [bu:t]
still quiet ['kwaɪət]
Stimme voice [vɔɪs]
stimmen: Das stimmt. That's right. [raɪt] • **Du brauchst ein Lineal, stimmt's?** You need a ruler, right?
stoßen push [pʊʃ]
Straße road [rəʊd]; street [stri:t]
streiten: sich streiten argue ['ɑ:gju:]
Strumpf sock [sɒk]
Stück piece [pi:s] • **ein Stück Papier** a piece of paper
Student/in student ['stju:dənt]
Studio studio ['stju:diəʊ]
Stuhl chair [tʃeə]
Stunde hour ['aʊə]; *(Schulstunde)* lesson ['lesn]
Stundenplan timetable ['taɪmteɪbl]
Subjekt subject ['sʌbdʒɪkt]
Supermarkt supermarket ['su:pəmɑ:kɪt]
süß sweet [swi:t]
Süßigkeiten sweets *(pl)* [swi:ts]
Sweatshirt sweatshirt ['swetʃɜ:t]
Szene scene [si:n]

T

Tafel *(Wandtafel)* board [bɔ:d] • **an der/die Tafel** on the board
Tag day [deɪ] • **drei Tage (lang)** for three days • **eines Tages** one day **Guten Tag.** Hello.; *(nachmittags)* Good afternoon. [gʊd_ˌɑ:ftə'nu:n]
Tagebuch diary ['daɪəri]
Tante aunt [ɑ:nt]
Tanz dance [dɑ:ns]
tanzen dance [dɑ:ns]
Tanzen dancing ['dɑ:nsɪŋ]
Tanzstunden, Tanzunterricht dancing lessons ['dɑ:nsɪŋ ˌlesnz]
Tasche *(Tragetasche, Beutel)* bag [bæg]
Tätigkeit activity [æk'tɪvəti]
tausend thousand ['θaʊznd]
Team team [ti:m]
Tee tea [ti:]
Teil part [pɑ:t]
teilen: sich etwas teilen (mit jm.) share sth. (with sb.) [ʃeə]
Telefon (tele)phone ['telɪfəʊn] • **am Telefon** on the phone
Telefonnummer (tele)phone number ['telɪfəʊn ˌnʌmbə]
Teller plate [pleɪt] • **ein Teller Pommes frites** a plate of chips
Tennis tennis ['tenɪs]
Termin appointment [ə'pɔɪntmənt]
Terminkalender diary ['daɪəri]
teuer expensive [ɪk'spensɪv]
Text text [tekst]
Theaterstück play [pleɪ]
Thema, Themenbereich topic ['tɒpɪk]
Tier animal ['ænɪml]; *(Haustier)* pet [pet]
Tierhandlung pet shop ['pet ʃɒp]
Tierpark zoo [zu:]
Tisch table ['teɪbl]
Tischtennis table tennis ['teɪbl tenɪs]
Titel title ['taɪtl]
Toast(brot) toast [təʊst]
Tochter daughter ['dɔ:tə]
Toilette toilet ['tɔɪlət]
toll fantastic [fæn'tæstɪk]; great [greɪt]
Top *(Oberteil)* top [tɒp]
Torte cake [keɪk]
tot dead [ded]
töten kill [kɪl]
Tour (durch das Haus) tour (of the house) [tʊə]

tragen *(Kleidung)* wear [weə]
trainieren practise ['præktɪs]
Traum dream [dri:m] • **Traumhaus** dream house
treffen; sich treffen meet [mi:t]
Treppe(nstufen) stairs *(pl)* [steəz]
Trick *(Zauberkunststück)* trick [trɪk]
trinken drink [drɪŋk] • **Milch zum Frühstück trinken** have milk for breakfast
Tschüs. Bye. [baɪ]; See you. ['si: ju:]
T-Shirt T-shirt ['ti:ʃɜ:t]
tun do [du:] • **Tue, was ich tue.** Do what I do. • **tun müssen** have to do • **tun wollen** want to do [wɒnt] **Tut mir leid.** I'm sorry. ['sɒri]
Tür door [dɔ:]
Türklingel doorbell ['dɔ:bel]
Turm tower ['taʊə]
Turnen *(Sportunterricht)* PE [ˌpi:‿'i:], Physical Education [ˌfɪzɪkəl‿edʒu'keɪʃn]
Tut mir leid. I'm sorry. ['sɒri]
Tüte bag [bæg]

U

üben practise ['præktɪs]
über about [ə'baʊt]; *(räumlich)* over ['əʊvə]
überall everywhere ['evriweə]
überprüfen check [tʃek]
Überschrift title ['taɪtl]
Übung *(im Schulbuch)* exercise ['eksəsaɪz]
Übungsheft exercise book ['eksəsaɪz bʊk]
Uhr 1. *(Armbanduhr)* watch [wɒtʃ]; *(Wand-, Stand-, Turmuhr)* clock [klɒk] **2. elf Uhr** eleven o'clock • **7 Uhr morgens/vormittags** 7 am [ˌeɪ‿'em] **7 Uhr nachmittags/abends** 7 pm [ˌpi:‿'em] • **um 8 Uhr 45** at 8.45
Uhrzeit time [taɪm]
um 1. um 8.45 at 8.45; **2. Es geht um Mr Green.** This is about Mr Green.; **3. um zu** to
umsehen: sich umsehen look round [ˌlʊk 'raʊnd]
und and [ənd, ænd]
unheimlich scary ['skeəri]
Uniform uniform ['ju:nɪfɔ:m]
Unordnung: alles in Unordnung bringen make a mess [ˌmeɪk‿ə 'mes]
uns us [əs, ʌs]
unser(e) our ['aʊə]
unten *(im Haus)* downstairs [ˌdaʊn'steəz] • **nach unten** down [daʊn]; *(im Haus)* downstairs
unter under ['ʌndə]
unterhalten: sich unterhalten (mit, über) talk (to, about) [tɔ:k]
Unterricht lessons *(pl)* ['lesnz]
unterrichten teach [ti:tʃ]
unterschiedlich different ['dɪfrənt]

V

Vater father ['fɑ:ðə]
Vati dad [dæd]
Verabredung appointment [ə'pɔɪntmənt]
verabschieden: sich verabschieden say goodbye [ˌseɪ gʊd'baɪ]
verängstigt scared [skeəd]
verbinden *(einander zuordnen)* link [lɪŋk]
Verein club [klʌb]
verfolgen follow ['fɒləʊ]
verheiratet (mit) married (to) ['mærɪd]
verkaufen sell [sel]
Verkäufer/in shop assistant ['ʃɒp‿əˌsɪstənt]
verkehrt *(falsch)* wrong [rɒŋ]
Verkleidung *(Kostüm)* costume ['kɒstju:m]
verknüpfen *(einander zuordnen)* link [lɪŋk]
verletzen hurt [hɜ:t]
vermuten suppose [sə'pəʊz]
verrückt mad [mæd]
verschieden different ['dɪfrənt]
verstecken; sich verstecken hide [haɪd]
verstehen understand [ˌʌndə'stænd]
versuchen try [traɪ] • **versuchen zu tun** try and do / try to do
verwenden use [ju:z]
viel a lot [ə 'lɒt]; lots of; much [mʌtʃ] **viele** lots of; many ['meni] • **Viel Glück (bei/mit ...)!** Good luck (with ...)! • **viel mehr** lots more • **Viel Spaß!** Have fun! • **wie viel?** how much? • **wie viele?** how many? **Vielen Dank!** Thanks a lot!
► S.175 „viel", „viele"
vielleicht maybe ['meɪbi]
Viertel: Viertel nach 11 quarter past 11 ['kwɔ:tə] • **Viertel vor 12** quarter to 12
violett purple ['pɜ:pl]
Vogel bird [bɜ:d]
Vokabelverzeichnis vocabulary [və'kæbjələri]
voll full [fʊl]
Volleyball volleyball ['vɒlibɔ:l]
von of [əv, ɒv]; from [frəm, frɒm] • **ein Aufsatz von ...** an essay by ... [baɪ]
vor 1. *(räumlich)* in front of [ɪn 'frʌnt‿əv]; **2.** *(zeitlich)* **vor dem Abendessen** before dinner [bɪ'fɔ:] • **vor einer Minute** a minute ago [ə'gəʊ] **Viertel vor 12** quarter to 12
vorbei sein be over ['əʊvə]
vorbereiten: Dinge vorbereiten get things ready ['redi] • **sich vorbereiten (auf)** get ready (for)
Vormittag morning ['mɔ:nɪŋ]
vorsichtig careful ['keəfl]
vorstellen: (jm.) etwas vorstellen *(präsentieren)* present sth. (to sb.) [prɪ'zent]
Vorstellung *(Präsentation)* presentation [ˌprezn'teɪʃn]; *(Show)* show [ʃəʊ]

W

wählen *(auswählen)* choose [tʃu:z]
wann when [wen]
warm warm [wɔ:m]
warten (auf) wait (for) [weɪt]
warum why [waɪ] • **Warum ich?** Why me?
was what [wɒt] • **Was haben wir als Hausaufgabe auf?** What's for homework? • **Was haben wir als Nächstes?** What have we got next? • **Was ist mit ...?** What about ...? • **Was kostet/kosten ...?** How much is/are ...?
waschen wash [wɒʃ] • **Ich wasche mir das Gesicht.** I wash my face.
Wasser water ['wɔ:tə]
Wechselgeld change [tʃeɪndʒ]
Wecker alarm clock [ə'lɑ:m klɒk]
Weg way [weɪ]
weg away [ə'weɪ] • **weg sein** *(nicht zu Hause sein)* be out [aʊt]
weggehen *(raus-, ausgehen)* go out [ˌgəʊ‿'aʊt]
wehtun hurt [hɜ:t]
weil because [bɪ'kɒz]
weiß white [waɪt]
weit (entfernt) far [fɑ:]; a long way
weitere(r, s): ein(e) weitere(r, s) one more [mɔ:]
weitergeben pass [pɑ:s]
weitermachen go on [ˌgəʊ‿'ɒn]
welche(r, s) which [wɪtʃ] • **Auf welcher Seite sind wir?** What page are we on? [wɒt] • **Welche Farbe hat ...?** What colour is ...?
Wellensittich budgie ['bʌdʒi]
Welt world [wɜ:ld]
wenigstens at least [ət 'li:st]
wenn *(zeitlich)* when [wen]
wer who [hu:]
werfen throw [θrəʊ]
wie 1. *(Fragewort)* how [haʊ] • **Wie bitte?** Sorry? ['sɒri] • **Wie heißt du?** What's your name? • **Wie**

spät ist es? What's the time? **wie viel?** how much? • **wie viele?** how many? • **Wie war ...?** How was ...? • **Wie wär's mit ...?** What about ...?
2. wie ein Filmstar like a film star [laɪk]
wieder again [ə'gen]
Wiederholung *(des Lernstoffs)* revision [rɪ'vɪʒn]
Wiedersehen: Auf Wiedersehen. Goodbye. [ˌgʊd'baɪ]
willkommen: Willkommen (in ...). Welcome (to ...). ['welkəm] • **Sie heißen dich in ... willkommen** They welcome you to ...
Wind wind [wɪnd]
windig windy ['wɪndi]
Winter winter ['wɪntə]
wir we [wiː]
wirklich 1. *(Adverb: tatsächlich)* really ['rɪəli]; **2.** *(Adjektiv: echt)* real [rɪəl]
wissen know [nəʊ] • **..., wissen Sie./ ..., weißt du.** ..., you know. • **Weißt du was, Sophie?** You know what, Sophie? • **Woher weißt du ...?** How do you know ...?
Witz joke [dʒəʊk]
witzig funny ['fʌni]
wo where [weə] • **Wo kommst du her?** Where are you from?
Woche week [wiːk]
Wochenende weekend [ˌwiːk'end] **am Wochenende** at the weekend
Wochentage days of the week
Woher weißt du ...? How do you know ...? [nəʊ]
wohin where [weə]
Wohltätigkeitsbasar jumble sale ['dʒʌmbl seɪl]
wohnen live [lɪv]
Wohnung flat [flæt]
Wohnungstür front door [ˌfrʌnt 'dɔː]
Wohnzimmer living room ['lɪvɪŋ ruːm]
wollen *(haben wollen)* want [wɒnt] **tun wollen** want to do
Wort word [wɜːd]
Wörterbuch dictionary ['dɪkʃənri]
Wörterverzeichnis vocabulary [və'kæbjələri]; *(alphabetisches)* dictionary ['dɪkʃənri]
Wovon redest du? What are you talking about?
Wurst, Würstchen sausage ['sɒsɪdʒ]

Y

Yoga yoga ['jəʊgə]

Z

Zahl number ['nʌmbə]
Zahn tooth [tuːθ], *pl* teeth [tiːθ] • **Ich putze mir die Zähne.** I clean my teeth.
zanken: sich zanken argue ['ɑːgjuː]
Zauberkunststück trick [trɪk] • **Zauberkunststücke machen** do tricks
Zeh toe [təʊ]
zeigen show [ʃəʊ]
Zeile line [laɪn]
Zeit time [taɪm]
Zeitschrift magazine [ˌmægə'ziːn]
Zeitung newspaper ['njuːspeɪpə]
Zentrum centre ['sentə]
Zeug *(Kram)* stuff [stʌf]
ziehen pull [pʊl]
Ziffer number ['nʌmbə]
Zimmer room [ruːm]
Zoo zoo [zuː]
zu 1. *(örtlich)* to [tə, tu] • **zu Jenny** to Jenny's • **zu Hause** at home **Setz dich zu mir.** Sit with me.
2. zum Beispiel for example [ɪg'zɑːmpl] • **zum Frühstück/ Mittagessen/Abendbrot** for breakfast/lunch/dinner
3. zu viel too much [tuː] • **zu spät sein/kommen** be late
4. versuchen zu tun try and do / try to do
5. um zu to
zuerst first [fɜːst]
Zug train [treɪn] • **im Zug** on the train
Zuhause home [həʊm]
zuhören listen (to) ['lɪsn]
zumachen close [kləʊz]
zumindest at least [ət 'liːst]
zurück (nach) back (to) [bæk]
zurückgeben give back [ˌgɪv 'bæk]
zurzeit at the moment ['məʊmənt]
zusammen together [tə'geðə]
zusätzlich extra ['ekstrə]
zusehen watch [wɒtʃ]
zustimmen: jm. zustimmen agree with sb. [ə'griː]
zweite(r, s) second ['sekənd]
Zwillinge twins *(pl)* [twɪnz]
Zwillingsbruder twin brother ['twɪn ˌbrʌðə]

Irregular verbs (Unregelmäßige Verben)

Infinitive	Simple past		Infinitive	Simple past	
(to) **be**	**was/were**	sein	(to) **make**	**made**	machen; bauen; bilden
(to) **begin**	**began**	beginnen, anfangen	(to) **put**	**put**	legen, stellen, *(wohin)* tun
(to) **come**	**came**	kommen	(to) **run**	**ran**	laufen, rennen
(to) **do**	**did**	tun, machen	(to) **say**	**said**	sagen
(to) **find**	**found**	finden	(to) **see**	**saw**	sehen
(to) **get**	**got**	gelangen, (hin)kommen	(to) **sing**	**sang**	singen
(to) **go**	**went**	gehen	(to) **sit**	**sat**	sitzen; sich setzen
(to) **have** (**have got**)	**had**	haben	(to) **stick on**	**stuck on**	aufkleben
			(to) **take**	**took**	nehmen; (weg-, hin)bringen
(to) **hurt**	**hurt**	wehtun; verletzen	(to) **tell**	**told**	sagen; erzählen
(to) **know**	**knew**	wissen; kennen	(to) **think**	**thought**	denken, glauben, meinen

Classroom English

Zu Beginn und am Ende des Unterrichts

Guten Morgen, Frau …	**Good morning, Mrs/Ms/Miss …** *(bis 12 Uhr)*
Guten Tag, Herr …	**Good afternoon, Mr …** *(ab 12 Uhr)*
Entschuldigung, dass ich zu spät komme.	**Sorry, I'm late.**
Auf Wiedersehen! / Bis morgen.	**Goodbye. / See you tomorrow.**

Du brauchst Hilfe

Können Sie mir bitte helfen?	**Can you help me, please?**
Auf welcher Seite sind wir, bitte?	**What page are we on, please?**
Was heißt … auf Englisch/Deutsch?	**What's … in English/German?**
Können Sie bitte … buchstabieren?	**Can you spell …, please?**
Können Sie es bitte an die Tafel schreiben?	**Can you write it on the board, please?**

Hausaufgaben und Übungen

Tut mir leid, ich habe mein Schulheft nicht dabei.	**Sorry, I haven't got my exercise book.**
Ich verstehe diese Übung nicht.	**I don't understand this exercise.**
Ich kann Nummer 3 nicht lösen.	**I can't do number 3.**
Entschuldigung, ich bin noch nicht fertig.	**Sorry, I haven't finished.**
Ich habe … Ist das auch richtig?	**I've got … Is that right too?**
Tut mir leid, das weiß ich nicht.	**Sorry, I don't know.**
Was haben wir (als Hausaufgabe) auf?	**What's for homework?**

Wenn es Probleme gibt

Kann ich es auf Deutsch sagen?	**Can I say it in German?**
Können Sie/Kannst du bitte lauter sprechen?	**Can you speak louder, please?**
Können Sie/Kannst du das bitte noch mal sagen?	**Can you say that again, please?**
Kann ich bitte das Fenster öffnen/zumachen?	**Can I open/close the window, please?**
Kann ich bitte zur Toilette gehen?	**Can I go to the toilet, please?**

Partnerarbeit

Kann ich mit Julian arbeiten?	**Can I work with Julian?**
Kann ich bitte dein Lineal/deinen Filzstift/… haben?	**Can I have your ruler/felt tip/…, please?**
Danke. / Vielen Dank.	**Thank you. / Thanks a lot.**
Du bist dran.	**It's your turn.**

Diese Arbeitsanweisungen findest du häufig im Schülerbuch

Act out your dialogue for the class.	Spielt der Klasse euren Dialog vor.
Add words to the mind map.	Füge der Mindmap neue Wörter hinzu.
Answer the questions.	Beantworte die Fragen.
Ask your partner questions.	Stelle deiner Partnerin/deinem Partner Fragen.
Check your answers.	Überprüfe deine Antworten.
Choose the best scene.	Wähle die beste Szene aus.
Collect ideas on the board.	Sammle Ideen an der Tafel.
Compare with a partner.	Vergleiche mit einem Partner/einer Partnerin.
Complete the sentences.	Vervollständige die Sätze.
Copy the chart.	Schreib die Tabelle ab.
Correct the sentences.	Verbessere die Sätze.
Draw a picture.	Zeichne ein Bild.
Fill in the verbs.	Setze die Verben ein.
Find the missing letters.	Finde die fehlenden Buchstaben.
Label your picture.	Beschrifte dein Bild.
Listen. / Listen again.	Hör zu. / Hör noch einmal zu.
Look at page ...	Sieh auf Seite ... nach.
Make a chart/a mind map/a page for your dossier.	Fertige eine Tabelle/Mindmap/Seite für dein Dossier an.
Match the letters and numbers.	Ordne die Buchstaben den Nummern zu.
Practise your dialogue.	Übt euren Dialog.
Prepare a dialogue.	Bereitet einen Dialog vor.
Put the pictures in the right order.	Bring die Bilder in die richtige Reihenfolge.
Read the poem.	Lies das Gedicht.
Right or wrong?	Richtig oder falsch?
Swap charts.	Tauscht die Tabellen.
Take a card.	Nimm eine Karte.
Take notes.	Mach dir Notizen.
Talk to your partner.	Sprich mit deinem Partner/deiner Partnerin.
Tell your partner about your picture.	Erzähle deinem Partner/deiner Partnerin etwas über dein Bild.
Use words from the box.	Verwende Wörter aus dem Kasten.
Which word is the odd one out?	Welches Wort passt nicht dazu?
What's different?	Was ist anders?
Work in groups of four.	Arbeitet in Vierergruppen.
Write the sentences.	Schreib die Sätze auf.

First names (Vornamen)

Ananda [ə'nændə]
Ann [æn]
Anna ['ænə]
Anne [æn]
Barnabas ['bɑ:nəbəs]
Becky ['beki]
Ben [ben]
Betty ['beti]
Bill [bɪl]
Billy ['bɪli]
Catherine ['kæθrɪn]
Dan [dæn]
Daniel ['dænjəl]
Dennis ['denɪs]
Dilip ['dɪlɪp]
Elizabeth [ɪ'lɪzəbəθ]
Emily ['eməli]
Emma ['emə]
Hannah ['hænə]
Harry ['hæri]
Henry ['henri]
Hip [hɪp]
Hop [hɒp]
Howard ['haʊəd]
Indira [ɪn'dɪərə]
Jack [dʒæk]
Jane [dʒeɪn]
Jay [dʒeɪ]
Jenny ['dʒeni]
Jim [dʒɪm]
Jo [dʒəʊ]
John [dʒɒn]
Johnny ['dʒɒni]
Jonah ['dʒəʊnə]
Kim [kɪm]
Larry ['læri]
Laura ['lɔ:rə]
Lee [li:]
Les [lez]
Liz [lɪz]
Mark [mɑ:k]
Mary ['meəri]
Michael ['maɪkl]
Michelle [mɪ'ʃel]
Mike [maɪk]
Nora ['nɔ:rə]
Pat [pæt]
Paul [pɔ:l]
Peter ['pi:tə]
Polly ['pɒli]
Prunella [pru'nelə]
Sanjay ['sændʒeɪ]
Sheeba ['ʃi:bə]
Sheila ['ʃi:lə]
Simon ['saɪmən]
Sophie ['səʊfi]
Spike [spaɪk]
Tim [tɪm]
Toby ['təʊbi]
Wanda ['wɒndə]
Winston ['wɪnstən]
Yoko ['jəʊkəʊ]

Family names (Familiennamen)

Barker ['bɑ:kə]
Baxter ['bækstə]
Baynton ['beɪntən]
Bonny ['bɒni]
Brown [braʊn]
Carter-Brown [ˌkɑ:tə 'braʊn]
Depp [dep]
Elliot ['eliət]
Green [gri:n]
Hanson ['hænsn]
Hitchcock ['hɪtʃkɒk]
Kapoor [kə'pɔ:, kə'pʊə]
King [kɪŋ]
Kingsley ['kɪŋzli]
Milligan ['mɪlɪgən]
Milne [mɪln]
Rackham ['rækəm]
Shaw [ʃɔ:]
Smith [smɪθ]
Thompson ['tɒmpsən]
White [waɪt]

Place names (Ortsnamen)

Bath [bɑ:θ]
Bristol ['brɪstl]
Cabot Tower [ˌkæbət 'taʊə]
Clifton Suspension Bridge [ˌklɪftən sə'spenʃn brɪdʒ]

Cooper Street ['ku:pə stri:t]
Cotham ['kɒtəm]
Cotham Park Road [ˌkɒtəm pɑ:k 'rəʊd]

Delhi ['deli]
England ['ɪŋglənd]
Frogmore Street ['frɒgmɔ: stri:t]
Germany ['dʒɜ:məni]
Hamilton Street ['hæməltən stri:t]

Hanover ['hænəvə]
Harbourside ['hɑ:bəsaɪd]
India ['ɪndiə]
The Industrial Museum [ɪnˌdʌstriəl mju'zi:əm]

Italy ['ɪtəli]
London ['lʌndən]
New York [ˌnju: 'jɔ:k]
New Zealand [nju: 'zi:lənd]
Paris ['pærɪs]
Paul Road [ˌpɔ:l 'rəʊd]
Portway ['pɔ:tweɪ]
Stockholm ['stɒkhəʊm]
Tokyo ['təʊkiəʊ]
Uganda [ju'gændə]

Other names (Andere Namen)

Aardman ['ɑ:dmən]
Halloween [ˌhæləʊ'i:n]
Hokey Cokey [ˌhəʊki 'kəʊki]
Madonna [mə'dɒnə]
Oxfam ['ɒksfæm]

Illustrationen

Graham-Cameron Illustration, UK: Fliss Cary, Grafikerin (wenn nicht anders angegeben); **Roland Beier**, Berlin (Vignetten vordere Umschlaginnenseite; S. 6/7; S.17: 1. Reihe u. unten; 22; 28 Mitte; 35 oben; 38 oben; 39 unten; 45; 54; 56; 58 Mitte; 62; 78 Mitte; 88; 93; 95; 99; 106; 108 Mitte; 109 unten; 112 unten; 113 oben Mitte u. unten; 118–120; 122–124 unten; 125–177); **Carlos Borrell**, Berlin (Karten vordere und hintere Umschlaginnenseite); **Johann Brandstetter**, Winhöring/Kronberg (S. 96–98; 124 Mitte); **Julie Colthorpe**, Berlin (S. 17 Mitte re.; 19; 21; 48 oben; 51; 52 Bild 5; 53 Bild 6)

Fotos

Rob Cousins, Bristol (wenn im Bildquellenverzeichnis nicht anders angegeben)

Bildquellen

Alamy, Abingdon (S. 41 Grandma Shaw: Eliane Farray-Sulle; S. 64: Janine Wiedel Photolibrary; S. 100 Bild 1: Rolf Richardson); Artquest, London (S. 67 oben re.); **Bank of England**, London (S. 67 banknotes, reproduced with kind permission); **Britain on View**, London (S. 101 Bild 4); BTZ Bremer Touristik-Zentrale Gesellschaft für Marketing & Service mbH (S. 125); **Corbis**, Düsseldorf (S. 9 Bild 3: Ariel Skelley; S. 52 Bild 4: LWA-Dann Tardif; S. 56Mitte; S. 60 u. 115 Yoko: Paul Barton); **Corel Library** (S. 21 unten Mitte; S. 86 u. 89); **Gareth Evans**, Berlin (S. 21 unten li.; S. 30; S. 59; S. 60 Mitte; S. 66; S. 70; S. 84/85 pinboard); **Folio Graphics Ltd**, Porirua (S. 113 oben li.: Kersten); **Brian Harris Photographer**, Saffron Walden (S. 101 Bild 6); **Bernhard Hunger**, Dettingen (S. 35 unten); **Juniors Bildarchiv**, Ruhpolding (S. 37 Bild E); **Keystone**, Hamburg (S. 9 Bild 4: TopFoto.co.uk); **Ling Design Ltd.**, Kent (S. 112 oben re.); **Mauritius**, Mittenwald (S. 80 li.: Torsten Krüger); Courtesy of **The Medici Society Limited**, London (S. 112 oben li.); **Werner Otto**, Oberhausen (S. 80 re.); **Picture-Alliance**, Frankfurt/Main (S. 62 hockey: dpa; basketball, tennis, judo, volleyball: dpa/dpaweb; football: PA_WIRE); **PunchStock**, Madison (S. 60 u. 115 Lars); **Shutterstock**, New York (S. 60 u. 115 Britta: Monkey Business Images; Sanjay: India Picture); **Statics Ltd.**, London (S. 113 oben re.: David Wojtowycz); **Hartmut Tschepe**, Berlin (S. 17); **Andrea Ulrich**, Bonn (S. 28 unten); Carita Watts, Sweden (S. 123); **Western Aspect**, Bristol (S. 100 Bild 2: David Harper)

Titelbild

Rob Cousins, Bristol; **IFA-Bilderteam**, Ottobrunn (Hintergrund Union Jack: Jon Arnold Images); **mpixel/Achim Meissner**, Krefeld (Himmel)

Textquellen

S. 99: "The Poetry United Chant" by Les Baynton from: *The Works.* Poems chosen by Paul Cookson. © Paul Cookson 2000, Macmillan Children's Books, London 2000; "Halfway down" by A. A. Milne from: *When we were very young.* © Egmont UK Ltd, London; "Rain" by Spike Milligan © Spike Milligan Productions, Ltd.